BACK ROADS
OF THE CAPE

David Fleminger

JACANA

"To my parents, for making me"

Segublication_info"> irst published in 2005 by
Jacana Media (Pty) Ltd.
10 Orange Street
Sunnyside 2092
Johannesburg
South Africa

Segil> © David Fleminger, 2005

All rights reserved

Segublication_info">ISBN 1-77009-066-5

Photographs by the author
Maps by Norma MacCallum
Author's photograph by Marc Shoul
Cover photograph: The Schoemanspoort road from Oudtshoorn is firmly deflected by the formidable Swartberg Mountains.

Printed and bound by Pinetown Printers

See a complete list of Jacana titles at www.jacana.co.za

Contents

Grit gets in your eyes on the dusty Rooiberg Pass

Introduction

HOW TO USE THIS BOOK

This is a book for people who like road trips, people who enjoy history and people who like to read. It is both a historical narrative that will help you make the most of your travels and a practical travel guide that will help you make the most of your history. A little bit of something for everyone, I hope…

But, essentially, I wrote this book because I love roads, all kinds of roads: in-roads, through-roads, old roads, and new roads. I especially like mountain passes because they offer great views, without any physical effort. I also love the dusty sand roads that wind through lonely tracts of forgotten land, leaving you with grit in your teeth and dirt in your hair. In fact, if I have the choice between two routes from A to B, I'll take the obscure back road every time, sometimes against my passengers' better judgement.

So, one of the big ideas behind this book is to encourage you to make the road trip a more integral part of your travel experience. The history of this country echoes along its byways and, if you take the time to slow down a bit, these echoes will ring loud in your mind. Roads document the great human story with an asphalt apathy, and function as both a chronicle and a requirement of human development. It doesn't matter whether your mode of transport is hatchback, sedan, 4x4 or armchair, the roads of South Africa are endlessly fascinating.

But why take longer to get from A to B? It goes against every tenet of our 'bigger, better, faster, more' mentality. Hitting the highway and careering down to Cape Town in the shortest possible time is a national hobby. But everything has a price and, road safety aside, the faster you go, the less you will see. Trust me, there isn't a single town in South Africa that won't reward an hour of two of your time. So,

slow down, I say, and stop more often. You never know what you will discover *en route*.

To help you plan your adventures accordingly, this book has been divided up into several sections. First, there are the main chapters, which distinguish between one region and another. Then, the opening pages of each section feature a map and some general orientation; including descriptions of the major through-roads, alternative routes and suggestions for round trips and interesting detours. The story of each region is then told, with sidebars detailing tourist attractions and historical titbits along the way.

All this is easier said than done. Writing a book of this nature is kinda like trying to catch a river in a plastic bag. It's a huge amount of material to squeeze into a very small space and, whenever you think you've got it all in, something splashes out and drifts away. Furthermore, anyone who lives in South Africa will tell you that ours is a very dynamic country. Things are changing all the time: place names, phone numbers and attractions are all in a constant state of flux. Even archaeological evidence and sociological nomenclature keep shifting, and new discoveries force us to revise constantly our understanding of the past.

To make matters worse, it is very difficult to be both accurate and timeless in one's descriptions of people and places. History is a slippery, subjective creature that continually squirms out of your grasp just when you think you have it pegged down. Nevertheless, I have tried to make this book as up-to-date as possible and all details were correct at the time of printing.

If any inconsistencies have inadvertently crept into the text, I most humbly beg the reader's pardon. And, if this book includes any glaring errors or omissions, I hasten to assure the reader that the fault is mine alone. However, if you have any comments, corrections or feedback about this book, please send them to me so that I can correct my oversights in any subsequent editions. My e-mail address is david@backroads.co.za.

THANKS AND ACKNOWLEDGMENTS

It has often been said that writing a book requires the support, money, time and energy of a surprisingly large collection of people. I can only affirm this common authorial assertion, and would like to express my extreme gratitude to all the people who helped me see this project through to fruition.

First, there are my parents who started schlepping me around the country from an early age. They instilled in me a love of travel and an appreciation of the limitless possibilities of the road. More specifically, I want to thank my father, Norman, for letting me put 25 000kms on the clock of his new 4x4 while I was researching this tome. And I'd like to pay tribute to my mother, who always made me sandwiches and hard-boiled eggs for *padkos*.

Then there is my publisher, Jacana, and Mike Martin, Chris Cocks and Lynda Harvey. They responded to my initial submission with alacrity and encouragement. Without their buy-in at a very early stage, this book might never have seen the light of day. I would like to thank Mike and Chris for all their faith and fortitude, and applaud Brett Rogers and Norma MacCallum for their excellent work on the layout and maps respectively. I also thank my scrupulous editor James McFarlane for his invaluable contribution.

Nic Griffin of Avis also deserves a tug of the forelock, as he agreed to sponsor the book based only on a proposal and a short writing sample. Without the generosity and support of Avis, I would not even have had the money for petrol!

When it comes to accommodation, the good people at Caraville really pulled out all the stops. Despite a challenging itinerary that criss-

An antler-studded stoep looks out on the Klein Karoo plains

crossed the country, Liska, Debbie and Grant at Caraville never failed to find me a comfortable bed at one of their affiliate hotels. Liska has since gone off to marry a farmer from Vryheid, and I wish them nothing but the best. I must also give a sincere 'thank you' to all the hotels and lodges that kindly offered to put me up. Details of these establishments can be found at the back of this book.

Thanks also go out to all the people at South African National Parks (SAN Parks), and Joep Stevens in particular. Their support was much appreciated, and I trust that SAN Parks will go from strength to strength.

Closer to home, sincere thanks must also go to: Hilary Fine, Sue Cohen, Lyanne Kopenhager and Marc Shoul, who read my manuscript and gave me comments; Johnny Katz from Foto Cats; Jaydon Immerman, Daryl Lieman, Violet Reve-Koyana, Enock, Greg and Monde who kept the home-fires burning while I was away; Samantha Saevitzon, who helped me when I was lost in the middle of nowhere; Debbie Fleminger, Lisa Perets, Anthony Rosmarin, Ivor Oudmayer, Mark and Micaeli Fleminger, Lisa Melman, Gillian, Lee, Shoki, Adam, Jacqui, Darren, Howard, Nick, Paul, Dave, Natalie, Lozza, Sagorin, Gabi, Gavin, Evan, Terry, Meira, Motti, Morris Bay, Molly, Sally, the Rybko's, Depth Animation, the Dog Walkers, the Mindsetters, the Witsies and all my family and friends, who have always been so supportive; Graham Ross, a true *padmaker* and road researcher, who generously sent me his comprehensive database on mountain passes; Hugo Legget, Anthony Paton and Lee Burger for insider information; and to everybody else I met during the course of my travels. I thank you all for taking the time to chat, give directions, dish some gossip or just share a moment. It is truly the strangers that you meet on the road who make travel so addictive.

I would also like to acknowledge all the South African writers who came before me. I read from a wide number of sources while writing this book, and I never failed to admire the passion, research and hard work that went into every word. In particular, I should mention the Godfather of South African travel writing, TV Bulpin. His eternal *Discovering South Africa* is the road-trip Bible and, although this hefty volume may be a tad old-fashioned, it is still a vast repository of information. Jose Burman is another veteran travel writer, and his benchmark book on mountain passes, *So High the Road*, bears his customary thoroughness. Graham Ross' superb book, *The Romance of Cape Mountain Passes*, was also an inspiration to me, and a catalyst for the entire Back Roads project. Finally, I heartily recommend Noel Mostert's epic tome, *Frontiers*, which contains a lot of valuable historical information. These and other useful titles are detailed at the back of this book.

Finally, I should like to thank the people of South Africa. Wherever I went, I revelled in the goodwill and indomitable spirit of our country. Despite the odds, we are really becoming a nation of friends. For that, above all else, I am glad.

Travel is one of life's true pleasures; a short escape from reality to a place where there are no consequences and no responsibilities. In South Africa, especially, travellers are spoiled for choice. In one day, you can drive from mountains to sea, or from bushveld to beaches. South Africa is, quite literally, a world in one country and I'm proud to be a part of that world. Thank God I'm an African.

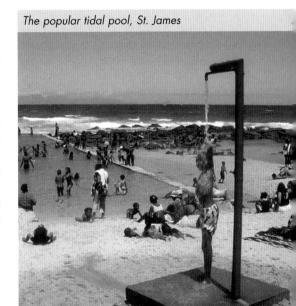
The popular tidal pool, St. James

Great boulders are worn down to pebbles by the eternal power of the sea

1. In the beginning

STARTING WITH A BANG!

We'll start at the very beginning, because it actually is a very good place to start. Unfortunately, since I am a bit of a completist, this means we have to go back billions of years to the creation of the Earth itself.

Now, this isn't the place for a theological debate on the origin of the universe, nor is it appropriate to plunge into an astrophysical description of the Big Bang itself. After all, this is just a humble travel guide. So, it will suffice to say that about 4 and half billion years ago, on the edge of the Milky Way galaxy, a spherical ball of molten rock found itself orbiting around a smallish, yellow sun.

This was the incipient Earth, spinning through space and covered by an expansive sea of hot, liquid rock. It was a fearsome, embryonic scene of fire and brimstone. However, as the little planet spun furiously, things started to cool down and the surface layer of liquid rock gradually solidified into hard stone; kinda like the skin that forms on warm custard.

Eventually, these sections of solid rock spread and grew together to form a hard outer crust, which surrounded the entire planet like a cocoon. Beneath the crust, however, the rock was still red-hot and molten. This vast, subterranean layer of magma still swaddles the Earth, and it is called the mantle. It extends downwards for thousands of kilometres until, at the very centre of the planet, the molten rock succumbs to the pressure and condenses into a small, solid core of the hottest stuff imaginable.

So, if you cut our planet down the middle, you will see the crust on the outside, the mantle in the middle, and the core in the centre. The crust is by far the thinnest zone of the three, roughly equivalent to the skin of an apple compared to the flesh of the fruit. The mantle is the thickest and most volatile zone. There the molten rock is under tremendous pressure, and this material regularly pushes itself up through cracks in the crust to emerge on the surface as volcanoes or lava flows. The core, at this stage, is divided into the Inner and Outer core, but its existence remains entirely theoretical as no one has actually seen the core, except for dodgy actors in cheesy sci-fi movies. And you can never trust Hollywood.

In any case, it is the crust that most interests us as a species because, on this thin membrane of jagged, brittle 'skin', humanoid forms of life entrenched themselves and proceeded to flourish. So, let's forget about the mantle and the core for a moment, and try to picture the surface of the Earth as it may have appeared billions of years ago…

THE MARCH OF LIFE

In the beginning, the Earth was not a Garden of Eden. There was no free water, no free oxygen, no oceans, no rivers, no birds, no trees; just steaming, barren ground and a petrified sea of jutting rocks. And yet, even in this relentlessly hostile environment, there was life.

The earliest fossils we have found show that single-celled organisms were present on Earth about 4 billion years ago. While this date might fly in the face of some Kentucky Fried Fundamentalists who still use the Bible as a scientific textbook, most rational thinkers now agree that the great cornucopia of life on Earth gradually grew out of these microscopic building blocks.

So, for ineffable reasons beyond our comprehension, these single-cell organisms slowly started arranging themselves into ever-more intricate forms of life. First, they developed into algae, then the algae gave rise to crustaceans, who diversified into fish, who begat amphibians, who split off into reptiles, and invertebrates, and birds, and mammals, and hominids, and so on.

All this development was sequential and incremental, taking place slowly over millions of years. Each new species of life was therefore a variation on, and departure from, those that had gone before. Later, we determined that the whole system of speciation is not random and is, instead, based on a series of natural principles which came to be summed up by pat phrases like 'survival of the fittest'. Eventually, this process was named Evolution.

A NEW WAY OF THINKING

By the late Victorian Era (around the turn of the twentieth century), common knowledge was being questioned and the status quo was under attack. Sigmund Freud's writing had opened up the Pandora's Box of a subconscious mind. Karl Marx had thrown the working-class cats amongst the Capitalist pigeons. Charles Darwin was championing a radical new scientific theory that seemed to deny the Bible. Clearly, the future wasn't what it used to be.

Unsurprisingly, all of this theoretical uncertainty sent the powers-that-were reeling against the ropes. Priests decried Darwin as a heretic, economists dismissed Marx as a pie-in-the-sky dreamer, and Freud was appropriately dismissed as delusional. But, despite all the hostility, this trinity of free-thinkers was largely responsible for dragging our planet into the modern era, even if it was kicking and screaming.

Out of the three, it was Darwin who was seen as the most egregious. A quiet but determined naturalist, Darwin had the gall to suggest that man was an evolutionary product, developed over millions of years, and had not emerged fully formed as Adam and Eve. It was a stance that outraged the solid stalwarts of European society who still believed that the Bible was the literal word of God, and that any attempt to interrogate the text was tantamount

to blasphemy. A hundred years later, Darwin's theories have won over most of his critics, but they continue to be divisive.

EVOLUTION

The Flat Earth Society notwithstanding, it is now accepted as fact that evolutionary change is a biological imperative. Evolution is a force of nature, an interactive process driven by the compulsion to survive and the adaptive response which allows us to do so in a changing environment. It's just as the great South African satirist, PW Botha, put it when describing the choice South Africans faced in the mid-1980s: 'Adapt or die'. This grim ultimatum could well be the mission statement for all life on Mother Earth.

You see, life is all about survival of the species and when the natural environment changes, life-forms must do the same if they want to endure. Therefore we can say that every living thing that we see today – trees, bugs, animals, plants and humans – is a biological adaptation to the exigencies of survival in a specific natural habitat. Or, more simply put, it's all a matter of cause and effect.

So, giraffes have tall necks because, in order to survive, they had to evolve an adaptation that would allow them eat the leaves that other grazing animals couldn't reach. Kangaroos developed those massive hind-legs so that they could leap effectively over the vast, flat plains of the Australian Outback. Predators, such as owls and lions, each developed an anatomical arsenal of specialised hunting equipment to help them catch their prey. And the relatively useless human species probably started walking upright so that we could leave the forests and traverse the grassy savanna, looking for food.

But all this evolutionary change took a long time – a very long time. In fact, it took over 4 billion years to get from single-celled organisms to the sophisticated mammals of today. This is an enormous time-span, one that cannot be easily grasped by the subjective human mind. So, to get an idea of the time-frame we are talking about here, imagine that one second equals one year. That would make each hour is equivalent to three and half millennia.

If this is our scale, then the Earth is one and a half centuries old, the first humans appeared within the last two months, the Christian era started about forty-five minutes ago and the average adult is less than a minute old. Therefore, in evolutionary terms, the cockroach is middle-aged, the coelacanth is a spring chicken, and human beings are cheeky upstarts who don't know their place.

ISOLATION TANK

But just how is a new species of life created? Why did the woolly mammoth develop into an elephant? How did the great apes give rise to the human species? And where the hell did a Duck-billed Platypus come from? In terms of evolutionary theory, it's useful to note that the most important requirement for the evolution of a new species is isolation.

Isolation occurs when members of a single breeding population get separated from one another. Once there is no longer any traffic between the groups, there can be no inter-breeding and this is the catalyst that causes one group of creatures to develop distinct new adaptations, designed to cope with the unique conditions of their distinct new habitat.

Physical boundaries (such as mountains, oceans or rivers) and environmental barriers (such as climatic zones and vegetation regions) are therefore an essential ingredient of the evolutionary process. If, for example, a population of proto-dogs was split in two by a mountain range, the pack on the cold side of the mountain might eventually grow a thicker coat than the pack on the warm side. And so it goes…

Isolation is such a prevalent evolutionary principle that it manifests itself in millions of little ways. Think about the strange lemurs of Madagascar, or the bizarre fauna of Australia, or the inimitable animals of the Galapagos Islands. All of these places have animal species which are found on a single isolated landmass, and nowhere else. In fact, it was the biological incongruity of the lizards which laze around on the Galapagos Islands that first spurred a young naturalist named Darwin to sit down and have a really good think about the origin of species.

This principle of Isolation doesn't apply only to animals; it applies to all living things. For example, in the Cape Floral Kingdom (also known as Fynbos) there are some plant species that are so rare they can be found only in a single valley. Now, it's not like these super-fussy flowers were once found all over the Cape Peninsula and have gradually shrunk back into one little protected habitat. The evolutionary truth is that these plants have evolved to suit the very specific micro-climate of their valley, with its unique combination of rainfall, sunlight, location and soil. Isolation has thus caused these plants to diverge from their floral 'cousins' and sprout into a new and distinct species that simply cannot grow anywhere else on the planet. How's that for specialisation? It's little wonder that the Cape Floral Kingdom has been declared a World Heritage Site of Natural Significance.

ROCKS AROUND THE CLOCK

The evolution of rocks is similar to the evolution of life, except that geology is an entirely reactive process whereas evolution is more pro-active. Broadly, the geological process works like this: existing rocks are exposed to the elements and worn down into smaller pieces by weathering agents, such as wind, water, ice and changes in temperature. These broken-down rock particles are then transported away from the source rock by the agents of erosion, such as water and wind.

Eventually, these bits of rock (ranging in size from specks to boulders) are dropped by the erosive forces and deposited in a new location, often at a river mouth or at the bottom of a lake or sea. Over the millennia, more and more rock particles get deposited on top of the older layers of sediment and, gradually, all these particles get cemented so tightly together that they compress to form a new layer of solid rock. This process is called sedimentation, and it generates sedimentary rock.

Since a new rock layer is formed from a mixture of particles that could have come from any number of different sources, it will probably have a different composition of minerals to any one of its source rocks. So, you could think of this as the geological equivalent of a new species. Sort of.

Additional rock 'species' can also be created by intrusions of molten rock, pushed up from the mantle into the crust. These intrusions of magma can cause a several things to happen, and are an important part of the geological process. So, if a flow of lava from the mantle reaches the Earth's surface, it will become an extrusive feature like a volcano. If, however, the lava flow remains intrusive (that is, below the ground) it will cool and solidify to form igneous rock.

These molten intrusions are usually forced up between the bedding plains of sedimentary rocks to create circular pipes, horizontal sills or vertical dykes of igneous material. The magma can also carry valuable minerals (such as

diamonds, formed in the pressure cooker of the mantle) into the upper reaches of the crust.

A third 'species' of rock is formed when the extreme temperature of a molten intrusion changes the chemical composition of any rocks that it contacts during the course of its subterranean journey. Any rock which has been changed by the heat and pressure of hot, molten rock from the mantle is called metamorphic rock.

Finally, when all the sedimentation is done and the intrusions are over, erosion or uplift could expose these 'new' layers of rock to the elements once again. And so the whole 'weathering-erosion-deposition-sedimentation-intrusion' process continues, through the ages.

As a result of all this breaking down and building up, the crust is like a huge layer-cake which has been nibbled by mice; in some places the recently applied icing is still visible on top, in other places the strawberry sponge is showing and, at certain spots, the cake has been eaten right down to the original chocolate basement.

It is this endless geological ebb and flow that has created the landscape and scenery of our planet as we know it today. This inscrutable

The hidden valley of Gamkaskloof, deep within the Swartberg Mountains

process is also responsible for depositing valuable minerals and ores under the ground. South Africa has been particularly blessed in this regard and, even though we only occupy half a percent of the world's land mass, we produce something like 50% of its strategic minerals. Now that's impressive…

THE GEOLOGICAL SEQUENCE OF SOUTHERN AFRICA

At the risk of presenting a very simple overview of a vast and complicated subject, I think that a brief discussion of the southern African geological sequence is probably useful to a contemporary traveller. After all, what's the point of admiring a mountain if you don't know what's going on inside?

GRANITE-GREENSTONE BELTS

Once upon a time, the Earth's crust was dominated by a big, hypothetical landmass made up of the oldest rocks on Earth – those that were created as the planet was first cooling down. At this stage, the Earth did not have any oceans, and there was very little free water in the atmosphere. Nevertheless, as soon as these ancient rocks had formed, they began to get worn down by the volatile climate and the howling wind. The weathering-erosion-deposition-sedimentation process had begun.

Subsequently, molten rock was pushed up into these most ancient sedimentary rock beds to form granite intrusions. This was the start of the Archean geological epoch, which lasted from three and a half to two and half billion years ago. The resulting 'granite-greenstone' belts of the Archean time period are the oldest identifiable rock systems on Earth and form the basement (or floor) for all subsequent geological activity.

Outcrops of these most senior 'granite-greenstone' belts can still be seen in the Barberton Mountain Land around Nelspruit, in the Murchison Range around Phalaborwa, and in other locations around Polokwane (Pietersburg).

THE WITWATERSRAND SUPERGROUP

After the Granite-Greenstones of the Archean Period were established, great basins began to form across the subcontinent, which slowly filled with shallow seas. By this time, water had begun to precipitate out of the sky, and many valuable minerals were washed out of the early rocks and carried into these prehistoric paddling pools. Here, the tiny particles of wealth were laid down along with bits of weathered rock to form pebbly conglomerates and, when the whole mixture had set, the result was a layer of sedimentary rock which contained the richest goldfields in the world. This sequence of rocks is called the Witwatersrand Supergroup.

THE VENTERSDORP & TRANSVAAL SUPERGROUPS

After our golden bounty was embedded in the Earth, there was a stormy period of intense volcanic activity, where thousands of broad lava flows covered the land. This was the foundation of the Ventersdorp Supergroup, which covered many of the older Witwatersrand rocks.

Between 2,6 and 2,2 billion years ago, the Ventersdorp lavas were again inundated by an inland sea and a new layer of sedimentary rock was deposited, called the Transvaal Supergroup. This section of the crust is notable for its well-preserved, dome-shaped stromatolites (petrified colonies of ancient algae, a very early form of life) and its caves, which were formed many years later when groundwater percolated through the Malmani dolomites in the upper part of the group

These caves, such as Taung, Makapansgat and Sterkfontein, subsequently became repositories for the bones of our early hominid ancestors and this 'Cradle of Humankind' has been declared a World Heritage Site. Harbouring evolutionary icons such as Mrs Ples, Little Foot and the Taung Child, they have yielded many important fossil finds into the hands of scientists such as Robert Broom, Ron Clarke and Raymond Dart. Taken together, the archaeological evidence gathered in these caves has confirmed

South Africa as one of the world's pre-eminent sites of early human development.

THE BUSHVELD COMPLEX & THE VREDEFORT DOME

After the Transvaal Supergroup came the Bushveld Complex, formed when a huge amount of molten rock was pushed from the Mantle into the upper reaches of the Transvaal Supergroup. This injection of rock into the easily-eroded sediments of the Transvaal Supergroup formed a layered igneous rock complex that covers an area of 60 000km², making it the largest in the world. The Bushveld Complex also just happens to contain 80% of the world's platinum. Yay for us!

But it wasn't all fun and games. About 2 billion years ago, a major meteorite slammed into the ground about 120km south-west of Joburg. The result is the Vredefort Dome, the earliest-known meteorite-impact site on Earth and the largest impact structure anywhere on the planet. A geologist's wet dream, the Vredefort Dome measures about 250km in diameter, and it has recently been declared South Africa's seventh World Heritage Site.

THE WATERBERG 'RED BEDS' & THE BUSHMANLAND GROUP

1,8 billion years ago, the Waterberg sediments were deposited over the older rocks of the Bushveld complex. The important thing about the Waterberg rocks is that they have a reddish colour due to the presence of iron oxides. This was the first indication that significant amounts of free oxygen were becoming present in our atmosphere. Rocks of a similar age and colour are found all over the world, and are collectively referred to as 'Red Beds'.

Then, things grew quiet for a couple of million years. Southern Africa was taking a breather. Nevertheless, there were a couple of geological highlights. The Pilanesberg volcanic complex (reportedly the largest alkaline volcano crater in the world) was formed near Sun City. Crustal instability in the south-western Cape was busy warping the rock strata. Oh, and let's not forget the intrusion of the diamond pipes at Cullinan, east of Pretoria.

Next up were the rocks of the Bushmanland Group. These were laid down about 1,5 billion years ago in a belt that stretched from Namaqualand to southern KZN. They contained deposits of zinc, lead and copper, and were metamorphosed by various volcanic intrusions. Although much of this 'metamorphic province' was subsequently covered by younger rocks, some of it is still visible (if much eroded) as the rolling, granitic landscape of The Valley of 1 000 Hills, near Durban.

THE CAPE SUPERGROUP

The Cape Supergroup was the next to form. Its base is the Malmesbury Group of sedimentary rocks, which formed about 600 million years ago in a chain of shallow basins along the south-west coast. 50 million years later, these sediments were intruded by the Cape Granites. Then, thousands of years after that, the partially eroded Cape Granites were covered by a series of shales and sandstones. This whole mess was subsequently crumpled and bent into the epic, twisted beauty of the Cape Fold Mountains.

As a final flourish, the uppermost layer of the Cape Supergroup was the Table Mountain Group, a cap of silver-grey sandstone made famous by the eponymous mountain and neighbouring cliffs of the Cape Peninsula.

Shortly after the formation of the Cape Supergroup (500 million years ago), crustaceans started to appear on the fossil record. They were followed by the first evidence of coral reefs and land plants, then by shells and fish skeletons. The first reptiles appeared about 300 million years ago.

THE KAROO SUPERGROUP

At the same time that the reptiles were creeping out into the evolutionary sunshine, the Karoo Supergroup started forming. It would eventually cover two thirds of South Africa, and representative Karoo rocks can be found in most sub-Saharan countries. They can also be found in South America, Antarctica, India and Australia. The Karoo Supergroup covered a turbulent time in the planet's history and deserves to be described in a bit of detail.

The lowest layer of the Karoo Supergroup is called Dwyka Tillite. Tillite is the motley collection of debris that is left behind when a glacier melts. This means that South Africa was once covered in thick glaciers and as cold as Scotland on a winter's day. These ice-sheets were formed while the continent was slowly migrating across the South Pole [see note on Gondwanaland, below].

Once the sub-continent entered more temperate climes, the glaciers melted and created a large, composite swamp over much of southern Africa. The rich organic life that flourished in these swamps and marshes would eventually consolidate into the substantial coal fields of the Ecca Group.

As the climate dried things out even further, the Beaufort Group was deposited on the river flood plains. This layer is rich in fossils from the animals that roamed the fertile landscape of the Permian Age. These included strange, 'mammal-like' reptiles, which were initially investigated by Andrew Geddes Bain (see chapter 8) and are sometimes thought of as the first dinosaurs.

On top of the Beaufort Group came the Clarens Sandstones. This is a beautifully roseate layer of rock, prone to spectacular erosion and wont to form graceful, curving overhangs and rounded bulges. This rock layer is most definitively observed in the Golden Gate National Park, near the town of Clarens, in the eastern Free State.

The Karoo Supergroup succession came to an end with a bang – or rather an eruption – of cataclysmic proportions. But before we talk about that, we must have a quick chat about Tectonic Plates.

WELCOME TO GONDWANALAND

In 1885, an Austrian geologist looked at the geological sequence and noticed that a specific sequence of rocks were common to Africa, South America, India and Australia. He then noticed that the fossil fern, *Glossopteris*, was also present on all these southern continents, but not in the north. Finally, he noticed that the scouring marks left behind by ice-sheets seemed to be contiguous across the same group of landmasses. This gave rise to one of the most audacious (and potentially ludicrous) scientific theories of recent time; second only to the absurd idea that man came from monkeys.

Briefly, it was theorised that these four continents (India, Australia, South America and Africa) were once all joined together in a huge landmass. This über-continent, it was then surmised, split up into the continents as we know them today.

This division wasn't imagined as a sudden, explosive action, but rather as a slow tearing-apart, in which the continents cut their terrestrial ties and started drifting away from each other. Appropriately enough, the geologist who thought up this fanciful idea was named Eduard Suess (not a doctor).

Suess called his proposed super-continent Gondwanaland, which kinda sounds like a prehistoric theme park. But don't laugh. The naming of Gondwanaland was the start of a startling scientific proposition which would significantly change the way we think about our planet.

Predictably, the initial reactions of his peers were cynical and Suess' theory was dismissed as preposterous. Subsequent researchers, however, weren't daunted. They picked up on his concepts and proceeded to prove that Suess was substantially right.

First, Alfred Wegener expanded the basic premise to include the Northern Hemisphere continents. He did this by proposing the existence of a single, great landmass, called Pangea. This idea was then further refined into two mega-continents, one called Laurasia (in the North) and the other called Gondwana (in the South). Later, exploration of the South Pole made it clear that Antarctica was also part of Gondwana, and this piece was added to the puzzle. A coherent picture was forming. But the question still remained: why did these two super-continents start breaking up late in the Triassic, 240 million years ago, just as the large dinosaurs were starting to appear?

It was a good question, and one that wasn't easy to answer. Eventually, however, geo-scientists made an important discovery that shed some light on the matter: the Earth's crust is not a single, continuous sphere that encircles the mantle like the skin of an orange. Rather, the crust is broken up into a series of distinct, interlocking plates that drift very slowly over the molten layer beneath, like a bunch of lily pads floating across the surface of a pond.

To give you a rough idea of just how much the Earth moves under your feet, consider that every year the cities of London and New York find themselves 1 cm further apart. This is a result of constant tectonic movement in mid-Atlantic.

The movements of these massive Tectonic Plates are usually imperceptible to humans, but the forces they generate are enormous. The boundaries where the plates meet are places of movement and mayhem, and plate tectonics are associated with earthquakes, orogeny (mountain building) and volcanoes.

For example, when the plates slide past each other, they might cause earthquakes like those experienced along the San Andreas fault line. When they move towards each other, they irrevocably collide, creating mountains like the Himalayas. When they move apart, they might create a line of volcanoes 1000km long, like the Pacific Ring of Fire. And when one plate is pushed under another plate, the subsiding rock melts and is re-incorporated into the mantle, thus equalising the whole, dynamic system.

This theory of 'Tectonic Plate Movement' finally explained the tearing-apart of Gondwanaland and the current distribution of the continents.

THE FORMATION OF THE DRAKENSBERG

It is estimated that Gondwana split apart between 250 and 200 million years ago, just as the last of the Clarens Sandstone suite of rocks was being laid down. As the super-continent broke up, however, the awesome power of the planet became manifest, and a wide flood of volcanic basalt boiled up from the mantle and swept across the land. When this molten basalt had cooled, the Karoo Supergroup found itself riddled with subterranean intrusions, and much of southern Africa was covered by a layer of solid rock up to 1 400 metres deep.

Inevitably, erosion started eating away at this vast swathe of flood-basalt almost as soon as it started to cool. Water ran off the summits and formed rivers, which cut steep valleys into the rock. Wind whipped at the stone and carried away the smallest fragments, piece by piece. Most importantly, changes in temperature made the rock fault and crack, and this caused large boulders to dislodge and tumble down the mountain slopes, resting at the bottom until they were picked to pieces by the eternal forces of wind and water. The Victoria Falls in northern Zimbabwe is just one of the many natural water features that cut through this flood-basalt and carried away the pieces.

Today, the sheer walls of the Drakensberg, the Lubombo Mountains in Swaziland and the Lesotho Highlands are the only mountainous remnants of this great volcanic flood. And, one day, they too will be gone. Even the mighty Natal Drakensberg is currently retreating at the stately pace of 1 cm every decade. John Keats was right; all beauty is transient.

FROM DINOSAURS TO MODERN MAN

After the formation of the Drakensberg, things settled down for a bit of consolidation. Around 200 million years ago, the seas started pooling into great oceans and the large dinosaurs became dominant. This was the Spielbergian period (formerly known as the Jurassic).

Mammals and flowering plants began to appear in the Cretaceous period (150 million years ago) and, in the late Cretaceous (100 million years ago), a few more diamond pipes were pushed up from the mantle. This occurred most notably at Kimberley, adding some more sparkle to our already lustrous mineral inventory.

The dinosaurs died out in the Palaeoscene (about 65 million years ago), probably as a result of a colossal meteorite impact event and the concomitant change in the Earth's climate. It was now time for the warm-blooded mammals to take centre stage.

Mammals proceded to rule the Earth until 5 or 6 million years ago, give or take. Then one particular mammal started gaining the ascendancy, as modern humans took their first shuffling steps into the light. Things would never the be same again.

In the meantime, new rock layers such as the Kalahari Group, coastal sediments, sandy beaches and river terraces were constantly forming, while older formations were wearing away. The level of the sea also fluctuated by more than 100 metres, and this constantly changed the appearance of our coastline.

And so, 4.5 billion years after the Big Bang, here we are. The landscape is familiar, the animals are well known (if a little bit endangered) and modern man stands proud and Pyrrhic, king of the Earth's crust.

But do not assume, just because we have arrived at our current, post-modern mentality, that the ancient processes of evolution and erosion have ceased. Quite the opposite. The forces of nature are ever-present, and the very land on which we walk is in a constant state of infinitesimal flux. Our activities can even speed up these inscrutable processes, as over-grazing leads to devastating erosion and human demands on the land drive unfortunate species into premature extinction.

Lichen splashes the rocks of the Garden Route with colour

A busker at the Cape Minstrel Carnival

2. Meet the locals

EARLY HUMANS

It is well established that South Africa has some of the most important early human fossil sites in the world. In fact, it is surmised from the fossil evidence of southern and East Africa (gathered in important sites such as the Sterkfontein Caves near Joburg, Taung in the North-West and Olduvai Gorge in Tanzania) that the human experience actually started on the Dark Continent some time between 5 and 7 million years ago, perhaps even earlier.

Unfortunately, the full scope of the human evolutionary saga is too vast to consider here, and new archaeological discoveries are constantly forcing us to revise our family tree. So, suffice it to say that the old 'relay race' theory, whereby each species of hominid smoothly passed the evolutionary baton onto the next generation, is no longer valid. It is now agreed that several different species of early humans shared the planet at any given time, muddying the waters of our genealogical heritage. All of this means that modern *Homo sapiens* must now ask themselves the eternal question, "Who's your daddy?"

Nevertheless, as palaeo-anthropologists slowly sift through the fossilised detritus of millennia trying to piece together the past, this is the story so far...

Between 7 and 5 million years ago, our earliest precursors and the great apes are presumed to have split off from a common ancestor. One stream subsequently became chimpanzees, our closest genetic relations, who share 98% of our DNA. Another stream became bi-pedal, which means they left the trees and started walking on two legs. Why we came down from the trees is difficult to determine. The thick, sub-tropical forests of Africa may have thinned out into grassy plains, or some other physical imperative may have forced a speciation event. Maybe it was just boredom, an early manifestation of the lingering dissatisfaction that seems to be a defining characteristic of our restless species. Perhaps even the proto-humanoid wanted to move to a better neighbourhood.

Despite some recent and inconclusive finds of very early proto-hominids (with unpronounceable names like *Sahelanthropus tchadensis*, *Orrorin tugenensis* and *Ardipithecus ramidus*), the first concrete archaeological evidence of a clearly human-like line surfaces in East Africa, between 3 and 4 million years ago. Most famously embodied by the discovery of 'Lucy' in 1973, these primitive primates are little more than bipedal scavengers, called *Australopithecus afarensis* (Southern Ape from Afar). Standing a little over a metre high, these fragile creatures were very probably the hunted, not the hunters.

Then, about 3 million years ago, specimens of *Australopithecus* turn up in southern Africa. They are slightly smaller and more delicate than their cousins in the north, and are called *Australopithecus africanus*. The Taung Child, Mrs Ples and the recently discovered Little Foot are the best-known representatives of this group. At roughly the same time, there was another species of early human on the scene. They were a thick-set bunch of critters, with flat faces and massive jaws for grinding nuts. Their friends know them as *Paranthropus* (or *Australopithecus*) *robustus*, and they are also found in East Africa under the family name, *Boisei*. These 'nutcracker' people lived for about 1 million years (not a bad evolutionary innings) and then abruptly disappear from the fossil record.

The archaeological evidence also shows that a third rudimentary human species was running around from about 2,5 million years ago: the *Homos*. The specifics of the *Homo* family tree are very difficult to discern, and it is not clear whether we descended from *Australopithecus* or whether we were always a distinct species. The controversy doesn't end there, as the various branches of the genus *Homo* are confusing and often speculative, but the broad progression goes like this: *Homo habilis*, *Homo erectus* and *Homo sapiens*.

Homo habilis (Handy man) was first identified by Louis and Mary Leakey from fossils found around Olduvai Gorge in Tanzania in 1960. This new species was distinct because they had started using stone tools (called the Olduwan Industry) to help with their daily activities. This was the start of the Early Stone Age, and *Homo habilis* may be our earliest direct ancestors. But very little is known about them and they are sometimes dismissively called a garbage-can species, made up of specimens that don't belong to any other category.

Around 2 million years ago, the first unquestionably human creatures start to appear. They are called *Homo erectus* (Upright man). Yes, after generations of nagging from their mothers, human beings were finally standing up straight. With bigger brains and an improved posture, *H erectus* were a very successful adaptation indeed, lasting for more than 1,5 million years and colonising the expanse of the Old World from Africa to Asia. For hundreds of thousands of years, the humble Mr and Mrs *H erectus* had their hands full; forming themselves into communities, hiding from hungry predators and mastering the intricacies of language, hunting, fire and stone-tool making (called the Acheulian Industry).

Then, about 200 000 years ago, the Middle Stone Age began with the appearance of *Homo sapiens* (Wise or Thinking Man). Once again, our anatomy had re-aligned itself, our tools had become infinitely more sophisticated and our diets were more expansive (including brain food like fish). For the next couple of hundred thousand years, *H sapiens* continued to develop

and faced down other *Homo* competitors such as the Neanderthals, until they finally became the last men (and women) standing. To emphasise this pinnacle of genetic refinement, it was once determined that our species should be re-classified *Homo sapiens sapiens* – so good, they named it twice. But this little nomenclaturial stammer has since been dropped.

The Middle Stone Age became the Late Stone Age around 35 000 years ago, about the same time that the Bushmen were starting to emerge as a recognisable culture in Southern Africa. These Late Stone Age people were no dummies: they used tools made of stone, bone and wood, they buried their dead, they painted on rocks, personal ornamentation was popular, and plant material was being used to make rope, nets and string. Bows and arrows became current about 10 000 years ago, as did agriculture.

Then, just to complete the picture, the Bronze Age began in the Middle East around 6 500 years ago, and the Iron Age started in the same region about 3000 years ago. I'm not sure what Age we're in now. I've heard it called the Information Age. But if that were true, we should all be much smarter...

Like their *H erectus* ancestors, *H sapiens* also had a plentiful supply of *wanderlust*. The 'Out-of-Africa' theory suggests that modern humans (who originated in southern Africa) started to spread north towards Europe sometimes after 100 000 BP (Before the Present). The reasons for this move are uncertain but, by 60 000 BP, they were spread across Europe and Asia. Around 25 000 BP, it is proposed that our intrepid ancestors crossed the Bering Straights from Russia into North America, walking on a land bridge that had been exposed by a recent ice-age. Finally, by 11 000 BP, we had reached Patagonia on the shores of Central South America.

Thus, in a relatively short time, anatomically modern humans had colonised the planet. And we've never looked back.

But we were not left unchanged by our extended migration. As the population of modern man multiplied and drifted apart, the ever-present laws of evolution and isolation began to assert themselves. Different types of *Homo sapiens* began to emerge in different parts of the world; each one exhibiting slight variations in their physical appearance, depending on their native environment.

Thus, we have the black man of Africa, the white man of Europe, the almond-eyed oriental and the 'Red-skin' of the Native Americans (who share their high cheekbones with distant Mongol cousins in Asia). Just like our animal counterparts, each one of these racial 'breeds' boasts special adaptations to equip them for life in their specific habitats.

This, in my view, means that our racial characteristics were formed as an evolutionary response to our ancestral breeding grounds. It makes sense when you think about it. It's surely no coincidence that humans who lived in the hot plains of Africa had dark skins full of melanin to stave off skin cancer and thick tufts of hair to keep the pounding sun off their scalps, while those who lived in the cold, snowy regions of Europe developed pale skins to let in all the sun and thin, hollow hair for insulation.

Yet, despite all the historical evidence to the contrary, these 'racial' groups do not represent two different species of human being. Whether you like it or not, we are all still *Homo sapiens*, each with the same biological fundamentals, requirements and characteristics. It's just that the packaging is different, like a cell phone with changeable covers.

In any case, the stage was now set. *Homo sapiens* had spread across the fertile Earth. Each group had developed physical, emotional and cultural traits of their own. Individual and communal identities were entrenched. And it seems that as soon as modern man reached the shores of Patagonia, 15 000 years ago, the world started getting smaller. It would only be a matter of time before there was a major clash of personalities.

THE BUSHMEN

Back in South Africa, the story of modern human beings starts with the Bushmen.

As far as we can tell, the Bushmen have been here for the last 25 000 years and probably even longer. They are the oldest identifiable human culture on the planet and, consequently, also one of the most abused. But, at first, the Bushmen were part of a perfectly balanced world.

In the beginning, there were no other humans in the land. There were only the wild plants, the wild animals and the small, dark Bushmen who hunted and gathered for their food. With no political borders to inhibit their freedom, and no other humans with which to compete, the Bushmen of old lived a life of gentle transhumanance; free to move with the great herds of game that roamed the plains of Southern Africa.

So, unencumbered by possessions, the Bushmen followed the migrations of buck from summer grazing near the sea, to winter pastures around the Drakensberg. Today, we can still see the evidence of their habitation, painted like a movie on the sandstone caves and overhangs of the Berg. Glorious hunting scenes, ecstatic dances and transcendental visions of strange creatures, half-man and half-antelope, can still be glimpsed in various stages of preservation. But the Mountain Bushmen themselves are long gone.

Still, for more than twenty thousand years, the Bushmen were a pristine example of the Late Stone Age human experience. They did not sow seed or build cities. They did not keep flocks or make war. Instead, the Bushmen lived simply as a part of their natural environment, adapting to the seasons and co-operating with the land. Their survival was based on maintaining a sustainable population, organised into small family groups, which hunted the great herds of game and gathered the edible plants proffered by the rich soil.

In many ways, the Bushmen were the poster-child for the recently rediscovered ideal of sustainable development; the only real example we've ever had of a people living in harmony with nature, instead of trying to conquer it. Even today, the remaining Bushmen try to live as a part of the natural process. They never claim too much for themselves, or behave as if they are more special than the other creatures around them.

But there's a paradox here. Modern Bushmen tribes are strongly characterised by the thirsty Kalahari and its sparse beauty. However, the desert isn't exactly the first place you would look for majestic hordes of game sweeping across the plains, or for fecund soil that will spontaneously sprout edible plants every season. Why, when you think about it, would the oldest human culture on the planet want to take root in a dry and dusty desert?

The truth of the matter is they didn't. While Bushmen have been living in the desert for thousands of years, carefully adapting to and learning from this challenging environment, the desert was never their heartland. Instead, the Bushmen of old lived in great contentment along the lush eastern coast of South Africa, and up on the great grasslands of the plateau.

So, why did they move? The sad truth of the matter is that, over the years, successive waves of land-hungry immigrants systematically wiped out the Bushmen. Specifically, it was the arrival of Khoikhoi, Bantu and European interlopers that slowly displaced the Bushmen from their homes around the Drakensberg, and those Bushmen who survived the increasingly ferocious onslaught did so only to be hounded up over the Escarpment, across the veld and out into the Kalahari to join their desert brethren. Here, the Bushmen nation was cast out and abandoned, left to survive as best they could on land that no one else wanted.

So, you could say that southern Africa's people of first origin are also southern Africa's people of first dispossession – the oldest landless people on Earth. But why were they chased away so vehemently, and why did the campaign against the Bushmen take on overtones of what we now call 'ethnic cleansing'?

The reason why everyone hated the Bushmen is because these plucky little Earth-warriors instinctively and violently resisted any attempt to usurp their traditional lands and lifestyle. They especially resented the narrow-minded arrogance of the white settlers, who took it as their right to waltz through the countryside with their hungry cows, taking over choice grazing land wherever they saw it. The first recorded attack by Bushmen on a white cattle farmer took place as early as 1701, only fifty years after the Dutch had landed at the Cape.

Although the Bushmen often outnumbered their pastoralist foes, they did not have the miraculous firepower of the Boers or the physical stamina of the Bantu. So, the Bushmen fought the enemy in the only way they could; by stealing away their cattle and burning down their farms. This was akin to kicking a man where it hurts the most but, instead of backing off, the Bushmen's acts of defiance only made their enemies more ruthless.

Thus, by the late 1700s, the gloves were well and truly off and the white colonists were enmeshed in a vicious struggle with the Bushmen holed up in the Sneeuberg mountains around Graaff-Reinet. The Bushmen in this region had been living there for centuries and refused to be pushed out by the invasive Trekboers. The Trekboers, in turn, refused to be turned back by a bunch of primitive little yellow men, but the Bushman attacks were devastating the new farms and settlements of the region. Something had to be done. The white man's solution was to turn genocidal.

This final solution to the Bushman problem was happily sanctioned by government, and regular commandos were organised to carry out the job. These bands of armed men rode out on horseback with the express purpose of exterminating any troublesome 'vermin' in the region, and the success of each sortie was measured by the body count. The Bushmen, for their part, would rather die than surrender, and proceeded to perish in great numbers before the bullets of the Boers. After several years of this ferocious policy, the Sneeuberg Bushmen were no more.

This battle for land then continued up the coast, as the Afrikaners entered Natal and the Zulu became increasingly territorial. The Bushmen were destined to bear the brunt of this escalating conflict and were, once again, dismissed by both sides as inveterate cattle thieves and worthless rascals. Thus, in several short decades, the mighty white Boers and the powerful Zulu pastoralists inadvertently combined forces to exterminate the immemorial Bushmen and, by the late 1800s, the Bushmen were gone from their stronghold in the Drakensberg too.

As a result of this wanton slaughter, much of the ancient Bushman lore has been lost. Today, the old recipes for their eternal paint pigments,

ancient ethnological beliefs, customs, language and lifestyle are all but unknowable. This needless waste is summed up in one saddening, maddening story of a lone, elderly Bushman who was shot dead in the foothills of the Drakensberg, late in the 1800s. When the killers recovered his body, they saw that the old man was wearing a leather belt, fashioned to hold small pots of pigment and a reed stylus. One of the last traditional Bushmen rock painters was gone forever.

So, how do we know anything about Bushman culture at all? Well, luckily, some Bushmen tribes have survived and maintained their traditional culture throughout much of the twentieth century. For decades, these isolated desert groups have been besieged by researchers and anthropologists intent on documenting every aspect of their lives; trying to study,

A Bushman by any other name

The semi-nomadic Khoikhoi thought very highly of their herds of cattle. In fact, they thought so much of their flocking prosperity that they named themselves 'Khoikhoi', a plural form meaning 'men of men'. By comparison, they named the herd-less Bushmen 'Sonqua', or 'Sanqua'.

The suffix 'qua' means 'people', but the meaning of 'San' is a little more obscure. Some say it means 'bush'; some say it means 'native' or 'aboriginal'; others say it is the plural form of 'forager'. In any case, the term 'Sonqua' was probably not meant as a compliment, and certain researchers broadly interpret the name as meaning 'men with nothing' or 'men-without', as compared to the confident re-iteration of 'Khoikhoi'.

The Bushmen, for their part, never had need to distinguish themselves from another tribe, and didn't seem to have a name for themselves with which to counter the derisive handle. Then, when the Bantu-speaking tribes moved into South Africa about 1000 years ago, they added another label to the linguistic confusion by calling the little people they encountered 'Twa' or 'Sarwa'.

Centuries later, the Europeans came along and gave everyone new names. The Sanqua were called the 'Bosjemans' or 'Bushmen'. The Khoikhoi were lumbered with the inflammatory name of 'Hottentot'; a term apparently derived as a mocking imitation of the Khoikhoi's peculiar, clicking language. The black tribes came to be lumped together under the hateful banner, 'kaffir' (which is Arabic for 'infidel' or 'unbeliever'). And the white men presumably named themselves, 'Master'.

As the influence of the white people ascended, the power of the black people waned, and whitey's lexicon of contempt became entrenched. So, with the eventual demise of the Khoikhoi as a distinct cultural group, the term 'Sonqua' went out of common use. That is, until it was resuscitated in the abbreviated form 'San' by earnest revisionists, eager to lift the academic idiom out of the colonial gutter. The term 'Khoi-San' was thus coined to collectively refer to the Khoikhoi and the Bushmen.

However, since the moniker 'San' is probably a condescending insult and the older, colonial term is actually quite accurate, I'm going to stick to the more flagrant nomenclature of 'Bushman' and political sensitivities be damned!

analyse and extrapolate the life of the Bushmen into a larger understanding of Late Stone Age people around the world.

This movement to lionise the Bushmen has been gaining ground ever since Sir Lourens van der Post wrote his revelatory narratives *The Lost World of the Kalahari* and *The Heart of the Hunter* in the late 1950s. But, for all the photographs, words and interviews that have appeared over the years, we have still only gained a vague insight into the complex mind of the Bushmen. One can't help but feel that we remain on the outside, looking in.

To add to our lack of certainty, very few documents were written about the Bushmen before the twentieth century took hold of the planet and changed things forever. In fact, we only have a single, reliable ethnographic document, which was transcribed verbatim from authentic Bushmen by sympathetic researchers, that predates the 1900s. This substantial volume lays out some basic facts about the Bushman's world and language, and it forms the cornerstone of our modern understanding of Bushman culture. Ironically, this invaluable text came to exist only because of a war!

In the early 1870s, the Koranna Wars were raging up in the northern Karoo. The Koranna were a mixed-blood tribe, made up of Tswana and Griqua, but the local Bushmen were inevitably caught up in the conflict too. As a result, several /Xam bushmen were taken prisoner by the British and sent to the Breakwater Prison in Cape Town. Here, they met the Prussian linguist, Dr Wilhelm Bleek, and his sister-in-law, Lucy Lloyd.

Bleek and Lloyd were fascinated by the archaic culture and strange language exhibited by these prehistoric people and, over the months that followed, they conducted extensive interviews with the prisoners. The data recorded by Bleek and Lloyd is now in the collection of the South African Museum.

Nowadays, the few remaining Bushmen are still living in the desert, clustered in small communities scattered across South Africa,

The Click Song

Ironically, the Bushmen left behind an important legacy to the indigenous populations who supplanted them – tongue clicks. When you listen to a Bushman speak his own language, it pops and sputters like the logs burning in the campfire. The Khoikhoi and Nguni people both picked up these linguistic trademarks, and incorporated the old Bushmen clicks into their new Ntu dialects.

For lazy Western tongues, the three pre-dominant click-sounds used today seem outlandish and difficult, but they are actually quite easy to master with a bit of practise. The clicks are also an integral part of the native pronunciation, and should be at least attempted by anyone wishing to read, speak or write about the native populations of South Africa.

Briefly then, the letter 'Q' is pronounced as a loud pop, made by flicking the tip of your tongue from your palette, down to your lower jaw. It has the daunting technical name of an 'Alveolar-palatal click'.

The letter 'X' is a hard 'tsk' noise made with the side of your tongue, like when you're calling a horse. It is also called a 'lateral click'.

The letter 'C' is a softer 'tsk', made with the front of your tongue, like the 'tsk, tsk,tsk' noise you make instead of saying 'Shame'. It is called a 'dental click'.

Contrary to popular belief, this vocal ability is not granted to black children at birth, along with a sense of rhythm. It is learnt behaviour, practised in school by classes of young learners who have to enunciate 'Xa', 'Xe', 'Xi', 'Xo', 'Xu' over and over again, like Latin students learning how to conjugate verbs. Eager to be more credible as an African, I now practice the same drill while driving in my car, and it is becoming more familiar to me. But I still have to concentrate every time I say 'Xhosa'.

Namibia, Botswana and Angola. For years, their needs have been ignored by governments, and their ancient way of life is about to disappear under the pervasive homogenisation of our modern age. But what can we do to stop this cultural extinction? Do we shrug and let the Bushmen wither away in front of our eyes? Do we declare them an 'endangered human species' and put them in a cultural zoo with a captive breeding programme? Do we stick them all in cultural villages and condemn them to a life of enforced antiquity? Or do we take account of their political autonomy and allow them to integrate into the modern world as they see fit?

I don't have an answer to this thorny sociological dilemma. But I do know that the death of the Bushman lineage after 30 000 years of uninterrupted existence is a terrible thing to contemplate. What is clear is that the time has come to collaborate with the extant Bushmen communities and to help them from becoming reluctant martyrs to progress.

THE KHOIKHOI

After the Bushmen came the Khoikhoi (also called Khoekhoe, Khoenkhoen or Koina). They were close cousins of the Bushmen, but had started keeping flocks of cattle and sheep. This early form of stock farming was picked up from the Cushitic cultures of Arabia, who were tentatively trading along the East African Coast in the time before the Christian Era.

Then, about 2000 years ago, these Khoikhoi people took their herds and moved south from northern Botswana into South Africa. They passed through the Bushman's realm without stopping, and headed on into the south and west. Here they chose to settle, spreading out along the southern Cape coast from East London to Cape Town, as well as in Namaqualand – a region still named after the Nama clan of the Khoikhoi.

Cattle and sheep were very important to the Khoikhoi. Their flocks gave them stability, status and security. More fundamentally, a regular supply of meat and milk greatly reduced all that inconvenient hunting and gathering, and it certainly added fuel to their physicality. For the Khoikhoi, cows became a form of currency with legs.

The Bushmen, for their part, didn't really mind the implied criticism. They may have got a little annoyed when the Khoikhoi herds got in the way of their traditional hunting routes and the Khoikhoi, in turn, might have been miffed when the Bushmen got in the way of their cows. But there was still plenty of land to go around and, by some kind of tacit agreement, the Bushmen focused their attention on the Natal side of the country while the Khoikhoi gravitated towards the Cape.

Once they had settled down, the Khoikhoi organised themselves into an extended clan structure, headed by chieftains. There were the Cochoqua and Guriqua in the near-north, the Chainouqua, Hessequa, Gouriqua, Attaqua and Houteniqua in the east, the Namaqua in the far-north, and the Goringhaiqua, Gorachouqua and Goringhaikona around the Cape Peninsula.

By all accounts, these different tribal groups spent many happy centuries tending their herds and extending their families, with only the occasional feud between the chiefs to keep things exciting. But the Khoikhoi's fate was not to be a happy one. They were the people destined to endure the first convulsive meetings with the Europeans who had started landing at the Cape from 1500 onwards. They were also the first indigenous nation to allow the yoke of white supremacy to be placed around their necks.

Almost from the first, the Europeans viewed the 'Hottentots' with ill-concealed disgust. The whites didn't approve of the Khoikhoi's facial features, their temperament, their dangling anatomy, their lack of clothing or their perceived dishonesty. They found the Khoikhoi habit of smearing rancid animal fat all over their bodies particularly abhorrent (despite the quite logical explanation that the stinking grease helped ward off fleas), and the Dutch were often tempted to shoot the whole bloody lot of them and be done with it.

On the other side of the fence, the Khoikhoi thought the white men were foolish, foppish and arrogant. They hated the way the Europeans swanned around the Cape like they owned the place, and resented the 'cultivated' European attitude that held the Khoikhoi up as nothing more than filthy, Godless savages. Most of all, they were afraid that the Europeans would steal their land, plunder their herds and chase the Khoikhoi away from their homes. It sounds like the Khoikhoi were pretty good judges of character.

So, predictably, the Europeans and the Khoikhoi did not get on. It was a volatile mixture of personalities that was bound to explode, sooner or later. And so it was, only a few decades after first meeting the white man, that incipient Khoikhoi nationalism resulted in several inglorious battles between the Dutch and the Khoikhoi. In the late 1600s and early 1700s, this popular wave of resistance gathered momentum, as the Khoikhoi became increasingly angry about the ever-more emphatic control exerted by the illegitimate colonial authorities at the Cape.

But it all started to come undone when the smallpox epidemic of 1713 decimated the Khoikhoi nation and destroyed their traditional family structures. By the late 1700s, the Khoikhoi had been wholly suppressed by force, disease and liquor, and they were doomed to become the white man's servant; gradually assimilating into the fabric of South African society and finally trickling away into cultural extinction.

THE BANTU

In pre-historic southern Africa, all was well with the world. The Bushmen and the Khoikhoi were living together in relative peace and quiet, game was abundant and life was sweet. But there was trouble brewing in the north. The Bantu were coming, and they were bringing the Iron Age with them.

The origins of the Bantu-speaking people are cloudy; hidden in the inarticulate depths of verbal prehistory. The current received opinion is that the Bantu originated in the jungles of West Africa, somewhere in the Cameroon region. Then, about 4 000 years ago, they started to migrate from their homeland, moving South and East in two great waves that washed against both shores of the continent and drifted back to meet in the middle.

Why the Bantu started moving is uncertain. It has been suggested that something, like a minute twitch in the Earth's axis, caused the climate to change and resulted in the desertification of the Sahara. This would have pushed people away from the region, stimulating the civilisations of the Middle East and fostering new ones in Sub-Saharan Africa. Or, maybe the exodus was sparked by political upheaval or population pressure. In any event, the Bantu diaspora had begun, and tens of thousands of people were on the move. The first wave of Bantu settlers eventually reached Southern Africa around 1 000 years ago.

As the long trail of Bantu emigrants fanned out from their homeland in search of greener pastures, they picked up the cattle culture and iron smelting techniques of the Cushitic people who were already plying the trade routes between Arabia and East Africa. The Bantu went on to spread this new technology wherever they went, and thus came the Iron Age to Africa.

The Bantu Language

The word 'Bantu' literally means 'people'. In the old days, the term was used by the South African government as a vague, racial epithet; a polite shorthand for 'darkie'. But this is a misnomer. 'Bantu' is actually a linguistic description, indicating a broad, common language group (called 'Ntu' by modern linguists). Many modern-day languages, found right across the African continent, have grown out of these ancient Ntu root words. Old-school South Africans are just going to have to get used to the fact that 'Bantu' is a legitimate linguistic classification, like Celt, Goth or Slav. So get over it!

NGUNI AND SOTHO

By 1000 BP (Before the Present), the Bantu had spread out across the breadth of Sub-Saharan Africa and established themselves as dozens of different tribes, each with their own dialect based on the broader Ntu language. The Southern Bantu stream that had finally reached South Africa subsequently split into two linguistic groups: the Nguni and the Sotho.

The Nguni-speakers became the Zulu, Xhosa, Ndebele and Swazi. The Sotho can be divided into the North Sotho tribes of the Tswana and the Pedi (led off by Chief Bagatla), and the South Sotho nation of the Basotho. The other tribal groups found in South Africa, such as the Tsonga/Shangaan and the Venda, have a different lineage, language and history to the Sotho and Nguni people.

The Sotho and Nguni cultures are similar, but distinct. The Sotho tribes tended to settle on the high grasslands of the interior, living in large towns of over a thousand people. The Nguni, meanwhile, preferred living in scattered villages along the coastal shelf, from Kosi Bay (on the border with Mozambique) down to the Fish River in the Eastern Cape. Both cultures kept cattle and sheep, but the Nguni were known to hold their herds in especially high esteem.

THE TROUBLE WITH COWS

It's strange to say this but, over the centuries, cows have caused more trouble in Africa than any other single political factor, including religion. These burdensome beasts never meant any harm. All they do is give milk, give birth and give meat. But a cow's insatiable desire for grazing land is usually matched by its owners' insatiable desire for more cows, and this vicious circle is bound to cause problems once the available land starts running out. In the years to come, it was cattle-borne conflict that pitted Bushman against Bantu, Dutchman against Khoikhoi, Xhosa against British and Zulu against Zulu. Just think how peaceful our history might've been if we were all vegetarians…

But it was already far too late for that kind of thinking. Meat and milk was our bread and butter and, by the start of the second millennium of the Common Era (1000 BP), there were Bushmen, Khoikhoi, Sotho, Zulu, Xhosa and their ever-expanding herds all jostling for space on the South African landscape. Things were certainly getting a little bit crowded.

Then, 500 years later the Europeans came barging in with all the delicacy of an enraged bull in a tiny china shop, and this is where our story really starts to pick up pace…

The Formation of the Basotho Nation

The Basotho nation was founded by King Moshoeshoe during the turbulent period from the 1820s to the 1870s, when Boers, Britons and blacks were locking horns over control of Natal and the interior. The great Moshoeshoe (pronounced Mo-shwe-shwe) was originally a member of the BaKwena sub-tribe of the Tswana nation but, during the on-going conflict in the region, he moved his people into the mountain fortress of Lesotho. Once he was safely ensconced there, Moshoeshoe offered succour to thousands of refugees and, in this rocky crucible, he formed the Basotho nation.

The lined face of a local speaks volumes, Prince Albert

Colonial colours fly over the Castle's ramparts, Cape To

3. Europe comes to southern Africa

THE PORTUGUESE AND THE SEA ROUTE TO THE EAST

In 1487, a sailor named Bartolomeu Dias set off in a little ship from the shores of Portugal. His goal was to find a sea route to the East. Superficially, this was a voyage of discovery; a brave journey into the great unknown; a mad, 'Branson-esque' attempt to be the first man to sail around the unknown bulk of Africa. More specifically, however, it was an investigative expedition with high hopes of mercantile returns.

PRINCE HENRY THE NAVIGATOR

The Silk Road to the East was already well established by the Fifteenth Century. This arduous overland route was the only way to bring valuable silks and exotic spices from the East (meaning India, South-East Asia and China) into Europe and, for centuries, shuffling caravans of camels and wagons traversed this route through the dry deserts and wild wastes of Asia, carrying their cargo of valuable goods to eager consumers in the West.

Even though the Silk Road was long and dangerous, the profits were high and many traders had become rich. Merchants were prepared to risk dehydration and banditry for the chance to fill their pockets, and many remote little towns grew into thriving trading stations, which supplied the camel trains with all their provisions.

With so much money at stake, the idea of an alternative sea route to the East was very desirable to any country that wished to cut out the middle-man and take the profits for itself. Several had already tried and failed. As early as 1291, the Vivaldi brothers from Genoa sailed out of Gibraltar, turned left and disappeared forever. Others followed intermittently.

Then, in the early 1400s, the Portuguese Prince Henry was made governor of the Algarve, a region that backs onto the Atlantic Ocean. Sitting in his palace, the determined Henry looked out over the water and made it his business to conquer the insouciant seas. Using any and all means at his disposal, Prince Henry was determined that Portugal would be the first to find a sea route to the East. His ambitious vision earned him the sobriquet, Prince Henry the Navigator – father of the Age of Discovery.

Under Henry's auspices, numerous expeditions were sent out to probe the mysteries of Africa's coast. At first, progress was slow. Ships tended to hug the shore and slowly inch their way South, like a blind man tapping along the walls of a strange room. Unfortunately, contrary winds and the jutting peninsula of Cape Bojador made extended progress along the African coast impossible.

It was only with the discovery of the trade winds, called *Volta da mer lago* (diversion to the deep sea) that Portuguese ships were able to round Cape Bojador and continue slowly along the West Coast of Africa. To catch this useful trade wind, ships had to sail far out into the Atlantic, almost to the (unknown) American shore, before a prevailing south-easterly gust pushed their vessels back towards the West coast of Africa.

Armed with this new-found knowledge, a succession of intrepid seafarers set off from Henry's station at Sagres, rounded the protruding Cape Bojador and slowly crept along the seemingly endless coast of Africa until supplies or morale ran low, and they were forced to scurry back home. Nevertheless, Henry's chosen navigators continued to chip away at the great unknown until their success was such that the Portuguese received a Papal sanction which gave them control over all lands that lay between Cape Bojador and the Indies – a remarkably arrogant edict considering the lack of cartographic knowledge at the time.

BARTOLOMEU DIAS

Prince Henry the Navigator died in 1460. He had not succeeded in sending a ship to the East, but his successors were just as keen to find that elusive sea route around the wild, dark continent that squatted below Europe. By 1483, the Portuguese had reached the Congo River. By 1486, they had erected a *padrao* (commemorative cross) on the Namibian coast. Then, in 1487, Bartolomeu Dias set off in his little caravel, a wooden sailing ship barely bigger than a tugboat, and headed out into the Atlantic. He and his crew were destined to become the first European sailors to round the southern tip of Africa.

Ironically, Dias accomplished this monumental feat quite by accident. As he neared the Namibian coast, a gale sprang up and blew his ship way off course to the south. When the winds abated, Dias turned east and sailed on, expecting to hit the African coastline once again. After several days of sailing with no sign of land, he turned north and sailed until he hit land somewhere on the Agulhas coastline, possibly at Gourits River Mouth. The date was February 3, 1488 and he appropriately named his landing place, *Dos Vaqueiros* – the place of the cow herders. This is the underwhelming story of how Bartolomeu Dias and his crew rounded the Cape, without even realising it.

Suitably emboldened by his navigational 'achievement', Dias continued sailing in an easterly direction up the coast. Then, when supplies started running low, he anchored in Mossel Bay, which he named after the traditional feast day of *Sao Bras* (Saint Blaise). Their arrival did not go unnoticed by the Khoikhoi locals but, undaunted, Dias and his men went ashore to get fresh water and food, and to put up a proprietary *padrao* on the shore.

A statue of the man himself at the Bartolomeu Dias Museum, Mossel Bay

This first meeting of European and native was ominous. The indigenes didn't like the look of Dias, and vice-versa. Then, as a result of some unspecified offence, the natives started throwing stones at the strangely dressed, pale-faced sailors. Dias responded by shooting one unlucky local with his crossbow. It was a regrettable pattern that came to be repeated endlessly over the next 500 years.

Understandably, Dias didn't hang around Mossel Bay after the little shooting incident and quickly sailed on, intent on finding the long-hidden sea route to the East. His crew, however, was reluctant to tempt fate any further. Tensions rose, and the risk of mutiny finally forced a grumpy Dias to turn around and return to Portugal. On his way back, Dias did manage to round the Cape intentionally, and stopped at what would become Hout Bay.

It was during this part of the voyage that Dias apparently gave the treacherous waters off Cape Town the fearsome name of *Cabo*

Tormentoso (Cape of Storms). But this was far too gloomy an appellation for the authorities back home, and the Portuguese spin doctors renamed it *Cabo da boa esperansa* (the Cape of Good Hope) to encourage further exploration.

Hundreds of years later, students from Wits University found fragments of Dias' *padrao* on the Kwaaihoek headland, near Mossel Bay. These ancient bits and pieces have now been reassembled, and are on display in the William Cullen Africana Library on the Wits Campus in Johannesburg.

VASCO DA GAMA

Armed with the new navigational information that Dias had collected on his trip, preparations were soon under way for another voyage, and another attempt to negotiate a sea route to the East. It took some time to set things up, however, and it was only ten years later, in July 1497, that a new captain set off with a small fleet of ships, designed with the help of Dias himself.

The captain's name was Vasco Da Gama and, as he sailed away from Portugal, he knew the pressure was on. Columbus had already found his way to Central America in 1492, and the Spanish were busy exploiting the New World as fast as they could. Nevertheless, Portuguese expectations for Da Gama's expedition were high.

Carefully following in his predecessor's footsteps, Da Gama rounded the Cape without major incident and, five months after leaving home, he found himself on the southern Cape coast, talking business with some natives. At first the gathering was friendly; trading was amicable, there was music and dancing and all seemed to bode well. Then, after a week or so, the natives grew restless and wanted to know when the Europeans were going to leave.

The Portuguese, for their part, had no intention of being told what to do by a bunch of darkies, and things quickly turned nasty. Da Gama and his men rushed back to the ship and fired their cannons onto the shore as a show of power. Then, as they sailed away, the Khoikhoi ran out of the coastal bush and knocked down

The Death of Dias and the Legend of the Flying Dutchman

In 1500, a few years after Da Gama came back to Portugal dripping with glory, that old sea-dog Bartolomeu Dias set out on another fateful expedition. He was still determined to see the East, that fabled land denied to him on his previous journey, but it was not to be. Once again, Dias sailed into a storm off the West Coast of South Africa and, this time, his ship sank, killing everyone on board. The Cape of Storms had taken its revenge. Dias was dead.

Soon, however, sailors began to tell stories of a ghost ship that sailed like a spectre through the choppy waters off the Cape. If you got too close to the vessel, they said, your ship would sink and you would join the undead crew, doomed to sail around the Cape forevermore.

The nationality of the ship changed from telling to telling, but this macabre maritime tale persevered through the years, appearing in plays, popular novels, songs and other entertainments of the day. One version even specified that the ship was actually a Dutch vessel, captained by Hendrik van der Decken, that was sailing back to Holland in 1641 when it sank. Other authors went on to add a Faustian sub-plot, where the Devil and the ship's captain struck a deal in which the dead man could escape his storm-tossed torment if he managed to find a faithful wife among the living. The contemporary irony of the story is that the Devil knew it was a sucker's bet, and the captain is still sailing the southern seas, looking for his ideal companion.

In the 1840s, the story of the ghost ship found its most memorable expression in Richard Wagner's opera 'The Flying Dutchman', and so it has remained. But next time you hear this spooky sea story, spare a thought for the restless spirit of Portuguese navigator Bartolomeu Dias; his spirit eternally trying to reach the fabled East but doomed, instead, to haunt the South African coast forevermore.

the *padrao* that Da Gama had just erected. It was probably the first instinctive example of African Nationalism in the face of European conquest – another portent of things to come.

One month later, Da Gama was still sailing up the coast, looking out at the verdant shore of South Africa's eastern seaboard. On Christmas Day, Da Gama and crew decided to name the land they were passing '*Natal*', in honour of Christ's nativity. It is a name that the region half-retains to this day. But, wary of the testy South African locals, Da Gama did not risk landing. Instead, he sailed on and finally anchored off the coast of Mozambique. The local Bantu tribes in this part of the world were much more tractable than the bolshy Khoikhoi, and Da Gama named the place *Terra de boa gente* (Land of the Good People).

From the shores of Mozambique, Da Gama discovered the convenient trade winds that blow from the east coast of Africa towards the west coast of Arabia every summer, only to reverse direction and blow back to towards Africa in the winter. This Aeolian fluke of nature was well known to the early Arabian sea traders, who had been plying their wares in Africa since 800CE, and had already established trading stations, such as Sofala, Zanzibar and Kilwa, along the east coast of Africa. This trade secret was now in the hands of the Europeans and they would make full use of it in the years to come.

Finally, in May 1498, after 11 months at sea, Da Gama landed at Calicut on the Malabar Coast of India. To celebrate, he seized 7 trading vessels and imprisoned their crews (according to one Arab source), and returned home with the good news and some booty. Within two years, Portuguese ships were sailing to the Indies with regularity.

For the next fifteen years, Portuguese ships continued reaching out across the Indies. First, trading posts were established at Socotra on the Red Sea, then at Hormuz on the Persian Gulf. These were followed by stations at Goa on the West coast of the Indian peninsula, Malacca in the East Indies (present day Malaysia) and

finally on the distant island outpost of Macao, just off the Chinese mainland. For good measure, they also kicked the Arab traders out of their old trading stations on the African coast and took control of the ancient settlements.

The Sea Route to the East was now firmly established, and the Europeans had ineluctably entered the building.

Ferdinand Magellan

Magellan was a Portuguese nobleman and a proud member of the Navy, seeing active service in battle and getting a gammy leg for his troubles. Then, after years of loyalty, he quarrelled with his superiors over a legal matter and was summarily dismissed. Suitably peeved, Magellan went over to the Spanish and immediately embarked on a journey to find a westward sea route to the Orient, one which would avoid the Portuguese stranglehold on the Eastern passage.

Magellan left Spain in 1519 with a fleet of 5 ships. Three months later, he landed at the bay of Rio de Janeiro and slowly started inching his way down the South American coast; testing out each inlet, hoping for a breakthrough into the Pacific. His crew soon became restive and wanted to return home, but Magellan firmly fought down the mutiny by killing one rebel leader, executing another and abandoning the third on the unknown mainland. Clearly, he was a man who would not back down from a challenge.

Eventually, in October 1520, he found the 'Straights of Magellan' around Cape Horn, and sailed into the open ocean once more. Things didn't get any easier, however. One ship sank and another vessel deserted before the diminished fleet reached Guam in 1521. Then, when they reached the Philippines, Magellan was abruptly killed in a skirmish with the natives. Only one of his 5 ships limped back to Spain, captained by Juan Sebastian de Elcano, in 1522. Nevertheless, Magellan had discovered the westward route to the Pacific, and the planet was about to become round.

THE CAPE OF GOOD HOPE

At first, there was very little European interest in the Cape of Storms. The waters around the headland were turbulent and so were the natives. Then, in 1503, Antonio da Saldanha accidentally found his way into Table Bay (which he modestly named Saldania), and the Cape began to gain some prominence. But, even though Table Bay was a useful anchorage (especially if the seas were stormy), it was still not a regular stop on the sea route east.

In fact, the Portuguese gave the whole South African coast a wide berth and established their refreshment stations along the humid shores of Mozambique. It's curious that they would choose these tropical latitudes, laden with the buzzing threat of malaria, as a base. But it was probably felt that the natives in South Africa were a bit too restless for their own good. Better angry mosquitoes than angry savages.

This lingering suspicion was consolidated in 1510, when a much-medalled Viceroy and a party of Portuguese noblemen, returning from the East, landed at the Cape. By this time, the local Khoikhoi tribes were getting pretty obstreperous with all the passing ships and, when the crew came ashore to trade for fresh supplies, the Khoikhoi were dismissive and rude. The distinguished assembly of knobs on board the ship decided that this insult could not be countenanced, and brashly went ashore to teach the savages a lesson in civility. This apparently included stealing cattle and kidnapping some Khoikhoi children to be sold into slavery.

The primitive heathen, however, met the punitive expedition head on. Using sticks, stones and their special war-trained cattle (!), the Cape Khoikhoi soundly defeated the Portuguese, and many well-born officers went down in a stampede of hooves, rocks and fire-hardened wooden spears. The loss was, understandably, a big shock to the European psyche and it added fuel for the glowing fires of anti-Hottentot sentiment.

Still, land battles notwithstanding, no one could challenge the Portuguese in their control of the seas. Portugal was becoming rich and it looked like it would always be the foremost sea-faring nation on the Earth. But everything runs in cycles, and Portugal's fortunes slowely started to sink as other European nations began to find their sea legs.

The turn-around started as early as 1522, when Ferdinand Magellan, sailing under the Spanish flag, found the westward passage to the Orient. Then, in 1580, Sir Francis Drake circumnavigated the globe for England. In the same year, Phillip II of Spain assumed the Portuguese throne and took control of the whole Iberian Peninsula. This, in effect, brought Portugal into a festering war between Spain and Holland. The Dutch and their British allies were consequently freed from any moral obligation to honour Portugal's monopoly over the trade route to the East. And the game was on.

Other setbacks were to follow for the Portuguese. First, England famously defeated the Spanish Armada in 1588 and decisively turned the tide of the war in their favour. Then, in 1595, a sailor who had travelled to the Indies on a Portuguese merchant ship published his memoirs. The book conveniently included a detailed account of Portugal's navigational secrets and other useful travel tips for marauding European nations keen on conquest. This was the last straw. Portugal's stranglehold on the oceans was effectively over.

THE DUTCH EAST INDIA COMPANY – VEREENIGDE OOST-INDISCHE COMPAGNIE (VOC)

The demise of Portuguese authority over the high seas facilitated the rise of the great chartered companies of the 17th century. These corporate entities were affiliated to, but independent of a ruling monarch, and each had complete control over the territories they chose to occupy in the course of their business interests.

At the time, many European monarchs seemed more interested in squabbling among themselves than in developing potentially lucrative trade routes. Well-connected businessmen thus negotiated legal charters with their respective monarchs, which gave free reign to even the most rampant corporate imaginations. Armed with these charters, investors set up trading companies with an expansive mandate to exploit new territories for fun and profit.

Since the chartered companies took on the financial risk of these endeavours, they were seen as an ideal way to increase a country's commercial activity without committing too many national resources. So, in essence, the chartered company was a free-wheeling, quasi-political authority, only concerned with the pursuit of profit – much like any modern-day corporation. In practise, however, the company charter was a law unto itself, and the companies functioned like institutionalised pirates.

Accordingly, the British East India Company (formed in 1600) and the Dutch East India Company (formed in 1602) were set up by canny capitalists who wanted all the power of government, with none of the hassles. The chartered companies could raise armies, wage war and impose their own rules on 'citizens', who were actually all employees working under contract. It was the kind of business plan that a modern-day CEO would kill for.

The Dutch East India Company, more accurately known as the *Vereenigde Nederlandsche Ge-Oktroyeerde Oost-Indische Compagnie* (VOC), was based in Holland and controlled by the venerable *Heeren Sewentien* (the Council of seventeen, or the seventeen Lords). This wealthy bunch of cronies were organised into six regional chambers, and functioned as the company's board of directors. They audited expenses, made policy and strategised future corporate endeavours – the most important of which was taking control of the lucrative sea route to the east.

To help them achieve this goal, the Dutch government gave the VOC a monopoly on the spice trade in East Asia, which included popular commodities such as cloves, nutmeg and pepper. The King also gave the VOC the power to colonise and subjugate local populations in any way that best suited the interests of the company. Thus empowered, the VOC were happy to wage a full-scale war against resistant natives who did want to go along with their ambitious plans. In one case, the VOC went so far as to kill the entire population of Banda, in Indonesia. They then brought in slave labour, and turned the whole island into a nutmeg plantation.

The VOC was clearly a ruthless corporation which would stop at nothing to make a buck for its members so, obviously, it was a huge success. In fact the VOC was so profitable, it helped launch the world's first stock market in Amsterdam.

With plenty of financial support and no discernable conscience whatsoever, the power of the VOC increased exponentially until finally, after fifty years of battling the entrenched stakeholders, it effectively controlled the sea passage to the Indies.

The VOC's base of operations was at Jakarta in Batavia (modern-day Indonesia), but the journey to the Indies was long and conditions on VOC ships were less than wholesome. A refreshment station was therefore needed to supply their ships with fresh water and meat.

The location of such a station was problematic. The Portuguese had chosen Mozambique as their halfway house and still maintained a presence there. Since the VOC didn't want to make too many waves back in Europe, they decided to leave the Portuguese to their malarial swamps and looked elsewhere for a suitable depot. Enter the Cape of Good Hope…

Table Bay had been intermittently used as an informal anchorage for British, Portuguese, French and Dutch ships almost since it was first discovered. But thus far, no one had stepped up to claim it as their own, despite several abortive attempts by over-eager British sailors.

Then, in 1647, a Dutch ship called *Niewe*

Haerlem was wrecked in the bay, and the survivors were forced to live in the lee of Table Mountain for nearly a year before being retrieved. When they finally returned to Holland, the Council asked one of the men, Leendert Janszen, to write up a report on the potential for using Table Bay as the Company's new refreshment station.

In his *'Remonstrantie'* to the venerable *Heeren XVII*, Janszen declared that they had been treated well by the local tribes, the water supply was good and the land was fertile. He whole-heartedly recommended using the Cape of Good Hope for any purposes the Company could devise. Thanks a lot, Leendert!

JAN VAN RIEBEECK ARRIVES AT THE CAPE

After the positive testimonials from the crew of the *Niewe Haerlem*, the VOC was prodded into action. And in 1652 – one hundred and fifty years after Bartolomeu Dias rounded the Cape – a former ship's surgeon with a dodgy hairdo sailed into Table Bay. His name was Jan Anthoniszoon van Riebeeck, and he was charged with the task of establishing a refreshment station for the VOC under the main face of Table Mountain. It was to be the first permanent European settlement in South Africa.

Van Riebeeck was born in Culemborg in 1619. He joined the VOC and worked his way through the ranks, until he was appointed commander of the newly proposed Cape settlement in 1651. Armed with his new promotion, he sailed off to his new home in a fleet of five ships, eager for the adventure that lay ahead.

On the fateful day of 6th of April 1652, the first three ships (the *Dromedaris*, the *Reijger* and the *Goede Hoop*) arrived safely with the new commander and his wife, a French Huguenot woman named Maria. The other two ships (the *Walvis* and the *Oliphant*) had some trouble and were delayed, after burying 130 people at sea.

Van Riebeeck's initial responsibilities sounded simple enough. Build a fort, plant a garden, and sell fresh supplies to the passing ships. The Dutch presence at the Cape was never supposed to be more extensive than that. Unfortunately, despite the best efforts of the parsimonious VOC, things soon got out of hand and, by 1676, the refreshment station had officially become a colony.

But success for the European invaders was far from guaranteed

In the beginning, things were tough for Van Riebeeck and the other company employees. These new settlers were a motley assortment of unimpressive men who had come from all over Europe, and they had to start from scratch in a wild land hemmed in by mountains. Rations were in very short supply and morale was low, partly because of the gruesome punishments meted out to employees in terms of the company's disciplinary regime. To make matters worse, the native Khoikhoi at the Cape were far from welcoming.

As soon as the Khoikhoi ascertained that this recent influx of whiteys had every intention of sticking around, relations with their new neighbours soured. The Hottentots, already despised as dirty savages by the Dutch, returned the compliment and often refused to trade with the untrustworthy white man. This meant that the company's stocks dwindled, and supplies of fresh meat and milk were not forthcoming.

Furthermore, the Dutch had no knowledge of the edible plants and roots that sprouted around the Cape, and the Khoikhoi were in no hurry to share their expertise. In any event, efforts to explore the coast beyond the fort were often dangerous, due to the predatory nature of both lions and the hostile tribes in the vicinity. Eventually, the settlers were forced to make regular trips to Robben Island where they collected eggs and penguin meat, which became part of their regular diet.

All in all, it was a pretty miserable existence for the Dutch, so far removed from the comforts and convenience of their motherland. For the first nine years of its existence, the little settlement charged with supplying fresh food to the ships in the bay was often too weak to feed itself.

Despite the successful cultivation of a small company garden next to the fort, hunger stalked the European outpost for much of its early history. Even the arrival of maize seeds, in 1655, and horses, in 1660, did not do much to ease the pressure. The arrival of sugar cane in 1672 did make a difference, however, but only because it allowed the farmers to distil their own liquor.

Things weren't helped by the chronic labour shortage at the Cape. The local Khoikhoi had no intention of working for the white man, but the Cape was not yet a colony and the Commander wasn't empowered to enslave the local population. The situation was so bad that Van Riebeeck started asking for slaves within a few weeks of his landing, but his constant requests fell on the VOC's deaf ears.

To compound his problems, Van Riebeeck was forced to rely on the services of wily interpreters, like the equivocal Herrie, to negotiate with the surly Khoikhoi. Furthermore, local resistance to the plundering Dutchmen mounted steadily as the Europeans took over more and more ancestral land in the name of the almighty Company. Still, the wealth and tenacity of Europe was on the side of the settlers and, despite all the odds against them, Van Riebeeck and his successors persevered.

Slowly, a little town began to grow up around the fort on Table Bay. It was to be called Cape Town, the Mother City. Which begs the question: Whose Mother City? Not the indigenous population, that's for sure. *Jou Ma se City*, more like…

AUTSHUMAO AND KROTOA – HERRIE AND EVA

Herrie, or Harry, is an interesting character in the early history of the Cape. He was there long before Van Riebeeck landed, and played a central role in the human drama that was to follow.

Herrie started out his life as a proud Khoikhoi chief called Autshumao (sometimes spelt Autshumato), with fat cattle and loyal subjects.

But he lost his herds and his prestige to a rival chieftain, and was left as the forlorn figurehead of a tribe of *strandlopers* (beach walkers).

These *strandlopers*, or 'Watermen', were a humble bunch of natives who roamed the coastal dunes, scavenging for food and living in flimsy huts. The Dutch recorded that there were about 60 to 80 Strandlopers around Table Bay when they landed, and Herrie was already their chief. For their part, Autshumao's *strandlopers* called themselves the *Goringhaikona*. This translates as 'children of the *Goringhaiqua*', who were the dominant Khoikhoi clan of the Cape Peninsula.

Before the Dutch arrived, however, the British had already shown some interest in acquiring the Cape. In 1631, they even tried to forge closer ties with the Peninsular Khoikhoi by convincing Autshumao to join them on a voyage to the East. When he returned, the newly christened 'Harry' was empowered with a few words of English and the informal job of postman, responsible for handling the infrequent mail from the passing British ships.

As Harry was not on good terms with the other Cape Khoikhoi, the British installed him and his followers on Robben Island which, at the time, was crowded with penguins and seals. After a few years, however, the *strandlopers* tired of their self-imposed exile and returned to the mainland, where Harry continued to collaborate with the British, Dutch and French ships that called at the Cape. So, when Van Riebeeck arrived in 1652, it made sense for the expedient and curious Harry to present himself and offer his services.

It had been a tough winter for the *Goringhaikona* that year and, when Harry knocked on the heavy door of the fort, he was accompanied by his orphaned niece, Krotoa. She was around six years old, a thin and fragile child, and exhausted by the difficult life of the *strandlopers*. Harry wanted Van Riebeeck to take her in, at least for the winter, and said that Krotoa could help with the housework and look after the Commander's children. Van Riebeeck agreed and gave her a room in his house. He renamed the child, 'Eva'.

Van Riebeeck also told 'Herrie' that, for the settlement to succeed, it needed fresh milk and meat. Herrie was initially concerned to hear that the Dutch were planning to stay. He was still smarting from the loss of his own beloved herd, and didn't want to help the new settler build up a rival flock in his own backyard. But Van Riebeeck was determined to have his own herds of cattle and sheep, and was prepared to pay the local chiefs for any animals they sent to the fort. Herrie quickly assessed the situation and saw an opportunity to regain some of his influence in local politics. He decided to become a go-between.

Cape Town city centre from Leerdam bastion, The Castle

At first, it wasn't an easy task. The Khoikhoi loved their cattle, and very few chiefs would sell their precious livestock to the white interloper. Van Riebeeck, however, was offering tobacco and liquor in exchange for cattle and, with a little prompting, the delights of European intoxication soon proved irresistible. Herrie sent out word of the offer to the local tribes and settled down at a nearby drift to wait. Then, whenever herd boys arrived with a few mangy sheep or couple of cows to trade, Herrie led them down to the Fort and brokered the deal with Van Riebeeck.

Herrie's motivation in all this is not clear. He had no qualms about playing Dutchman off against Khoikhoi for his own perceived gain, and he relished his position as the only person who could speak both a European language (English) and Khoikhoi. But he was also a proud Khoikhoi chief who disliked the stuffy, overdressed Europeans and their superior attitude. Nevertheless, Herrie and Van Riebeeck continued to work together, forging a precarious working relationship that was fraught with distrust and suspicion.

Eva, for her part, was fitting in very nicely. She was learning Dutch, wearing European clothes and going to Church with the Van Riebeeck family every Sunday. Within the walls of the Fort, Eva was growing into a pretty young lady, but she was also growing increasingly distant from her native culture. Her frame of reference was becoming more European than Khoikhoi, and her loyalty to her tribe was ambiguous. Like an alpine climber caught with one foot on either side of a widening crevasse, Eva was being pulled apart by the conflicting demands of her two families.

By 1658, Herrie was becoming alarmed. Van Riebeeck was building up a large herd of shiny animals. Eva was in danger of going over to the other side. The Fort was becoming larger and more permanent every day. And the Company had just allowed a group of 'free citizens' to take over fertile land along the Liesbeek River, formerly grazed by the Khoikhoi. Something had to be done to stop the white man's advance. Herrie felt it was time to go on the offensive.

His plan was simple but effective. At the time, Mrs Van Riebeeck was about to have her third child. On the day after the birth, everyone from the fort was in church, giving thanks. The Company's cattle were out on the dunes, under the care of a single young herdboy. In a carefully timed raid, Herrie's supporters killed the young boy and stole most of the cattle. At the same time, Herrie went to the Fort, ordered Eva to pack her bags and hurried her out the door. By the time the Europeans came out of church, Herrie was over the hills and far away. With one bold move, he had regained his herds, his niece and his self-respect.

Within a year, however, the tide had once again turned against Herrie. His old habits of double-dealing and agitation had not made him many friends among his fellow Khoikhoi, and he could not maintain the momentum of his daring escapade. Eva returned to the fort, begging forgiveness, and Herrie was eventually caught. He and some accomplices were sent to Robben Island as its first prisoners, in 1659.

By this time, however, another Khoikhoi leader had been recruited by the VOC and sent to the Indies for 'education'. He was called Doman and he returned from his voyage speaking Dutch, but full of scorn and hatred for his erstwhile masters. Once back at the Cape, Doman quickly threw off the white man's clothes and started giving voice to the nascent nationalism of the Khoikhoi.

With his fiery speeches and angry denunciations of the white man's arrogance, Doman quickly became the figurehead of a popular Khoikhoi rebellion that threatened to overwhelm the tiny fort. This has now become known as the First Dutch-Khoikhoi War of 1659.

Skirmishes became frequent and lethal for both sides and, with neither party prepared to back down, the conflict was becoming brutal. In desperation, Van Riebeeck sent a boat to recall Herrie, hoping that the arch manipulator could pull one out of the hat for the settlers. When

The eponymous vista from Table View

Van Riebeeck and Herrie met, however, a frail and stubborn Chief Autshumao refused to help the Dutch commander. Instead, he called Van Riebeeck a thief and told the Commander to return the ancestral lands that he and his farmers had stolen.

With a sigh, Van Riebeeck refused and sent Herrie back to Robben Island. The battles continued unabated and, for several months, the farmers along the Liesbeek River were constantly terrorised by Doman's warriors. Back in Holland, the Company's confidence in their new territory was evaporating.

But Van Riebeeck was a shrewd strategist

and realised that he couldn't fight fire with fire. Instead, he decided on a more lateral approach and started building a cordon around the Cape Peninsula that would cut off the Khoikhoi from their traditional winter grazing. After all, the Hottentots had started the war, so it was clearly nothing less than they deserved.

Accordingly, Van Riebeeck ordered the construction of fortified outposts along the Liesbeek river, and planted a wall of fast-growing Wild Almond hedges to keep the Khoikhoi out. A large gate was also built across the main ford in the river, and this redoubt was manned twenty-four hours a day so that no Khoikhoi could pass through the gate without the commander's permission. This, finally, seemed to have the desired effect and hostilities subsided somewhat. Parts of this 300-year-old bitter almond hedge can still be seen around Cape Town, with a particularly good section growing apace in Kirstenbosch Gardens.

So, with the establishment of the new cordon, things grew quiet until, one day, word reached Van Riebeeck that Herrie had escaped from Robben Island. In the dead of night, the old man and one of his fellow prisoners had stolen some oars and a leaky old boat, discarded by the wardens as hopelessly unseaworthy, and rowed themselves back to the mainland. This remarkable feat earned Autshumao the distinction of becoming one of the very few prisoners to effect a successful escape from the fearsome island. One of the modern tourist ferries that now plies the route from the Waterfront to Robben Island is named in his honour.

As soon as Van Reibeeck heard this troubling news, he grew anxious and sent out search parties to find the irritating old Hottentot. But they all came back empty-handed. Herrie had disappeared into the interior. Then, Van Riebeeck got some good news from Eva. Herrie was with Doman, and they were ready to discuss peace. Doman had been badly wounded in a recent skirmish and the other chiefs were growing tired of the bloodshed. More importantly, the Khoikhoi

wanted to revert to their traditional patterns, and longed to graze their cattle on the fertile banks of the Liesbeek once more. For this, they needed the Commander's permission.

Using Eva as a mediator, a meeting was duly arranged between a confident Van Riebeeck, a weary Herrie and a glowering Doman. It was an acrimonious affair all round, with each side accusing the other of being aggressive and greedy. Nevertheless, it was agreed that the other Khoikhoi chiefs would come to the Fort and meet with Van Riebeeck to discuss the matter further.

When it was time for this great indaba, Van Riebeeck calmly told the horrified Khoikhoi that the Dutch had no intention of leaving, and that the ancestral land of the Khoikhoi was gone forever. The land was forfeit to the Company as a spoil of war, and they would only let the Khoikhoi graze their flocks on the Dutch side of the river if everyone agreed to the Dutch terms of armistice, which included forfeiting many heads of tribal cattle. The Khoikhoi refused and returned to the far side of the river, empty-handed. Van Riebeeck was triumphant.

Meanwhile, the medical officer at the Fort found himself falling in love with the young Eva. He was a Danish man called Peter Havgard (named Pieter van Meerhof by the Dutch), and he was moved by the plight of the luckless girl. Eva had been singled out by Doman as the worst kind of traitor, spurned by her tribe and ostracized by the white people at the fort. So, it's not surprising that Eva was receptive to the overtures from the swashbuckling doctor. Eva eventually fell pregnant with Van Meerhof's baby, and this made the situation even more delicate.

Then, in 1662, while Van Meerhof was away on an expedition to the north, Doman and Herrie both passed away. Eva was devastated. Herrie might have been anywhere between sixty-five and eighty-five years old when he died. An era had ended.

By this time, Van Riebeeck's tenure at the Cape was also coming to an end. He had succeeded in establishing a refreshment station at Table Bay and finally received a prestigious transfer to Batavia in 1662. Before he left, however, he gave orders that Eva should be baptised, and that the union of the Khoikhoi girl with the Danish doctor should be legitimised. Although inter racial marriage was not illegal at this time, the next Commander was not likely to be very sympathetic to the young couple, and Van Riebeeck wanted to get everything signed-off before he left.

The baptism was a bitter-sweet affair for the Khoikhoi girl, and the couple did eventually get married in 1664, by which time they had conceived a second child to follow their first-born daughter, Pieternella. But their union was not entirely happy. Money was short, Eva was withdrawn, and Van Meerhof often volunteered to go on long, exploratory expeditions into the unknown interior of Namaqualand.

These journeys earned the couple extra money, but Eva became increasingly lonely and difficult whenever Pieter was away. Even their children did not make her happy and, to add to the pressure, Pieter was becoming frustrated with the paucity of opportunities at the Cape. He longed to leave the African shore and take his family to the East, where he felt they would be happy and prosperous. But Eva vowed that she would never leave her homeland and the couple continued living in a stalemate.

Meanwhile, money continued to be tight for the small family and the poorly-paid Company doctor looked forward to any kind of promotion. Unfortunately, the new governor, a German called Zaccharias Wagner (or Wagenaer, in Dutch), had other ideas and ordered Pieter and his family to Robben Island, where he was to take up the post of Superintendent. By this time, the couple had three children and the windy island, populated with thuggish guards and hardened criminals, was a far from ideal kindergarten.

Nevertheless, Wagenaer promised Pieter that this service would be much appreciated by the Company and could, in due course, lead to his desired re-assignment to the East. Pieter accepted the post, and the Van Meerhofs lived on the wretched rock for three long years. Eva's only consolation during this miserable time was that Pieter no longer went on long exploratory trips away from his family. But she still missed the halcyon days of her youth when she was tucked away in the warm Fort and fussed over by her foster parents, Van Riebeeck and his wife.

The Mother City, as seen from the Robben Island ferry

As the years passed, Wagenaer moved on from the Cape and his successor, a dandified man called Van Quaelberg, had no understanding or appreciation of Eva and Pieter's situation. It looked like they were destined to remain on Robben Island, prisoners in everything except name. Then, the message came from the Castle. The Commander had an important job for Pieter. Van Meerhof quickly rowed across the sea to the mainland, and went in to see Van Quaelberg with high expectations. The task was to accompany a slaving expedition to Madagascar, and to bring back a fresh batch of workers.

It wasn't quite the East, but Van Meerhof was elated. If all went well, he would soon get his family off the barren island and, perhaps, even be transferred to Batavia. Eva was devastated that her husband was leaving once again, but she did get a chance to return to the mainland and await his return. The year was 1668.

Sadly, while ashore in Madagascar, Pieter and a number of the crew were killed by the locals. Apparently, the natives had taken umbrage at the mission to kidnap their people and rape their women. Go figure.

This left Eva in a terrible position. She was stranded with three kids and no husband in a hostile, alien environment. She couldn't return to her own people, and her intimate involvement with the early years of the fort was all but forgotten. To numb her pain, Eva predictably turned to the white man's poison: alcohol. As she sank further into the barrel, her children were taken away and given to white foster-parents. Eva was eventually declared a public nuisance and was sent back to Robben Island as a prisoner. She died, alone on the rock, in 1674. She was 31 years old.

To complete this part of the story, we should mention that Pieternella van Meerhof, the child of Eva and Pieter, went on to marry a man called Daniel Zaayman and had a child of her own, Magdalena. Jan van Riebeeck died in Batavia in 1677, and his wife, Maria, died in Malacca. Her gravestone can still be seen in the old fort above the town.

The sun sets on the modern city streets of Cape Town

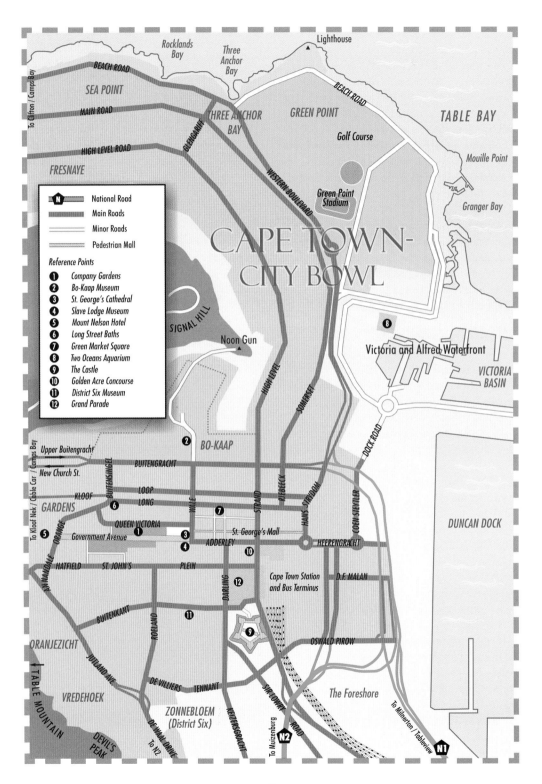

CAPE TOWN-
CITY BOWL

National Road
Main Roads
Minor Roads
Pedestrian Mall

Reference Points

1 Company Gardens
2 Bo-Kaap Museum
3 St. George's Cathedral
4 Slave Lodge Museum
5 Mount Nelson Hotel
6 Long Street Baths
7 Green Market Square
8 Two Oceans Aquarium
9 The Castle
10 Golden Acre Concourse
11 District Six Museum
12 Grand Parade

Rocklands Bay
Three Anchor Bay
Lighthouse
BEACH ROAD
SEA POINT
MAIN ROAD
THREE ANCHOR BAY
GREEN POINT
BEACH ROAD
TABLE BAY
Golf Course
Mouille Point
HIGH LEVEL ROAD
FRESNAYE
GLENGARIFF
WESTERN BOULEVARD
Green Point Stadium
Granger Bay
SIGNAL HILL
Noon Gun
Victoria and Alfred Waterfront
VICTORIA BASIN
DOCK ROAD
Upper Buitengracht
BO-KAAP
New Church St.
BUITENGRACHT
BUITENSINGEL
KLOOF
LOOP
LONG
WALE
STRAND
RIEBEECK
HANS STRIDOM
COEN STEYTLER
DUNCAN DOCK
GARDENS
ORANGE
QUEEN VICTORIA
St. George's Mall
Government Avenue
ADDERLEY
HEERENGRACHT
HATFIELD
ST. JOHN'S
PLEIN
Cape Town Station and Bus Terminus
D.F. MALAN
BUITENKANT
DARLING
ROELAND
ORANJEZICHT
OSWALD PIROW
JUTLAND AVE.
DE VILLIERS
TENNANT
TABLE MOUNTAIN
VREDEHOEK
DE WALL DRIVE
ZONNEBLOEM (District Six)
KEIZERSGRACHT
SIR LOWRY ROAD
The Foreshore
To Clifton / Camps Bay
To Kloof Nek / Cable Car / Camps Bay
To Muizenburg
To N2
To Milnerton / Tableview
AN MANDALE
DEVIL'S PEAK
HIGH LEVEL
SOMERSET
N2
N1

4. Cape Town – The City Bowl

ORIENTATION

The heart of Cape Town is the City Bowl. This is a large scoop of land, bounded by the harbour of Table Bay in the north and the main face of Table Mountain to the south. This famous flat-topped rock, known by the locals simply and definitively as 'The Mountain', provides an unforgettable backdrop for the City. It's the view that launched a thousand postcards.

On either side of The Mountain are two thrusting arms which reach out to cradle the City Bowl. To the left of the Table is the ominously named Devil's Peak, clearly identified by three unsightly cylindrical buildings rising up from its base. Local wags have dubbed these architectural abominations 'the Tampon Towers'. To the right of The Mountain is the sphinx-like peak of Lion's Head, which leads down to the rump of Signal Hill. Lion's Head is linked to The Mountain by a narrow saddle of high ground called Kloof Nek.

Cape Town's city centre is located in the middle of this great bowl, an abrupt stand of high-rise buildings cowering under The Mountain's lofty heights. Fanning out from the CBD, and rising up the lower slopes of its mountainous embrace, are the increasingly desirable suburbs of Vredehoek, Oranjezicht, Gardens, Higgovale, Tamboerskloof and the Bo-Kaap.

It's quite easy to explore the City Centre of Cape Town as it's reasonably small and ideally suited for pedestrian perambulation.

The city centre itself is roughly delineated as a square, formed by the streets of Buitengracht, Wale, Adderley (which becomes Heerengracht) and Coen Steytler. Long Street roughly cuts the CBD in half, and is arguably the most interesting retail boulevard for visitors to explore.

At the corner of Adderley and Wale (the latter named after two gentlemen of the Walloon persuasion who used to live there, apparently), you will find the Company Gardens, South Africa's own version of Washington's Smithsonian Mall. Greenmarket Square (the popular fleamarket) is close by, and the Castle can be found on the other side of the Grand Parade car park.

When you first arrive in Cape Town, the main highway deposits you at the intersection of Buitengracht and Coen Steytler, right at the corner of the city centre, close to the harbour. From this point, you can turn sharp right to the

Proteas and a smile at the Flower Market

V & A Waterfront, or you can go up Buitengracht Street along the upper edge of Downtown.

If you continue along Buitengracht you can:
➡ Turn right at Somerset Road towards Sea Point, and from there follow the superlative Victoria Road that runs right around the Cape Peninsula *[see Chapter 5]*.
➡ Turn right into Strand Street, go past De Waterkant Shopping Centre and take the scenic High Level Road to Sea Point *[see Chapter 5]*.
➡ Turn left into Strand Street and drive down to The Castle. The interesting Gold of Africa Museum is on the corner of Strand and Buitengracht.
➡ Turn left down one of the side-streets (try Shortmarket) towards the centre of town, for some cosmopolitan shopping.

At the intersection of Buitengracht and Wale Street, you will find the legendary Harley's Liquors, the only bottle store in Cape Town that never seems to close. To your right is the Bo-Kaap, the traditional 'coloured' neighbourhood which climbs steeply up the slopes of Signal Hill. Turn left into Wale Street if you want to head towards the City Centre, the Company Gardens and the Slave Lodge.

If you continue along Buitengracht, you soon some to an intersection with Buitensingel.

Turn left here if you want to drive along the top of town, past the Mount Nelson Hotel, through the suburb of Gardens and onto De Waal Drive, which leads back into the highway network. If you still continue along Buitengracht, the road goes through a bit of an identity crisis before becoming Kloof Nek Road. This road takes you up to the Nek between Table Mountain and Lion's Head. At the summit of this road, you can turn right to the Signal Hill lookout or left to the Cable Car station. You can also go straight over Kloof Nek and down to Camps Bay *[see Chapter 5]*. Lunatics sometimes run a half-marathon up this road, and psycho's have been known to have a street-luge race down it!

For a good alternative view of The Mountain, head out on the main highway and follow signs for Paarden Eiland, and the suburbs

Greenmarket Square

The centre of Cape Town's urban attractions is arguably Greenmarket Square. This cobblestone quadrangle was originally the city's open-air fruit and vegetable market. Now, it is the centre of Cape Town's newest agricultural activity: milking tourists. But don't let that put you off. Greenmarket Square is an energetic fleamarket with hundreds of stalls that offer African masks, ethnic fabrics, jewellery, crafts, wind chimes, more African masks, sculptures and even some African masks. The evergreen Purple Turtle Bar and Grill is adjacent to the Square and offers travellers Internet facilities. The Long Street African Craft Centre is also nearby.

St George's Mall

Just below Greenmarket Square is a long pedestrian walkway, called St George's Mall. This is a bricked thoroughfare with sidewalk cafes, hawkers, buskers and office blocks on either side. You'll find all the major banks, service providers and chain stores somewhere on the Mall, and it's a good place to go if you want to knock off a few errands in one location. One block down from the mall, across Adderley Street, is the Golden Acre Shopping Centre, and whatever you can't find in St George's, you'll find at the Golden Acre.

View of the City Bowl from Lion's Head

Masks and crafts at Greenmarket Square fleamarket

of Milnerton and Table View. The windy strip of beach on this side of Table Bay offers panoramic views of the City Bowl, and the seaside road continues up the West Coast to the resort towns of Bloubergstrand and Langebaan.

ESCAPE TOWN

What can I say about Cape Town? It's beautiful, dammit. Absolutely, gob-smackingly gorgeous: the City Bowl framed by The Mountain, the Atlantic seaboard with its palatial apartments clinging onto sheer walls of rock, Hout Bay, Noordhoek Beach, the tapering talon of Cape Point pointing out towards the deep sea. It's all bloody beautiful.

You may have picked up that my praise of the Mother City is tempered with a little bit of reluctance. There are two reasons for this. Firstly, I love dissing Cape Town. And, secondly, I am jealous.

As a Joburg boy, born and bred, I have a lingering resentment of all the natural beauty that abounds on the Cape Peninsula. It's not that I think Joburg is ugly. It's just that Cape Town is so blatantly pretty, I somehow feel like someone is rubbing my nose in it.

Secondly, and more perversely, I just enjoy pissing off the Capetonians. Now, I know that it is wrong to class any group of people as a 'they', but I can't help it. As a devoted Gautie (or Vaalie, as we used to be called), I refuse to add fuel to the already insufferable fire of white Cape Town's smug self-satisfaction, and I will

take any chance I get to burst their prissy little bubble of European sophistication.

But I don't want this discourse to degenerate into a petty provincial squabble, so I won't say that Capetonians are lazy, rude, self-indulgent and unfriendly. I also won't say that Capetonians are a cliquey bunch of stuck-up tightwads or that, by and large, the *Kaapenaars* are as cold as a bucket load of dead fish.

Capetonians, for their part, may counter with the common Cape perception that Joburgers are crass, flashy and unspiritual. But I won't let that rile me, and I will refrain from telling the Capetonians where they can stick their precious Mountain.

I will also not point out that the Cape Town is actually a wannabe European city-state, rather than an active part of the New South Africa. Nor will I mention that if they keep charging exorbitant prices for food and accommodation, their new-found popularity will quickly melt away. The once-booming Cape film industry has already stumbled as a result of greed and price gouging, and tourism may be going the same way. Still, I can't really blame Cape Town for climbing on board the gravy train. It's not like it has a strong industrial sector, or jobs, or anything like that.

But let's move past all this regional rancour. The rivalry between *Slaap Stad* and *Egoli* is well established, and it can be quite entertaining as long as things don't get taken too seriously. You see, I don't really believe that everyone at the

Long Street

Long Street is the entertainment artery of the City Bowl. Along its course, you will find chi-chi homeware stores, retro-funk fashion boutiques, antique shops tucked away in old-fashioned arcades, dozens of restaurants, African craft markets, pool halls, nightclubs and so on. During the day the shopping is excellent and, when it gets dark, it is one of the most reliable places to go for a night out.

Long Street is always happening, especially around the top end of town where you will find stalwart venues like Kennedy's Jazz Café, Mr Pickwicks (for late night food), the strangely named Joburg Bar, and various other drinking spots that come and go with the Season. If you're hungry, try the sidewalk schwarma stand (which is an institution) or the outstanding Royale, which has an extensive range of gourmet hamburgers.

At the top of Long Street, you will see the Long Street Baths, a rather humble Victorian building that houses a lovely indoor swimming pool and Turkish Bath. It's not a substantial building, like the Melbourne Baths in Australia, but South Africa was never a very prosperous colony, and the British only did as much as was required to maintain a basic level of civility.

As is usually the case in developing countries, this playground of the haves is also home to a large population of have-nots. The street kids of Long Street are something of a legend, and have resisted many attempts by the council and private philanthropists to 'clean them up'.

Cape is allergic to work, any more than I believe that all Greeks are genetically pre-disposed to opening up a corner café. Still, it's good fun to deflate the ego of a city that is so resolutely self-involved. And if the Capetonians want to fight back, all I can say is 'bring it on, you softies.'

THE CASTLE

The story of Cape Town itself begins at The Castle. It was the first thing the VOC set about building and, for 150 years, it was the seat of Dutch government at the Cape. Life in the town was thus based around The Castle, which gave the huddled settlement some semblance of protection. Outside the walls of this 17th century Pentagon a slovenly little city began to grow.

But the current Castle is not actually the original fort built by Van Riebeeck. The first Cape Town Fort was built across the road, on the site of the Grand Parade (once a military parade ground, but now just a parking lot). This

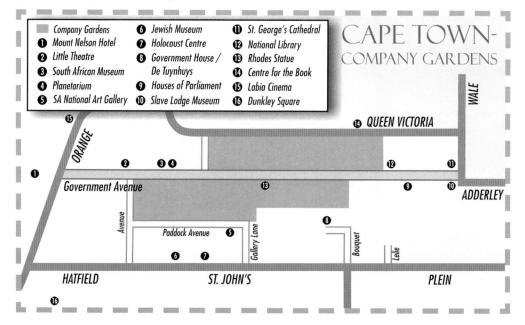

Company Gardens	⑥ Jewish Museum	⑪ St. George's Cathedral
❶ Mount Nelson Hotel	⑦ Holocaust Centre	⑫ National Library
❷ Little Theatre	⑧ Government House /	⑬ Rhodes Statue
❸ South African Museum	De Tuynhuys	⑭ Centre for the Book
❹ Planetarium	⑨ Houses of Parliament	⑮ Labia Cinema
❺ SA National Art Gallery	⑩ Slave Lodge Museum	⑯ Dunkley Square

CAPE TOWN-
COMPANY GARDENS

old earth fort is long gone, and the current stone Castle of Good Hope was built in its present position between 1666 and 1674. It is, presumably, a much grander affair than Van Riebeeck's initial, makeshift battlements.

The current Castle is a five-sided stone structure with each external wall measuring 175 metres long and 10 metres high. The bastions on each corner of the Castle are named after the various titles of the Prince of Orange, Holland's ruling monarch. *Leerdam* contained the kitchens, *Buren* housed the officers, *Oranje* contained the arsenal, *Nassau* had the powder magazine and *Catzellenbogen* accommodated the garrison. The prison cells are underground.

The Castle

Today, the Castle is a museum detailing life at the Cape under the VOC. There are guided tours at 11:00, 12:00 and 14:00, and the tour lasts about 30 minutes. The Castle also offers an art gallery, a military museum, several catering options and a lovely central courtyard with great views of The Mountain. A walk around the high ramparts of this 17th century Pentagon is a particular highlight of any visit to the Castle.
- *The Castle Museum: 021 787 1249*

THE COMPANY GARDENS
From the Castle, it is a short walk back into town where you will find the site of Van Riebeeck's original Company Gardens. These carefully cultivated orchards were once used to grow fresh fruit and vegetables for the hungry garrison housed at the Fort. Today, about half the original gardens still remain as a shady botanical park, right in the heart of Cape Town's CBD.

At the centre of the gardens there is a resonant statue of Cecil John Rhodes, pointing to the north with unashamed imperial ambition. Erected in 1910, the immortal caption on the plinth of this statue optimistically reads "Your hinterland is there". I think he meant to inscribe 'My hinterland is there', but was prevented by a false sense of propriety.

Walking Tour through the Company Gardens

The Company Gardens are a leafy place, where squirrels flick from tree to tree, while locals laze on the lawns. But the gardens are more than a pleasant park. This green lung is a central courtyard around which can be found many of South Africa's most important museums and buildings. The South African Museum, The Planetarium, The National Art Gallery, The Slave Lodge Museum, The National Library, The Jewish Museum and Holocaust Centre, and even the Houses of Parliament abut the commonage of the Company Gardens, and all can be visited by the eager traveller.

The Company Gardens begin at the corner of Adderley and Wale streets, right behind the gorgeous sandstone walls of St. George's Cathedral. This is the mother church of the Anglican community of South Africa, and was once the seat of Archbishop Desmond Tutu, the outspoken clergyman who caused the Nats so much grief. The cathedral has a relief by Anton van Wouw and the largest stained glass window in South Africa. Adjacent to the main chapel is The Crypt, a subterranean jazz club which offers breakfast and lunches in atmospheric surroundings.

From behind the cathedral, the gardens run as a rectangular park towards the mountain. They are bisected by the pedestrian thoroughfare known as Government Avenue. At the far end of the gardens you will find the Mount Nelson Hotel, colloquially called The Nellie. This gracious relic of the colonial era still serves a spiffing High Tea.
- *The Mount Nelson Hotel: 021 483 1000*
- *Cape Town Jewish Museum: 021 465 1546*
- *Cape Town Holocaust Centre: 021 462 5553*
- *Houses of Parliament tours: 021 403 2460/1*
- *SA National Gallery: 021 467 4660*
- *Slave Lodge Museum: 021 460 8240*

THE SLAVE LODGE MUSEUM
The Slave Lodge is an interesting museum situated at the corner of Adderley and Wale Street, on the edge of the Company Gardens. Built in 1679, this building was used to house the slaves who were imported from Batavia (modern-day Indonesia) and East Africa by the VOC. Over the years, these slaves were destined to mix and blend with the white settlers (and each other) to form the Cape coloured community – a spicy genetic

Table Mountain

The famous white 'tablecloth' of cloud that pours over the top of The Mountain has two causes: one mythological and the other meteorological. Both are quite interesting. First, let's get the bare-arsed facts out of the way.

The Tablecloth and the South-Easter

Quite simply, the tablecloth on Table Mountain is caused by the famous south-easter wind.

During summer, this prevailing wind howls through the streets of Cape Town, slamming car doors and flailing at the trees. It is a hearty, gusty wind that can knock you off your feet once it really gets going, and locals affectionately call it the Cape Doctor. This is ostensibly because it blows all the pollution and sickness out of the city, but it also describes what you'll need if you ever get hit by a fly-away tree branch.

Technically speaking, this is how the south-easter works: In the summer months a belt of high-pressure cells (called anti-cyclones) move north over the oceans, nearing the Cape Peninsula. This weather system pumps air up towards the southern coastline, but this air gets trapped by the mountains which line the coast. As the pressure starts to builds up, the air is pushed along the mountains, looking for a release. At Cape Hangklip, near Hermanus, all this 'compressed' air is suddenly let loose. It corners hard around the Hottentots Holland mountains at breakneck speeds and races out over the expanse of False Bay.

As it travels over the sea, the hurtling south-easter picks up lots of moisture. Then, it slams into the mountains of the Cape Peninsula. Some of this moisture-laden air is subsequently pushed up the back of Table Mountain. This causes the air to cool as it rises and, when conditions are right, the water particles suspended in the air condense into a fine water vapour. This is what pours over the edge of the Table in a gracious billow of cloud, threatening to swamp the city below. But this doesn't happen. Even though the tablecloth tumbles over The Mountain in a thick plume, the water evaporates in the warmer air and it never reaches the city.

The mythological explanation of The Mountain's tablecloth is much more entertaining.

The Story of Van Huncks

Once upon a time, there was a rough old man named Van Huncks who lived on the slopes of Devil's Peak. He used to be a

The main viewing platform on top of Table Mountain

pirate in the early 1700s before retiring to Cape Town and, in his twilight years, Van Hunks liked to climb up the slopes of The Mountain for a bit of peace and quiet. Here, cradled in the solitude of the mountain heights, he would take out his pipe and puff away to his heart's content.

One day, a mysterious stranger appeared and asked if he could try some of Van Huncks rum-soaked tobacco. Van Huncks was sociable and, like all smokers, was only too happy to share his addiction with another like-minded soul.

As the two men puffed and chuffed on their pipes, they got to chatting. In a moment of braggadocio, Van Huncks immodestly declared that he was the best pipe-smoker in the whole Cape Colony. His companion raised an eyebrow and asked if Van Huncks was prepared to bet on that. The stranger said that he was a big smoker too, and reckoned he could out-smoke old Van Huncks. The challenge was accepted, and both men filled the bowls of their pipes and started puffing.

The smoking contest lasted for many days. As Van Huncks and his companion smoked themselves into a stupor, clouds of dense fumes belched down the mountain sides. Eventually, the stranger could take no more and conceded defeat. Van Huncks was gracious in his victory and shook the strange man's hand. As the loser dejectedly turned to leave, he adjusted his big overcoat and Van Huncks caught a glimpse of a long tail and a cloven hoof. He had been playing games with the Devil himself.

So, next time you look up at The Mountain, and a majestic waterfall of cloud is pouring off its flanks, you can either say that the south-easter is blowing lots of moisture-laden air up the back of the mountain, or you can say that Van Huncks and the Devil are at it again. My money's on Van Huncks.

Signal Hill and Lion's Head

Once you have done your time on The Mountain, return to Kloof Nek and go straight over the road, following signs for Signal Hill. This will take you to the very popular Signal Hill viewsite, which is perfect for sundowners. Bring along a bottle of your favourite plonk, and enjoy the views out over Sea Point to Robben Island.

For the more energetic, a walk up Lion's Head is highly recommended. It's a relatively short hike that can be handled by most people in a reasonable state of health, and it offers wonderful views of The Mountain and the Atlantic Seaboard. Tramping up Lion's Head for a full moon party is also very popular, and on clear summer nights, several hundred people could find themselves assembled on the flat, narrow summit. The Lion's Head walk starts at the big tree, just before the Signal Hill lookout.

Table Mountain and the Cable Car

Next to Robben Island, a trip up Table Mountain is the most essential feature of any Cape Town itinerary. The cable car service has been running since 1929 and, so far, over 15 million people have taken the ride up to the top of the Tafelberg. The smart, new, revolving cable car has been operating for a few years now, and the journey is both memorable and thrilling. Just be prepared to wait your turn. Every year, over 800 000 people visit 'The Mountain' and the crowds can be hectic.

But it's all worth it, as the views from the top of The Mountain are just awesome. Take the time to walk around the paved walkways and check out the vistas on both sides of the tabletop. Guided walks depart at 10:00 and 12:00 and, surprisingly, they are free! A return ticket to the top, however, will cost over R100 per adult.

On the summit, a well-stocked cafeteria serves wine and meals, and patrons can dine al fresco on a patio overlooking the Atlantic seaboard. Sipping on your dry-white and rubbing shoulders with the nations of the world is a great way to enjoy a sundowner, and sunsets from the main viewing platform inevitably earn a round of well-deserved applause from the happy crowds. A 'shop at the top' sells a predictable assortment of tourist tat.

If you would like to see more of The Mountain, there are dozens of walks and climbs up to the summit. SAN Parks is also establishing a multi-day walking trail which will lead from Cape Point all the way across the Back Table to the Cable Car Station. It sounds fantastic. This hike has been made possible by a new initiative which has united all the conservation areas around Cape Town into a unit called the Table Mountain National Park. This stretches from Signal Hill in the north to Cape Point in the south, and includes a protected marine area that extends from Mouille Point, below Signal Hill, all the way around the Peninsula to Muizenberg.

- Cable Car Weather and Info Line: 021 424 8181
- Table Mountain National Park: 021 701 8692
  www.tmnp.co.za

Gazing at The Mountain from Lion's Head

The imperial salute of Cecil John Rhodes, Company Gardens

concoction that has grown to become one of the Cape's most vibrant cultural assets.

In 1811, after the Dutch had left, the Slave Lodge was renovated and became government offices for the new British administration. It was virtually abandoned when the British left in 1910 and, after surviving a demolition threat in the first half of the 1900s, the old Slave Lodge was declared a national monument in 1966.

True to its name, the Slave Lodge Museum is intent on offering an insight into the lives and impact of slaves at the Cape. Although slavery was not considered kosher in progressive seventeenth-century Holland, the Cape was Company property and therefore had its own set of rules. Accordingly, the first slaves started arriving within a few years of Van Riebeeck's landing, and this signalled a consolidation in the racial attitudes of the settlers. White now equated to master, and dark equated to servant. The implications for the indigenous tribes of the region were hard to ignore.

The reason the Cape required the services of the slaves is because the local Khoikhoi were unwilling to work for the white man, and

The South African Museum + Planetarium

Founded in 1825, the South African Museum is the oldest museum in sub-Saharan Africa. The planetarium is adjacent to the main museum building and charges a separate admission fee. All the museums in Cape Town are run under the auspices of the Iziko Organisation. Iziko is the Xhosa word for 'hearth', a place where people traditionally gather around the warm fire to share stories.

However, as is the case with many other old institutions, Iziko has its hands full trying to pull the South African Museum out of the old Nationalist mode of educational discourse and into the new way of thinking. As a result of this on-going modernisation, the museum is a bit of a mixed bag.

Highlights are the newly refurbished exhibit on the Bushmen and the eerie Lydenberg Heads, a fascinating relic of a little-known tribal culture. The other cultural exhibits are still very old fashioned, but are bolstered by extensive displays of implements and traditional costumes.

There are also many halls filled with melancholy rows of stuffed animals displayed in dusty glass boxes, their glassy eyes eternally staring out at the passers-by. These are the Natural History displays, and there doesn't seem to be a single creature on the subcontinent that was not killed and mounted by the zealous curators of the museum. Dozens of animal skeletons, an extensive fossil collection, a coelacanth and an extinct quagga foal in formaldehyde are also on display.

The highlight of the museum, however, is unquestionably the Whale Well. This vast, airy atrium in the centre of the building houses several whale skeletons, suspended dreamily from the roof as if swimming in a huge tank of invisible water. The size and beauty of these creatures is greatly appreciated, as you walk slowly along the ascending ramps to view their mammoth intricacy. With the soft sounds of whale song in the background and the awesome scale of the largest mammal on Earth overhead, the Whale Well alone is worth the price of admission.
• The South African Museum:021 481 3800 / www.museums.org.za/iziko
• Planetarium: 021 424 3330

proved unreliable when they did. This meant that there was no effective resident labour force, and a manpower vacuum in the growing Dutch settlement soon became apparent. Additionally, the VOC had been exposed to the native slave-owning classes in Batavia, and this had helped turn their heads.

So, to help ease the white man's burden, the VOC ordered a couple of shiploads of slaves from the West Coast of Africa. But these captives didn't behave much better than the intransigent Hottentots. Furthermore, the Dutch West India Company (the VOC's sister corporation) had cornered the market in West African slaves and didn't want to share. So, the VOC looked along its own sea route to the East and, between 1658 and 1808, 63 000 slaves were brought to the Cape from East Africa, India, Madagascar and Batavia.

This human inventory was variously owned by the VOC itself, VOC employees, free burghers and a small number of free blacks. Although house slaves were seen as a status symbol, and some female slaves even ended up as the wives of white men, conditions for the general work force

were harsh. The eerily familiar Slave Code of 1754 makes the situation quite clear:

- All slaves are to go barefoot and carry passes.
- No slave is permitted to carry a gun or alcohol.
- Any slave who assaults a free burgher will be chained and whipped.
- Any slave who raises a hand to a master will be put to death without mercy.
- Slaves may be beaten for stopping on a street to talk to each other, for meeting in a group on public holidays, during church services or in taverns.
- After dark, all slaves are to carry a lantern. No singing or whistling is allowed at night.

As was generally the case with slave-owning cultures (like America or Apartheid South Africa) life was often relentlessly grim for the human cargo locked up in the Slave Lodge. On the plus side, however, slaves at the Cape were graciously given one day off each year. This was granted on the second of January. Three centuries later, the descendants of the slaves

The Cape Minstrel Carnival in full flight

still celebrate this traditional day of rest as *Tweede Nuwe Jaar* (second new year).

THE END OF THE KHOIKHOI

But whatever happened to the Khoikhoi? They did not assimilate readily with the Dutch or the slaves, yet they no longer exist as an identifiable cultural group. So where did they go?

Well, for years after the European Invasion, this uncooperative bunch of 'savages' continued living in their traditional tribal groups, happily tending their flocks and annoying the white man at the Cape. Unfortunately, fate had a nasty trick up its inscrutable sleeve, and the Slave Lodge was to be its facilitator.

In 1713, a Dutch fleet docked at the harbour after a gruelling voyage in which many of the crew had been stricken with smallpox. Miraculously, all the victims had survived the usually fatal disease, and the fleet's commander calmly sent the crew's dirty laundry to the Slave Lodge for some much-needed washing. This was not a good idea.

From the epicentre of the Slave Lodge, the virulent smallpox virus spread like wildfire through the settlement. Slaves and masters both started dying at such an alarming rate that the demand for coffins outstripped the supply of wood. After a few traumatic months, the plague had run its course through the streets of Cape Town, but it continued to spread unchecked into the countryside.

The Khoikhoi, wholly unprepared for such a filthy European disease, had little resistance against the onslaught and were effectively decimated. In the aftermath, traditional clan structures fell apart and Khoikhoi society was left in tatters. The back of the Khoikhoi nation had been broken and further outbreaks of the disease only compounded the problem. The remaining Khoikhoi were eventually forced to become drifters, looking for work in the farms and towns of the white settlers.

So ended the independence of the Cape Khoikhoi. Henceforth, the Khoikhoi became known as the white man's servant and, in the years to come, they fought many wars against the indigenous black population on the white man's behalf. The Khoikhoi have subsequently ceased to exist as an identifiable social grouping. The moral of the story: don't wash your dirty laundry in public.

THE BO-KAAP

From the doors of the Slave Lodge, you can see up Wale Street into the colourful heart of the Bo-Kaap. Pronounced *Boo-uh Kaap*, this is the traditional heartland of the Cape coloured community, and it echoes with the sounds of their laughter and the sighs of their suffering.

The Bo-Kaap is a tightly packed suburb that starts above Buitengracht Street and creeps up the Eastern slopes of Signal Hill. The steep streets of this distinctive district are crowded with cars, kids and slightly decrepit rows of pastel-coloured houses.

Although first developed in the 1760s as a place for poor people to live, the Bo-Kaap's close proximity to the City always marked it out as something special. When the slaves were finally emancipated in the 1830s, most of them quickly moved into the Bo-Kaap and here they lived for many years, producing the so-called 'so-called coloured' community of the Cape.

Then, in the 1930s, the city council undertook The Great Task.

The Great Task was an early example of forced removals, intended to rid the City Bowl of blacks and other undesirables and move them to the sandy wasteland of the Cape Flats. It was also a convenient way to make more room for the expanding CBD. You see, prior to the 1930s, the black population lived in backyards and slums around the city. Many of these slums were owned by members of the city council and, once the deportations were underway, the city fathers quickly began knocking down the old houses to make way for expensive new developments on their now-vacant land.

True to the Capetonian spirit, however, this Great Task ran out of steam and was never completed. Thankfully, the Bo-Kaap also went on to survive apartheid and did not suffer the same fate as the now-vacant District 6. Today, it remains a thriving, full-blooded coloured stronghold. And yet, the Bo-Kaap is now facing its greatest threat yet – gentrification!

You see, slowly but surely, the Bo-Kaap is becoming fashionable. It's starting to attract a certain kind of yuppie intent on moving in, redecorating and having dinner parties. Property prices are ballooning, and Porsches are being parked on the pavement. Oh well, there goes the neighbourhood.

The crowded, chaotic streets of the Bo-Kaap

The Noon Gun

A visit to the Noon Gun Battery on top of Signal Hill is worthwhile. Every day at noon, one of two old cannons is fired with a bang that can be heard right across the City Bowl. It's a centuries-old tradition, originally instituted to give the ships in the bay a way to synchronise their unreliable clocks, and the guns are the oldest regularly fired cannons in the world. Although they are fired by a remote switch located in the SA Astronomical Observatory, you can still drive up to the Battery and experience the puff of smoke and loud retort that signals the arrival of mid-day in Cape Town. As if under starter's orders, Capetonians usually take the Noon Gun as a signal to knock off from work and race to a restaurant for an extended lunch.

Unfortunately, the little museum that used to be located at the Battery has been dismantled and its exhibits sent to the Naval Museum in Simon's Town. This is a pity. The views from the Noon Gun Battery are superb, and much more could be done to attract visitors to this little-seen (but much-heard) part of Cape Town's maritime history.

The Bo-Kaap

For the visitor, there are quite a few things to see and do in the Bo-Kaap. A good first stop is the Bo-Kaap Museum. This is a small installation that explains the history of the area, and the museum also houses a superb photographic exhibition.

Then, go get something to eat from one of the wonderfully unpretentious restaurants. This is the best way for open-minded gourmands to try some of the distinctively spicy Cape Malay cuisine. While Cape Town has ritzier places to eat Bobotie or Bredie, these old establishments reek of authenticity and offer a friendly welcome.

Two stalwarts of the Bo-Kaap eating scene are Biesmiellah's (which also has a take-away section) and the Noon Gun Tea Room, which offers an extensive set menu. Situated right at the top of the Bo-Kaap, the Noon Gun Tea Room has the added attraction of a marvellous view out over the City Bowl, and is a short walk away from the Noon Gun itself.
- *Bo-Kaap Museum: 021 481 3939*
- *Noon Gun Tea Room: 021 424 0529*
- *Biesmiellah's: 021 423 0850*

The Arrival of Islam at the Cape

The Bo-Kaap is a predominantly Muslim community, and the arrival of Islam at the Cape is an interesting story. The venerated Sheik Yusuf is generally considered to be the father of Islam in South Africa. He was born in the Hantam district of Batavia, and grew up to become the leader of a native rebellion against Dutch colonial expansion. As was generally the case with combative indigenes, Yusuf was captured in 1686 and sent to Ceylon. He was later exiled to Cape Town in 1694 and died in 1699.

A devout Hanafi Muslim, Yusuf was soon joined by other religious practitioners, including the Soofi cleric, Abu Bakr Effendi. Together, these revolutionaries spread their message of salvation through the receptive slave population at the Cape. The first mosque in South Africa was built in the Bo-Kaap as early as 1794. Sheik Yusuf is buried at Faure near Somerset West, and his kramat (shrine) can still be visited.

THE V&A WATERFRONT

Before we talk about the retail wonderland that is the modern Victoria and Alfred Waterfront, let's go back a little and look at the original shoreline of Table Bay.

When the Dutch landed at the Cape, the coastline of Table Bay looked very different to that of today. Back then, the sea came to within a few dozen metres of the Castle walls, and the original mooring for ships was at a little inlet called *Roggebaai*, located more or less at the end of today's *Heerengracht* (Gentleman's Canal). The original fresh water stream (suitably called the Fresh River), which the early ships used to replenish their water barrels, used to enter the sea at this point. The Fresh River now runs, unseen, through the storm drains under Adderley Street.

At *Roggebaai* (meaning either Ray or Rocky Bay), the big ships would sit at anchor, a short distance off-shore, while smaller boats ferried goods and people back and forth. This wasn't an ideal set-up, however, as strong winds and big waves often drove the bobbing fleets into the rocks. When this happened, the crew inevitably went to the nearest tavern and got wrecked a second time.

The first part of the solution was to build the Alfred Basin in 1860. Named after Queen Victoria's second son (who was present to tip the first load of stone into the breakwater), this little man-made harbour was soon too small to handle the Cape's increased shipping, and the larger Victoria Basin was soon commissioned. In 1913, a lovely wooden pier and promenade was also established at the bottom of Adderley Street, but this was later demolished to make way for an even bigger harbour development, the Duncan Dock, which was completed during the Second World War.

While the Duncan Dock was being built, the harbour was dredged all the way down to its rocky bottom, and the huge volume of sand that they removed from the harbour was then dumped into the former Roggebaai inlet to create a large, level concourse. This is the Foreshore, a rather barren strip of reclaimed land that runs south from the Castle towards the ugly highway overpass and the modern harbour beyond.

When the larger-still Ben Schoeman Dock was built later in the 20th Century, the old Victoria and Alfred basins fell into disuse. The adjacent waterfront became a run-down area of old warehouses, hobos and hookers. Then, in 1988, it was announced that the old V&A Waterfront was to be re-created as a multi-purpose venue with shopping malls, restaurants, yacht moorings, upmarket hotels, office blocks, apartment complexes, an aquarium and loads of other useful stuff. Even the old Breakwater Prison complex was converted into the new University of Cape Town (UCT) Business School campus.

Thankfully, the new Waterfront development was carried out with sensitivity and style. Many of the old warehouse facades have been retained and converted into attractive shopping centres filled with jewellery, curios, clothes and coffee shops. While it has its detractors, who deplore the rampant commercialism of the complex, the V&A Waterfront is an excellent place to stroll around. The Two Oceans Aquarium, an Imax Theatre and the Maritime Museum are all part of the complex, and it's also the place where you catch the ferry to Robben Island.

ROBBEN ISLAND

San Francisco has Alcatraz, and we have Robben Island. But this rocky little lump in the ocean off Cape Town is much, much more than just another famous prison. It is a symbol of righteous resistance, of awful oppression and of triumphant tolerance. It's also one of Cape Town's premier tourist attractions.

Today, a trip to Robben Island is tragic and uplifting at the same time. Although the early Dutch Settlers ate most of the seals that gave the island its name (*Robben* is Dutch for 'seals'), Robben Island is an emotional touchstone for the nation and a tacit lesson for the planet as a whole.

Most people visit the island because of its relationship to Nelson Mandela, but it has a long history of housing famous political prisoners who were condemned to years of bleak incarceration, far away from the land of their birth. For example, in the mid-1800s, several Xhosa chiefs, such as Maqoma, Stokwe and Mhala, were imprisoned here as a result of their refusal to accept British domination of their homelands in the Eastern Cape. In the 20th century, Robert Sobukwe, the founder of the Pan Africanist

A giant seagull menaces the V&A Waterfront

Robben Island

I first visited Robben Island in 1989, as part of a special school tour. It was still a functioning prison back then, and my recollections are of a dark and dismal place where the miasma of despair hung thick in the salty air. Now, Robben Island has been rehabilitated into a tourist attraction and the inmates have, literally, taken over the asylum.

Accordingly, the hulking old ferry that used to lumber over the choppy seas to the small harbour on the island has been replaced by sleek, new, high-speed boats that whisk hordes of tourists to-and-fro in comfort. The boat ride itself is remarkable for the breathtaking views that it offers of The Mountain and the city which squats at its feet.

Once on the island, everybody clambers off the boat and onto one of two waiting busses. Like a well-oiled machine, the busses take you on a slightly frustrating journey around the island while the guide points out some of the famous sites, including the lime quarry where Mandela and his comrades hacked the days away. Limestone from this old quarry was used to pave the streets of 17th century Cape Town, and it has also been used to carve the 'Freedom of Speech' monument, due to be erected in Church Square, Pretoria. I felt that this part of the excursion was a bit annoying because you aren't allowed to leave the bus and, while this might give you a taste of the curtailed liberties endured by the previous inmates, it's hardly conducive to sight-seeing.

When we returned to the main prison complex, I was glad to get off the bus and into the prison cells. Each guide on this part of the tour is a previous in-mate of the prison, and their recollections of life under the old regime are bitter-sweet. As we sat in one of the communal cells, our guide gave us quite a forthright and somewhat angry description of life as he knew it on Robben Island. The motley audience of whiteys and foreigners listened with solemn deportment as our guide described the paltry rations and daily humiliations heaped on the inmates. One poppie adjusted her high-heel shoes guiltily, while American tourists tut-tutted as if they understood.

After the communal cell, we were lead to the prison courtyard where Mandela kept his small garden. And then came the main attraction: the row of single cells where Mandela and his fellow Rivonia Trialists were held. A flurry of flash photography followed, and there was only time for a final debriefing in the toilets before we were released and sent back to the ship.

As I walked back to the harbour, I had the choice of taking a stroll along the sponsored boardwalk to watch the penguins, or browsing the extensive gift shop on the quayside. At the appointed time, I climbed on board for the return journey home, and watched with rueful irony as the next busload of voluntary inmates began their journey through the portals of Robben Island.

So, in many ways, Robben Island is a slick tourist machine, processing people like Disneyland during summer vacation. In other ways, it is an important excursion that should be experienced by all South Africans so that we can better understand the traumatic realities of our history. The round trip costs R150 per person and takes about 3 and a half hours. Don't miss it.
* *Robben Island Information: 021 413 4200 / www.robbenisland.org.za*

Congress, spent so many years alone in a little house on the island that his speech became impaired. And, in the 1970s, just about every major black political activist spent some time on the rock. Back in those dark days, who could have predicted that the prison roll call would one day sound like the minutes of a cabinet meeting?

Although its isolated proximity to the Cape made it a natural place to put people who weren't wanted, Robben Island wasn't always a prison. It's true that obstreperous Khoikhoi (including the troublesome Herrie) were sent there by the Dutch, but the island was also used as a leper colony, a whaling station and as a naval base during World War Two.

But it is Nelson Mandela who has given the desolate little island its enduring place as a World Heritage Site of Cultural Significance. The twenty-seven years that our beloved Madiba spent behind bars in this brutal facility are a testament to the strength of the human spirit, and a reminder of what can be accomplished by the righteous.

DISTRICT SIX

One of the most ignominious chapters in Cape Town's history is the legacy of forced removals that ripped the city apart in the 1950s and 1960s. This was an era of oppression and ideological barbarity that swept over the whole of South Africa, as guided by the smiling face of HF Verwoerd and the Nationalist party. And it

The rusty barbed-wire fence that encircles the Robben Island prison compound

was all done on the flimsy excuse that it would be best for the native populations to be allowed to develop separately, for their own good.

Accordingly, the official policy of the time was to remove all non-whites and other 'undesirables' from the white cities to pre-ordained townships where, like the Bushmen in the desert, they would be left to survive as best they could on land that no one wanted. In practise, it was a cold, callous process that was carried out with all the ruthless efficiency of Hitler's *kindertransport*.

Two of the best-known forced removals in South African history were from Sophiatown (in Joburg) and District Six in Cape Town. As case studies, they have a lot in common: both areas were home to thriving mixed-race communities, situated close to their respective city centres. Both were chaotic, overcrowded suburbs riddled with criminals. And both were home to proud and independent people who cherished their freedom, their music and their unique lifestyle. As such, these areas were a slap in the face to the dour, hateful Nats who wanted a white dominion untainted by the filth of miscegenation. Sophiatown and District Six were consequently bulldozed into oblivion.

From the ashes of Sophiatown, a new white suburb arose. It was called *Triomf* (Triumph), perhaps the most distasteful and contemptuous place name ever awarded to a suburb. But at least in Joburg they built a new suburb on the rubble of the old. The streets of District Six, by comparison, were not re-developed and stood largely empty for years, a weird urban wasteland just a few k's outside the heart of the Mother City. As a final irony, both suburbs have been turned into successful protest musicals, which toured the world's stages and helped galvanise international attitudes against the Apartheid regime.

Today, District Six is being rebuilt in an appropriate style, and the sights and sounds of 'Fairyland' live on in the District Six Museum. It's a touching and important installation that documents the suburb's unique character, history and ultimate destruction at the hands of Apartheid's architects. The original inhabitants may have been moved to the Cape Flats and other desolate locations, but the soul of 'Distrik' Six (and Sophiatown) is slowly being reclaimed with the return of some former residents.

Cape Town City Bowl contacts:
- *Cape Town Tourism: 021 426 4260*
  www.tourismcapetown.co.za
- *V&A Waterfront: 021 408 7600*
  www.waterfront.co.za
- *Two Oceans Aquarium: 021 418 3823*
  www.aquarium.co.za
- *Gold of Africa Museum: 021 405 1540*
  www.goldofafrica.com
- *District Six Museum: 021 461 8745*
  www.districtsix.co.za
- *Grand West Casino: 021 505 7777*
  www.grandwest.co.za
- *Canal Walk Shopping Centre: 021 555 4444*
  www.canalwalk.co.za
- *Ratanga Junction Theme Park: 0861 200 300*
  www.ratangajunction.co.za
- *Tygerberg Zoo: 021 884 4494*
  www.tygerbergzoo.co.za
- *Cape Town International Airport: 021 937 1200*
  www.acsa.co.za

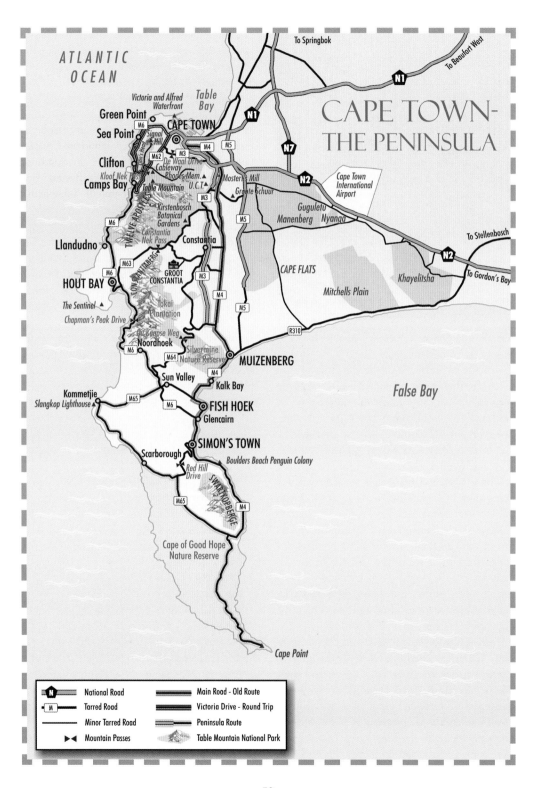

CAPE TOWN-THE PENINSULA

ATLANTIC OCEAN

To Springbok
To Beaufort West

N1

Table Bay

Victoria and Alfred Waterfront

Green Point
Sea Point
CAPE TOWN
Signal Hill
Clifton
Camps Bay
Kloof Nek Pass
De Waal Drive
Cableway
Rhodes Mem.
Table Mountain
U.C.T.
Twelve Apostles

Mostert's Mill
Groote Schuur

N7

N2

Cape Town International Airport

Guguletu
Manenberg
Nyanga

To Stellenbosch

Kirstenbosch Botanical Gardens
Constantia Nek Pass
Constantia

Llandudno

Orange Kloof

M6
M63
M62
M3
M4
M5

GROOT CONSTANTIA

CAPE FLATS

Khayelitsha

To Gordon's Bay

HOUT BAY
The Sentinel
Chapman's Peak Drive

Tokai Plantation
Ou Kaapse Weg

Mitchells Plain

N2

Noordhoek

Silvermine Nature Reserve

MUIZENBERG

R310

False Bay

Sun Valley
Kalk Bay

Kommetjie
Slangkop Lighthouse

FISH HOEK
Glencairn

SIMON'S TOWN
Boulders Beach Penguin Colony

Scarborough

Red Hill Drive

SWARTKOPBERG

Cape of Good Hope Nature Reserve

Cape Point

M64
M65
M6
M4

Legend

N	National Road		Main Road - Old Route
M	Tarred Road		Victoria Drive - Round Trip
	Minor Tarred Road		Peninsula Route
►◄	Mountain Passes		Table Mountain National Park

5. Cape Town – The Peninsula

ORIENTATION

The Cape Peninsula is shaped like a claw, curving out into the sea between Table Bay and False Bay. It is a magnificent headland, with extravagant mountains, dramatic seascapes and attractive suburbs all competing for your attention.

The main road around the Peninsula runs from the City Bowl through the Atlantic Seaboard suburbs of Green Point, Sea Point, Clifton, Camps Bay, Llandudno, Hout Bay and Noordhoek to Kommetjie. From here, the road veers inland to rejoin the sea on the False Bay side of the Peninsula. From there, you can turn South towards Cape Point, or turn North and drive up the False Bay coast to Muizenberg. From Muizenberg, you can take either the M3 highway or the robot-riddled Main Road (The M4) back to Cape Town, through the Southern Suburbs. The round trip is about 150 k's, including the detour to Cape Point.

Our route starts at the edge of the City Bowl as a humble thoroughfare called Somerset Road. As Somerset curves around the foot of Signal Hill, it changes its name to Main Road, and leads through the high-rise suburbs of Green Point, Mouille Point and Sea Point. After Sea Point, the road does a little dog's leg and changes its name, once again, to Victoria Drive. Also known as the M6, Victoria Drive then continues across the precarious cliffs of Clifton to the rarefied atmosphere to Camps Bay.

At Camps Bay, you can either follow signs for Kloof Nek, which will take you up to the Cable Car Station and then down to the Cape Town City Bowl [see Chapter 4], or you can continue with Victoria Drive, along the coast, to Llandudno. At this point, the road rises over a low nek between the Twelve Apostles and the Little Lion's Head, and descends to Hout Bay.

Hout Bay is actually a very isolated settlement with only three land-based access routes: Constantia Nek (M63) to the Southern Suburbs; Victoria Drive to Camps Bay and Sea Point; and, greatest of them all, Chapman's Peak Drive (M6) to Noordhoek.

After Noordhoek, you have four options. You can:

➡ Take the M66, through the Silvermine Nature Reserve and down *Ou Kaapse Weg*, to join the M3 highway above Muizenberg. This road is part of the annual Cape Argus Cycle Race, and offers cyclists a lovely (if very steep) ride.

➡ Take the M65 East, through Sun Valley and Clovelly, to the village of Fish Hoek on the False Bay coast [see Chapter 6].

➡ Take the continuation of the M6 to Glencairn, a little town to the south of Fish Hoek.

➡ Or, continue on the road around the Peninsula by taking the M65 West, to Kommetjie and Scarborough.

After Scarborough, the road turns away from the sea, and you can either take the spectacular Red Hill Drive down to Simon's town on the False Bay coast [see Chapter 6], or continue with the M65 towards land's end at Cape Point. The False Bay section of the drive is discussed more fully in the next chapter.

THE FIRST ROADS IN SOUTH AFRICA

The first roads in South Africa came with the Europeans. Before the VOC landed on our shores, footpaths, game trails and bare feet got you just about anywhere you wanted to go. Wheeled transport was unknown, and there was simply no need for roads.

In retrospect, it is strange that Africa never really got hold of the wheel as a useful concept. I suppose it's just a matter of necessity being the mother of invention, and subsistence farming doesn't really require a wagon to take goods to market. In any event, the various mountain ranges that cut the country into slices were not easily crossed by wagon wheels – a geographical reality well appreciated by road builders in the years to come.

So, it was only when Van Riebeeck and crew disembarked with notions of corporate enterprise that the business of road building slowly began in South Africa. But making roads was not an initial priority for the new commander. As has already been discussed, the early years of the VOC settlement at the Cape were tough. There was little food, no support and no infrastructure. The only commodity that was not in short supply was wood.

Tall stands of trees covered the slopes of Table Mountain, and getting timber for building or heating was simply a matter of chopping down a likely-looking specimen and dragging it down to the fort. However, trees cannot be carried by man alone, and timber must be transported on a wagon to achieve any kind of economy of scale. Wagons, in turn, need roads, and so began the history of road building in SA.

DIE OU WAGEN PAD NA 'T BOS / THE OLD WAGON ROAD TO THE FOREST
The *Ou Wagen Pad na 't Bos* was the first European-made road in the country. It started at the Castle and slowly stretched out into the trees, growing longer as the demand for wood increased and the proximity of nearby timber dwindled. At first, the road extended around the landward slopes of Table Mountain, hugging the treeline as far as was convenient at the time. Over time, however, it grew until it finally stretched all the way to the False Bay coast at Muizenberg.

It appears that the old 'waggon road to the forest' was begun soon after Van Riebeeck

landed. The rough-hewn route started at the Fort and wound around the *Windberg* (Windy Mountain, now known as Devil's Peak). It was then extended through Rondebosch and Newlands, and so into the Kirstenbosch forest. By 1687, an offshoot of the road reached as far as the new winter harbour of Simon's Town.

Interestingly enough, the approximate route of this woodcutter's road, much trodden and now tarred, remains in place today, 350 years after it was first hacked out of the trees. In fact, the *Ou Wagen Pad na t' bos* is still very familiar to the modern people of Cape Town, although it has been given a new name. It's now called the M4 or, more appropriately, Main Road.

MAIN ROAD / THE M4
The M4 starts at the southern corner of the Castle. Despite the antiquity of its origins, driving along Main Road today takes you on a fascinating journey right through the pulsing, bi-polar heart of modern-day Cape Town.

Initially, Main Road leads from the City Bowl, around the bulk of Devil's Peak, through the crowded, honking streets of Woodstock, Salt River, Observatory and Mowbray. Pedestrians, pots and pans, taxis, hawkers, general merchants, carpet sellers and pawn shops fill your eyes, while the beat from a sound system outside a shop (or inside a car) offers a thumping bass as aural counterpoint to the urban landscape.

The architecture is that of a ramshackle old High Street, with crumbling shops and ancient flats jostling for place between the newer commercial developments of the 1970s and 80s. This part of the road is an arresting drive, especially at rush hour when the traffic is heavy and the going is slow.

Then, the tenor of the road changes as it passes the very large Groote Schuur Hospital. This is the great medical institution where a slightly mad visionary named Dr Christiaan Barnard, performed the world's first heart transplant back in 1967.

Once past Groote Schuur, Main Road leaves

Stone lions give their stern benediction to a wedding at Rhodes Memorial

behind the cacophonous city centre *aria* and enters the quiet *recitative* of the Southern Suburbs. Not to be confused with the Southern Suburbs in Joburg (which are rather, shall we say, proletarian), the Southern Suburbs of Cape Town are the sedate and settled heart of the suburban bourgeoisie.

Although I have one Cape Town friend who says he'd rather live in Joburg than in Claremont, this part of town contains Mostert's Mill, the Rhodes Memorial, the Presidential residence of Groote Schuur, the Baxter Theatre, Cavendish Square Shopping Mall, Kirstenbosch Gardens, Newlands Cricket Ground and The University of Cape Town (UCT), perhaps the most beautiful university campus in the world.

As you pass through Rosebank, Rondebosch, Newlands and Claremont, the Mountain turns its back and shows off the crags and crevices of its Southern flanks. Grand houses, leafy avenues and discreet shops gradually take over from the bustle of the city, impressing on the visitor that most crucial element of Capetonian society, class distinction.

This gentility is short-lived however, and the Southern Suburbs soon give way to the colourful reality of Wynberg, firmly located on the other side of the tracks. The honking gets louder, the houses get smaller and the shops get bigger as you move into the western fringes of the Cape Flats.

Main Road continues in this fashion through Plumstead, Dieprivier and Retreat until it eventually reaches False Bay near Muizenberg. From here, Main Road continues along False Bay all the way to Simon's Town. However, there are other ways to get to Muizenberg and following Main Road all the

Rhodes Memorial

Despite the colonial overtones, Rhodes 'Mem' is a nice little detour. It offers the visitor a pretty tea garden and grand views over the city towards Bloubergstrand. Built in 1912 by Rhodes' favourite architect, Sir Herbert Baker, the monument is a suitably austere and impressive testament to the Colossus of Cecil John Rhodes. Made from blocks of Table Mountain granite, the memorial is all neo-classical columns, staircases and stone lions perched on pediments. It's a favourite place for wedding pictures, and for students intent on bunking class.

Groote Schuur Residence

In 1657, the Dutch East India Company started building 'De Schuur' at Rondebosch. It was a large barn, designed to store all the Company's grain and other produce, and it was constantly in use for the next 200 years. In 1812, the building got an upgrade and was re-named 'Groote Schuur', meaning the Great Barn but, by the late 19th century, the venerable old building was falling into disrepair.

Then, in 1893, Cecil John Rhodes bought the building and its extensive estate, which ran from the eastern slopes of Devil's Peak all the way to Constantia Nek. By this time, Rhodes was already filthy rich from his exploits on the diamond and gold fields, and had been instated as Prime Minister of the Cape in 1890. Flush with his overwhelming success, Rhodes decided that Groote Schuur should be his new official residence and, after a chance meeting with an untried British architect named Herbert Baker, Rhodes commissioned him to design a grand new residence, fit for a king.

Baker's architectural vernacular mixed barley-twist chimneys, natural stone, dark wood panels, shady verandas and gracious gables. It was to become a trademark style which made Baker one of the most influential architects in South Africa's history. He went on to design the Union Buildings in Pretoria, and many of the grand 'Randlord' mansions on the Reef.

Rhodes, meanwhile, was busy furnishing his new palace with the finest furniture, books, silver, glassware and porcelain that he could find. There were Delft tiles on the skirtings, souvenirs from the Great Zimbabwe ruins on the mantelpiece, 17th century Flemish tapestries on the walls and a huge bathtub carved from Paarl granite. Today, the interior of the house remains much as Rhodes left it, and the magnificent gardens are still redolent with Plumbago, Rhodes' favourite bloom.

Once he was safely ensconced in his refurbished barn, Rhodes began to entertain lavishly. He would also open his estate to the public every weekend, declaring that he liked to fill his grounds with people rather than wild animals. But Rhodes, inevitably, became the victim of his own hubris, and had to resign from his post as Prime Minister after getting involved in the disastrous Jameson Raid; a foolish attempt to overthrow the sovereign government of Paul Kruger's South African Republic, in 1895.

Nevertheless, despite his ignominious fall from political grace, Rhodes was still as rich as Croesus and he continued to live at Groote Schuur until his death in 1902. Rhodes bequeathed his grand estate to his adoptive country, and the Groote Schuur homestead was given to the government as the official residence for all future South African leaders. The rest of the property was given to 'the people of South Africa', and Kirstenbosch Gardens, the Universtity of Cape Town campus and the Groote Schuur Hospital were all built on the grounds of Rhodes' old estate. In fact, the UCT post office still respectfully uses the post mark 'Rhodes' Gift'. The remainder of the estate, once in private hands, has now been incorporated into the Table Mountain National Park.

When a liberated Nelson Mandela became the first president of a multi-racial South Africa, he too moved into the Victorian eminence of Groote Schuur and lived there, as if to the manor born. Tours around the residence can be booked, whenever the current President is not in residence.

• Groote Schuur Estate (Table Mountain National Park): 021 689 4441 / www.tmnp.co.za
• Groote Schuur / Genadendal Residence (tour bookings): 021 686 9100

way is slow and inconvenient. I would suggest driving along Main Road until you see the signs for Constantia. Then, nip onto the M3 highway, which runs parallel to Main Road, and zip down to Muizenberg where you can pick up Main Road once again.

CLOOF PASS / CONSTANTIA NEK

Formerly content to chop down trees along the foot of the mountain, the loggers responsible for keeping Cape Town stocked with wood were faced with an inevitable problem. As demand for timber grew, supplies started running low on the

Kirstenbosch National Botanical Gardens

The headquarters of the National Biodiversity Institute, Kirstenbosch is one of 8 National Botanical Gardens around South Africa. It is also the flagship of the institute and, as befits such a prestigious installation, these lovely gardens are a treat for the horticulturalist and botanically illiterate alike.

After passing through the hands of many owners, this property was eventually bought by the ubiquitous C J Rhodes as part of his Groote Schuur Estate, and was bequeathed to the city in 1895. In 1913, it was established as the National Botanical Gardens and now boasts 5000 thriving plant species. The respected restaurant is always popular, and the snazzy visitor's centre has a coffee shop, book shop and garden centre.

The beautiful grounds of the 528 hectare Kirstenbosch complex run up the side slopes of Table Mountain, and strolling around the complex is a great way to spend an afternoon. The sculpture garden is a highlight, and other themed areas include the Fynbos Trail and the Fragrance Garden. A Braille Trail for the visually impaired has also been laid out. Kirstenbosch is a convenient starting point for some of the popular walking routes that lead up to the top of the mountain.

- *Kirstenbosch National Botanical Gardens: 021 762 1166 / www.nbi.ac.za*

accessible slopes around the Castle. Additional trees had to be found. These were discovered growing in great abundance on the Western side of the mountain in a valley called, with customary imagination, Hout Bay (Wood Bay).

But there was a problem. If they wanted to get trees out of Hout Bay, they would have to get wagons in, and this meant building a road from one side of the range to the other. In 1666, Commander Wagenaer (Van Riebeeck's successor) gave the order, and a bunch of soldiers went out with 'some crowbars, picks and shovels in order to make a road'. This rough dirt

track grew into the lovely road that runs from the Groot Constantia wine estate, over Constantia Nek, and down into Hout Bay. Originally called Cloof Pass, this was the first mountain road constructed in South Africa.

But don't be in a hurry to drive over the pass. First, take a few hours to drive around Constantia and explore the one of the oldest wine routes in the Cape. When you have had enough of all the wining, follow Constantia Road up the mountain, past the shopping centre and the tour buses, to Constantia Nek.

The road climbs quite gently at first, but soon succumbs to the contour lines and starts

The sculpture garden at Kirstenbosch

twisting up the final ascent to the summit of the Nek – a low-lying saddle that connects the back of Table Mountain to the Vlakkenberg and Constantiaberg. Once over the Nek, the road winds in and out of the rumpled mountainside, descending the narrow valley of the Disa River. This delightful vale gradually widens out to reveal the enchanted Hout Bay Valley.

CONSTANTIA WINE ROUTE

Today, Constantia is both an idyllic suburb of modern Cape Town and home to some of the oldest wine estates in the Cape. The land was originally granted to Dutch Governor, Simon van der Stel, in appreciation for his services to the Company and, as a special reward, he was allowed to select the site of his new homestead. Being a very thorough person, van der Stel tested soil all over the Peninsula until he found the ideal composition that would give his grapes the best flavour.

The huge new farm he finally chose was named *Constantia*, apparently in honour of a young woman named Constance who had helped convince the thrifty Company to give away such a prime piece of real estate. By 1685, Van der Stel had built a grand homestead on his new farm, and was busily planting 70 000 grape vines, among them Muscadel and Steen. Unfortunately, Van der Stel died before his efforts bore fruit and, with no descendants living in South Africa, his picture-perfect farm was split up and sold off.

Years later, in 1778, Hendrik Cloete bought the piece of land that had become known as Groot Constantia. The property was run down and the vines were mostly dead, but, together with his neighbour and relative Johannes Colyn, Cloete restored Van der Stel's old manor house and replanted thousands of grape vines. The estate went on to produce two of the greatest wines in the history of viticulture: the white and red Constantia wines. This nectar was so renowned that kings, generals and dukes kept it in their cellars for special occasions. Writers such as Dickens, Jane Austen and Alexander Dumas all mentioned Constantia wines in their books, and Napoleon drank a

Constantia Wine Route

Spread out like a quilt over the undulating hips of Table Mountain's south-eastern flanks, the pretty Constantia Valley is the heart of the 'mink and manure' set of Cape Town. The whole area fairly glows with complacent civility, and the Groot Constantia wine estate is especially venerable, with Simon van der Stel's restored manor house adding to the general air of maturity. Today, Groot Constantia offers wine tasting, a museum, good dining and a stroll among the vineyards. Nearby, other wine estates, like the ever-optimistic Buitenverwagting (Beyond Expectation), Klein Constantia, Alphen and Steenberg, can also be visited. And after a heavy day of wine tasting, the mountain walk through Cecilia Forest to the Kirstenbosch Gardens is an enticing way to stroll off the booze.

- *Groot Constantia Museum:*
  021 795 5140 / www.grootconstantia.co.za

Watching the sunset from Victoria Drive

bottle every day while he was exiled on St Helena.

Sadly, the recipe for the original Constantia wines has been lost, and the few remaining bottles aren't giving away any secrets. Nevertheless, the Constantia Valley still produces a number of fine wines from the few vineyards that haven't been taken over by suburban housing, and the Constantia wine route is bound to please those who like a spot of plonk.

VICTORIA DRIVE

By the mid-1800s, Cape Town was growing apace and the need for improved access routes became apparent. Accordingly, a rough track was built from the City Bowl over Kloof Nek down to Camps Bay, and then along the coast to Hout Bay. These early roads were rather rudimentary and in 1884 it was decided that road-meister Thomas Bain should be called in to build a proper road along the Atlantic Seaboard. The road was completed in 1888, using convict labour and funding from the Cape Town Divisional Council.

The result is the glorious Victoria Drive and, despite various improvements, it still substantially follows Bain's original course. The road begins in the high-rise suburb of Sea Point.

SEA POINT

With its lovely promenade along the water's edge and once-decorous blocks of flats, Sea Point used to be the Riviera of the Cape Peninsula. Unfortunately, this little bit of paradise has seen better days and, today, Sea Point is a crowded residential area with high-density housing and the smell of urban decay leaking slowly out onto the streets.

But Sea Point is also a vibrant, colourful suburb with a long High Street filled with every kind of shop, restaurant and consumer service imaginable. The various delis and eating houses along Sea Point Main Road are legendary, as are the porn shops and brothels that throb redly in the night sky.

At night, Sea Point turns into an urban wonderland, full of screeching stray cats and drunken car guards. As a youngster, I remember spending many happy December holidays on the streets of Sea Point, hanging around outside Steers and eating burgers from Saul's Saloon. Those were the days. Now its more like

Beachball on Clifton First, looking onto Clifton Second

'Hillbrow-by-the-sea', but Sea Point still has a resident population that is very proud of their little enclave, and the steep streets leading off Main Road have a special charm of their own.

But it's Main Road that defines Sea Point, for better or for worse, and walking along the main drag is bound to be an adventure – especially on New Year's Eve, when you are likely to get a face full of shoe polish, slapped on by the playful locals. 'Happy Happy', indeed.

Sea Point does not have a beach, as the sea runs right up to the stone ramparts of the Promenade, but this hardly seems to matter. The pedestrian walkway along the water's edge is gorgeous, lined with green lawns, comfy benches and a drooping string of fairy lights. A stroll along the Prom is remarkably pleasant, and a dip in the large salt water pool of the Sea Point Pavilion is a good way to cool off.

The Promenade also has a little secret hid away at its southern extremity. Here you will find a rare geological exposure that that has drawn the attention of the world's scientists for hundreds of years. Even the estimable Charles Darwin came to inspect the site during his visit to South Africa, in 1836.

Snoozing on Clifton First Beach

At the end of Sea Point, Main Road does a small left/right and turns into Victoria Drive. Wedged between the steep sides of Lion's Head and the crashing waves of the Atlantic, this two-lane thoroughfare is a marvel of engineering and a delight to drive. However, it is woefully inadequate for the purposes of modern road transportation and, in season, Victoria Drive becomes one long, winding traffic jam as everyone (and their mates from Joburg) converge on the trendy beaches of Clifton and Camps Bay.

If you want to miss the traffic, try taking Kloof Road, which runs high on the cliffs above and parallel to Victoria Drive. This useful road

View of Camps Bay from Kloof Nek Road

leads from Sea Point up to Kloof Nek, or down to rejoin Victoria Drive just before Camps Bay. Either way, the views from the car are unsurpassable, and both Victoria Drive and Kloof Road take you on a trip through the heart of opulent Cape Town, as epitomised by the high-life of Clifton.

CLIFTON

With unimpeded sea views to the West, the endless sunsets of Clifton are justifiably famous. While, at first glance, the suburbs of Bantry Bay and Clifton are the zenith of Capetonian real-estate, this section of the Atlantic Seaboard had humble beginnings.

At the end of the First World War, several cottages were built on these sea-facing cliffs as emergency housing for veterans returning from the war. Over the years, more of these little bungalows were erected, and they came to be inhabited by alternative, hippie types and ordinary families just trying to make ends meet. It was a homely community where everybody knew everybody else, and one of my friends tells the story of how his parents (both Clifton natives) used to meet on the beach every day after school until they fell in love.

Soon, however, the views from the cliffs started attracting big money. The little bungalows were sold off, one by one, to be replaced by increasingly expensive houses, flats and apartments, clinging precariously to the sheer rock face. Nowadays, Clifton is one of the best addresses in Cape Town, and a holiday flat in Clifton is the ultimate status symbol of the land-locked yuppie.

Accordingly, the tiny, secluded beaches that fill the rocky clefts in the shore line have become status symbols in their own right. Clifton First, Second, Third and Fourth Beaches are among the most frequented and socially overheated shingles on the Peninsula. In season, hordes of inlanders descend the steps to Clifton First and parade themselves on the warm sands, as hundreds more spend hours looking for parking on the road above. This is not to say that anybody actually goes swimming at Clifton. The water's too cold and the hair-do's too expensive. But who cares? The Clifton beaches are, indeed, stunning.

While even penguins shun the Clifton surf because it's too chilly, the sunsets are gorgeous. Many people stay on the beach until well into the evening, making the most of Cape Town's

Plenty of palm trees but no parking on the Camps Bay beachfront

late summer sun, which sinks below the waves only at nine in the evening. Furthermore, Clifton's beaches are nestled into the rocks and are protected from the whipping wind that often plagues the other Peninsula beaches. So, if it's a windy day in town, rest assured that the beautiful people will be strutting and pouting quite happily in the sheltered coves of Clifton.

If you still don't know whether or not to brave the titivating flocks of Clifton, consider the added attraction of taking the walk over the rocks from First to Fourth beach. At sunset, this ramble is a visual treat, and the scenery's quite pretty too.

CAMPS BAY

After the delights of Clifton, Victoria Drive leads out of the cliffs into Camps Bay. First established as a farm called *Ravensteyn*, this once-remote outpost was re-named after Frederick von Kamptz, an invalid sailor who cleverly married the widow of the farm's original owner. Camps Bay is now one of the most exclusive suburbs in Cape Town, and with good reason.

Simply put, Camps Bay has three things going for it: location, location and location. Cradled between Devils Peak and Table Mountain, with the achingly beautiful range of the Twelve Apostles stretching off to the South, Camps Bay has parlayed its exceptional setting into a large and very expensive enclave.

Thankfully, Camps Bay beach is open to all and a sunset stroll along the beach is memorable. Smooth rocks, golden sand and exotic palm trees fringe the sea, as the sun sinks and turns the sky orange, red and rosy. Silhouettes of happy walkers pass before your eyes and, should you turn around, the mountains are there to complete the picture. For surfers, the adjacent cove of Glen Beach offers some reliable breaks.

But even paradise has its downside, and Camps Bay beach can be very windy and very busy. Furthermore, the beachside strip of shops and pricey restaurants is always packed and often jammed solid with cars. To make matters worse,

Cape Town is positively infested with models and assorted Euro-trash who have made Camps Bay their home away from home. The local watering hole, frivolously named Caprice, is the High Temple of these Beautiful People and the place to be if you want to sample the Scene.

LLANDUDNO

After leaving Camps Bay, Victoria Drive runs along the foot of the Twelve Apostles towards Llandudno. Surprisingly, development is curtailed on this lovely stretch of coast, and regular picnic spots have been built alongside the road so that you can stop to admire the view. Much to their credit, this is something that the Capetonians do with regularity. For those who are prepared to brave the icy waters of the Atlantic, the beaches of Oudekraal and Bakoven can be found along this part of the road.

The next residential suburb is Llandudno, an upmarket village of large homes that has established itself around a small beach, surrounded by enormous boulders. Sandy Bay, the only nude beach on the Peninsula, can be reached from the southern end of Llandudno. However, Llandudno is a largely residential area and facilities for the day tripper are limited. The beach does have its devotees, however, and who can blame them?

HOUT BAY

From Llandudno, Victoria Road leapfrogs over a low nek and winds down into the self-styled 'Republic' of Hout Bay. With its small fishing harbour and large township, Hout Bay is a beautiful place to explore.

The traditional centre of town is the old harbour pier. From here you can catch a ferry to see the seals on Duiker Island, you can stroll along the beach, or you can buy some *fres' fis'* from Mariners Wharf (reputedly the first harbour-front emporium in SA). On the other side of the beach, there are a number of retail developments that offer restaurants, galleries, craft shops and every other sort of tourist necessity.

The sprawling, controversial township of Imizamo Yethu also offers tours through its ramshackle streets and, as much as the residents of Hout Bay wish it could be moved somewhere else, a trip through the location offers a critical counterpoint to the lush prosperity of the big homes in the valley.

For the historically minded, Hout Bay has two forts and a museum. These forts, one on either side of the Bay, have recently been restored and now boast working cannons – just in case the Americans try to invade. Additionally, there are horse rides in the vicinity, as well as the well-known World of Birds. The beach itself is lovely, but the water's bloody freezing and the wind can be fierce.

THE 'ALL ROUND THE CAPE PENINSULA' ROAD

By 1913, motorised transport was becoming quite common in the Cape. But there still weren't that many roads around the Peninsula. There was access to Hout Bay via Constantia Nek or Victoria Drive, and Main Road ran along the landward side of Table Mountain down to Simon's town. But there was no road joining False Bay to the Atlantic Seaboard.

Then, with a diplomatic flourish, it was decided that an 'All Round the Cape Peninsula Road' should be constructed. This project was generously funded by the national government (perhaps as compensation for moving the national capital to Pretoria), and work soon began on an assortment of new roads. De Waal Drive, Red Hill Drive, the road from Simon's Town to Cape Point, the road from Kommetjie to Cape Point, and Chapman's Peak Drive from Hout Bay to Noordhoek were all built during this time, using convict labour. Within a few years, a road harness had been thrown around the muzzle of the Cape Peninsula.

CHAPMAN'S PEAK DRIVE

Chapman's Peak is one of my all-time favourite drives in the world, ever! And if I overstate my case with childish enthusiasm, I'm allowed, because Chapman's Peak Drive has made me gasp since I was kid.

Unsurprisingly, the Chapman's Peak road pass was very difficult to build. In fact, the nine-

The amazing coastal road to Scarborough

kilometre road was completed only in 1922, nearly ten years after it was first proposed. The reasons for the delay were obvious; this was a very steep and rocky mountain. A dispute over the routing didn't make things any easier. Some people wanted the road to go over the summit, while others wanted to make a lateral cut into the cliffs. Finally, the latter option was chosen and a track was hacked into the sheer mountain face, under the supervision of Robert Glenday.

The result was a plucky little road that ran halfway between the high peaks and the sea below; balanced on a narrow ledge formed by the transition zone between a layer of Cape Granite and the sedimentary rocks of the Graafwater Formation immediately above. This original route was both a miraculous piece of engineering and a scenic masterpiece to boot. Once it was completed, Chapman's Peak quickly gained a reputation as a day drive of extraordinary appeal.

The road begins on the eastern side of Hout Bay. At the foot of the pass, there is a bronze statue of a leopard, sculpted by Ivan Mitford-Barberton in 1963. The statue is a little tribute to the leopards who used to live in the area as recently as the 1930s. Elephants were also common in the Hout Bay Valley, but the last two were shot way back in the 1830s.

After this melancholy monument to Wildlife Past, Chapman's Peak Drive continues past the little inlet of Flora Bay (which happens to be my mother's maiden name) and through the new toll booth, currently charging around R20 per car. Then, the road starts to climb in a slow, rising arc that curves up from the bay, hugging the mountainside.

At the summit of the climb, there is a parking area where you can stop for a eye-filling view of the Sentinel, Karbonkelberg, Little Lions Head, the Back Table and Chapman's Peak itself; the unbroken bowl of mountains which form a protective cup around the beautiful Bay of Wood.

For a few bleak years, this is where the road ended, as a number of serious rock falls forced

Noordhoek

For many years, Noordhoek was a sleepy little village at the end of Chapman's Peak. Now it is a prosperous sleepy village that offers restaurants, craft shops and overpriced real estate to eager tourists. Horse rides on the beach, the Red Herring Trading Post and Noordhoek Farm Village are all good reasons to stop here, but the main attraction is the quiet country atmosphere and the staggering stretch of sandy beach that curves for 8km, from Noordhoek all the way to Kommetjie.

• *Noordhoek Tourism: 021 789 2812*
• *Noordhoek Beach Horse Rides: 021 783 1168*

the council to close the pass in 2000. The fate of the old road seemed uncertain, and residents of Hout Bay had to make do with Constantia Nek and Victoria Drive as their only links to the outside world. Thankfully, a remarkable rehabilitation project was completed in 2003 and a safer Chapman's Peak is once again open to traffic.

So, now we can continue as the road cuts through a jutting spur, swings to the left, and runs at a slight decline along a precipitous cliff face that plunges straight down to the sea. The vista is extraordinary as you drive along the formidable wall of rock, suspended between the sky and the deep blue sea. There can be few other roads in the world to compete with Chapman's for unadulterated visual drama

Kommetjie

On the far end of Noordhoek beach lies the village of Kommetjie (Little Bowl). Slightly more built up than the devotedly rural Noordhoek, Kommetjie is best known for surfing, seafood and Slangkop lighthouse. Nearby Long Beach has one of the best surfing breaks in Cape Town, and it attracts many city folk looking to unwind after a hard morning at the office. Imhoff's Gift Farm and several large craft centres can also be found in the area.

(although the Big Sur highway along the Californian coast does comes close). Then, all too soon, the last thrusting promontory is rounded and the road calmly descends to the charming village of Noordhoek.

In the old days, Chapman's Peak Drive was entirely exposed on the cliff face, largely following the original route staked out in 1915.

The new, improved road is now cut into the mountain's face, tucked away in a half-tunnel treated to look like rock. Dozens of huge chain nets have also been suspended above the road, like giant baseball-mitts, to catch the tumbling boulders. While this renovation has been accomplished with great skill and sensitivity, one can't help but think that the new road lacks some of the visceral impact of the old pass. But it's still an awesome drive to have at our disposal, and it's good to have Chapman's Peak back.

By the way, next time you drive Chapman's Peak, spare a thought for the poor, deluded individuals who voluntarily use this pass as a form of competitive exercise. Since Chapman's Peak has been reopened, both the Two Oceans marathon and the Cape Argus cycle race have reverted to their original route over the pass, thus proving that sound mind and sound body have absolutely nothing to do with each other.

Cape Peninsula contacts:
- Hout Bay Tourism: 021 790 1264
- Hout Bay Holidays: 021 790 1194
  www.houtbayholiday.co.za
- Mariner's Wharf: 021 790 1100
- World of Birds – 021 790 2730
  www.worldofbirds.org.za
- Chapman's Peak Toll Plaza: 021 791 8220
  www.chapmanspeakdrive.co.za
- Table Mountain National Park:
  021 701 8692 / www.tmnp.co.za

Misty Cliffs and Scarborough

As you continue along the M65 towards Cape Point, the road rises steeply and traverses a mountain spur (offering good views out over Slangkop lighthouse and the adjacent caravan park). It then decends back to the coast and heads off towards Misty Cliffs and Scarborough. This stretch of road runs right along the sea, offering sublime views of the pristine coastline. There are very few houses out here; just a small cluster at Misty Cliffs and a larger conglomeration of holiday homes in Scarborough. Scarborough also offers a restaurant and pub. The main attractions of this drive, however, are the limitless sea and a refreshing absence of human habitation.

Even dogs live the highlife in Camps Bay

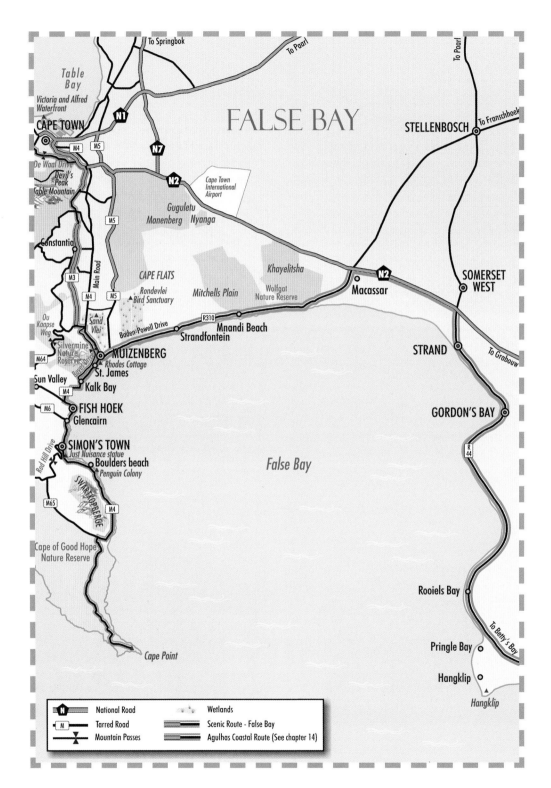

FALSE BAY

Table Bay
Victoria and Alfred Waterfront
CAPE TOWN
To Springbok
To Paarl
To Paarl
STELLENBOSCH
To Franschhoek

De Waal Drive
Devil's Peak
Table Mountain
Cape Town International Airport
Guguletu
Manenberg Nyanga

Constantia

CAPE FLATS
Khayelitsha
SOMERSET WEST

Ou Kaapse Weg
Rondevlei Bird Sanctuary
Mitchells Plain
Wolfgat Nature Reserve
Macassar

Sand Vlei
Baden-Powell Drive
Mnandi Beach
Strandfontein

Silvermine Nature Reserve
Sun Valley
MUIZENBERG
Rhodes Cottage
St. James
Kalk Bay

STRAND
To Grabouw

FISH HOEK
Glencairn

SIMON'S TOWN
Just Nuisance statue
Boulders beach
Penguin Colony
SWARTKOPBERGE

GORDON'S BAY

False Bay

Cape of Good Hope Nature Reserve

Rooiels Bay

Cape Point

Pringle Bay
To Betty's Bay

Hangklip
Hangklip

	National Road		Wetlands
	Tarred Road		Scenic Route - False Bay
	Mountain Passes		Agulhas Coastal Route (See chapter 14)

6. False Bay

ORIENTATION

There are two ways to get from the City Bowl to the False Bay coast. The first is the old Main Road (the M4), which is riddled with robots [see Chapter 5]. The other is a highway called the M3.

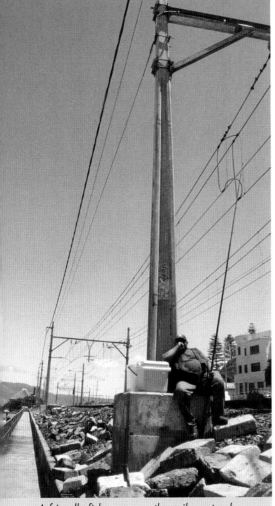

A friendly fisherman on the railway tracks between Muizenberg and St. James

From Cape Town, the M3 is lifted up the slopes of Devil's Peak, parallel to the old Main Road. It speeds along, leading past the University of Cape Town, until it abruptly hits a robot and turns into a busy suburban road, which curves through the bustling Southern Suburbs. Claremont, Bishopscourt, Cavendish Square shopping mall, Kirstenbosch Gardens and the Newlands Forest are all close by. If you are intent on reaching False Bay, a bit of patience may be required before you clear the last robot and the road becomes a highway once again.

> ### Mostert's Mill
> *One of the most distinctive landmarks on the M3 highway, this old windmill was built in 1796 on the farm Welgelegen. It is the only working Dutch windmill in the Cape, and tours can be arranged.*
> •*Mostert's Mill: 021 762 5127*

Once the M3 has regained its composure, you will pass the turn-off for Constantia. Take this off-ramp if you want to drive through the old vineyards, over Constantia Nek and into Hout Bay [see Chapter 5]. Otherwise, continue on the M3 as the highway levels out and heads straight, past the unassuming suburbs of Tokai, Bergvliet (Mountain Stream) and Ladies Mile, before terminating at a T-junction near Muizenberg.

At this point, you can follow signs for the *Ou Kaapse Weg*, which leads up a steep pass, through the Silvermine Nature Reserve, to Noordhoek [see Chapter 5]. Or you can do a left and right onto the old Main Road (the M4), coming down from the city towards Muizenberg.

When you get to Muizenberg, you can go to the beach by turning left off Main Road onto

Baden-Powell Drive. You can then continue on Baden-Powell, past the beach, and journey along the intriguing coastal road that runs along the top of False Bay, all the way to Gordon's Bay in the East [see Chapter 14]. If you want to explore the other villages scattered along the False Bay side of the Peninsula, continue on Main Road past St James and Kalk Bay, towards Fish Hoek.

From Muizenberg, Main Road squeezes its way through a narrow passage between the sea and a line of low mountains. This is a tight fit, as houses and the railway line push up against the road from all sides. In season, this constricted coastal road gets more congested than a fat man eating dumplings. So be warned.

A good alternative route is via Boyes Drive, which joins Muizenberg to Kalk Bay. This scenic road runs high across the mountainside, offering the most superlative views out over the golden expanse of False Bay. Boyes Drive also offers historical sightseers a good look at the grave of Sir Abe Bailey, the famous Randlord, and Sandvlei, the fertile wetlands where the Battle of Muizenberg took place.

After driving through the vibrant village of Kalk Bay, the next town you will reach is Fish Hoek. From here, you can either take the access road up to Sun Valley and Noordhoek [see Chapter 5], or you can continue along Main Road to Simon's Town.

> From Simon's Town, you can:
> ➡ Turn around and drive back to Cape Town.
> ➡ Take Red Hill Drive (which offers great views over Simon's Town harbour) to Scarborough and Kommetjie. This will take you back to Cape Town along the Atlantic Seaboard [see Chapter 5].
> ➡ Keep driving South on the M4, until you reach the gates of Cape Point Nature Reserve.

FALSE BAY

False Bay is so named because many sailors returning from the East used to mistake Cape Hangklip (near Hermanus) for Cape Point. As a result of this little navigational error, the ships would turn right, expecting to sail up the Atlantic seaboard towards Table Bay. Instead, they found themselves trapped in the broad, watery dead-end of False Bay. Turning a ship around in the prevailing winds that blow across the bay was not an easy task, so the name 'False Bay' was more cautionary than it was affectionate. But, whatever the etymology, it's a misleading name for a spectacular bay.

False Bay begins at the very tip of Cape Point and leads in a vast, sweeping curve all the way around to Gordon's Bay at the foot of the Hottentots Holland Mountains, 35km to the east. It is a huge and challenging expanse of water, riven with powerful currents and hungry sharks. Only two people have ever succeeded in swimming from one side of False Bay to the other, and both said it was bloody hard.

The main attractions of False Bay are the charming seaside villages on the western side of the bay, and the extravagantly golden beach that runs unbroken for 30-odd k's towards the misty mountains in the east. The quintessential seaside resort of Muizenberg is Cape Town's gateway to this region.

MUIZENBERG

Muizenberg is an exquisitely faded resort town with a long history. It all began in 1673, when Sergeant Muys set up a garrison in the shade of what has became known as Muizenberg Mountain. From this position, he was ordered to patrol the False Bay coastline and to stop the farmers of Constantia from trading illegally with rogue ships. All in all, it was a cushy job and nothing much went on for the next 120 years. One of the original buildings of Muys' garrison still stands, reputedly the oldest habitable building in False Bay, and has been turned into De Post Huys museum.

Then, False Bay suddenly hit the headlines in 1795, when the Battle of Muizenberg broke out. This was a brief skirmish between the Dutch and the British, and it ushered in the

The iconic Victorian bathing boxes on Muizenberg Beach

Muizenberg Beach

Rudyard Kipling coined the phrase, 'white as the sands of Muizenberg, spun before the gale'. He was spot-on about both the white sands and the gale. Muizenberg is a windy beach, but it is also the best swimming beach on the Cape Peninsula.

Famously characterised by the brightly coloured rows of Victorian bathing boxes that line the main swimming area, Muizenberg is a great place for a paddle. This wide, sandy beach descends gently beneath the waves in a long shelf, the surf is gentle, and the shallow sea is excellent for kids and waders.

The water's nice too! In summer, the warm Moçambique Current gets pushed into the bay by the prevailing south-easter wind, and this makes the water much warmer than at the icy Atlantic beaches, just on the other side of the Peninsula. In winter, however, the cold Benguela current takes over and the water temperature drops. But this is when the surf is at its best, and Muizenberg is well known for its dependable breaks. Many professional surfers cut their teeth on the rolling breakers of False Bay.

There are only two problems with Muizenberg beach: the wind and the bluebottles. Both are inevitable in the summer and should be taken as proof that every pleasure in life comes at a cost. But why nitpick? A leisurely stroll along the beach, with your feet splashing in the warm waters of False Bay, is a rare treat.

I have many happy memories of Muizenberg. As a child, our family would drive down each year for three weeks at the nearby Sandvlei Caravan Park, and from this base we would spend our summer holiday playing in the sea and having picnics on what my father called 'Chicken-Bone Beach'.

On the grassy banks outside the beachfront we used to watch Punch and Judy shows, while eating our granadilla ice-lollies. Then we'd ride the little train through the dark tunnel that smelt of mildew and urine. Or we would rent row-boats and paddle around on the murky waters of a small concrete pond. Today, all that is gone. But the legendary Putt-Putt course is still open and the big water slide is still operational. A good kids' playground has also been built on the site of the old railway.

Muizenberg offers most of the modcons you would expect from a seaside village, including a backpackers', well-established surf shops, several restaurants and a modest shopping centre opposite the park. But, I have heard of big plans for Muizenberg's dilapidated art-deco beach front, so keep an eye out for new developments.

Muizenberg

Apart from the beach, Muizenberg is blessed with many museums: Rhodes' Cottage, the Police Museum, the Old Magistrate's Court, Het Posthuys Museum, a toy museum and the Natale Labia Museum. The latter, which is housed in an elaborate, pink baroque mansion, is a satellite of the National Gallery and houses fine art. Just as a point of clarity, that's 'Labia'. Pronounced 'Lah-bia' and not 'Lay-bia', which would be a different kettle of fish entirely. The Labia Cinema in the City Bowl is named for the same Italian noble family and, despite its misleading name, shows art-house films.

Before you start your exploration of old Muizenberg, arm yourself with the excellent walking-tour booklet, published by the Muizenberg Historical Society. It describes the old homes of the rich and famous still scattered along Millionaire's Mile, and maps out a good route for you to follow.

If you don't feel like walking, take the train which runs along the coast from Muizenberg to Simon's Town. It starts at Muizenberg's beautiful red brick and sandstone station, built in 1912, and stops at each of the villages along the coast.

first, temporary British occupation of the Cape [see Chapter 11].

Once the British had arrived for good, in 1806, their penchant for picturesque seaside resorts found its ideal expression along the beautiful beach at Muizenberg and, over the years, the town grew as a holiday annex to Cape Town. Then, in 1899, Cecil Rhodes bought a little cottage on the edge of Muizenberg, and gave the place his implicit stamp of approval. The flood gates opened and all manner of well-to-do folk moved in. Many of their stately mansions can still be seen standing proudly on the 'Millionaires Mile', which runs from Muizenberg to St James along the main road.

But everything started to change when the old Queen died in 1901. The Victorian Age was coming to a shuddering end, and Victoria's successor, King Edward, was fated to preside over the final heyday of the British Empire. When the First World War erupted in 1914, the death knell rang for the Imperial system, and the British Motherland went into terminal decline. The golden age of Britain was officially over. Then, the rot set in.

As the world marched into the twentieth century, Muizenberg fell into a state of gentle decay. Many of the houses and holiday flats

The sun sets on the golden sands of Muizenberg

Rhodes' Cottage

Rhodes' Cottage, Cecil John's holiday home, is still standing alongside Main Road, and it is an interesting place to visit. It was in this humble beachside retreat that the arch-imperialist died of respiratory illness, at the age of 49, and it resonates with a tranquil power.

Rhodes lived a remarkable life. He was the son of a British vicar, and arrived in South Africa as a sickly child of thirteen, hoping that the climate would improve his health. That was in 1866. By the time he died in 1902, he had made a fortune on the diamond fields, founded the De Beers diamond monopoly, made another fortune on the Gold Fields of the Transvaal, been elected Prime Minister of the Cape Colony in 1890, urged the British government to take over the territory of Bechuanaland (Botswana), and formed the British South Africa Company which controlled the vast territory now known as Zambia and Zimbabwe. He also set up the Rhodes Scholarship system, which helps people from around the world to study at Oxford University, his alma mater.

One shudders to think what the tenacious Rhodes would have accomplished if he had lived another 30 years. Never mind painting the map of Africa red, he might have re-conquered America! But it was not to be. The poor health of his early years returned, and was compounded by the stress of being a Victorian Bill Gates. Rhodes outlived his beloved monarch, Queen Victoria, by only a single year, seemingly unable to continue without his most cherished justification. Today, his seaside cottage is a quaint little museum that displays Rhodes' spooky deathbed and other memorabilia from his larger-than-life career.

Muizenberg – St James Walkway

If you don't feel like swimming, take the excellent walk from Muizenberg to St James along the specially constructed sea-front walkway. Built from public funds and private donations, this is a lovely promenade along the shoreline, mere meters above the frothing sea. From this walkway, it's common to see seals basking on the rocks, and you are bound to meet some interesting locals lounging on the memorial benches that dot the 1,5km walk. At the other end of the Promenade, you will find the pretty resort suburb of St James. The beach at St James has it own short row of Victorian bathing boxes and a popular tidal pool.

The local council did, occasionally, try to upgrade things and, in the 1980s, the beachfront promenade was lumbered with a rather ugly Pavilion and freshwater swimming pool. But nothing seemed to help. The whole country was caught in the downward spiral of national uncertainty, and urban regeneration was still a long way off.

Now, with the explosion in Cape property prices since 1994, Muizenberg is finally starting to wake from its slumber. House prices are rising exponentially, and the row of ruined old buildings on the beachfront has apparently been sold to developers. One can only hope that they maintain the outstanding art deco facades of the

A birds-eye view of Kalk Bay Harbour

were being used only one month of the year and, despite the bustle of the December season, the place became something of a ghost town for the rest of the time. The entrancing art deco buildings on the Western side of the beachfront became decrepit, and the once-grand hotels became fleapits.

Looking up the False Bay coast from Boulders Beach

Kalk Bay

Kalk Bay is a busy village filled with antique shops, eating places, homeware stores and boutiques. Highlights include: Cape 2 Cuba restaurant, situated right on the railway tracks and decorated in a frenzy of Castroesque chic; The Brass Bell, a local institution and a good place to enjoy a raucous seafood basket and a couple dozen beers; the Harbour House bar; and the bustling Adelphi Café, great for a quiche, croissant and a cup of coffee. If this all sounds a bit too mainstream for you, drive into the quaint fishing harbour and enjoy an authentic meal of deep-fried calamari and linefish from Kalkies. During the snoek season (June/July), Kalk Bay harbour is a flurry of activity, and you can buy your very own piece of fres' snoek from the back of a bakkie.

If you are keen on walking, speleology or botany, there are a number of walks from Kalk Bay that will take you up into the fynbos-covered mountains, where you can explore the numerous caves that riddle this part of the coastal hills.

• *Kalk Bay Harbour: 021 788 8313*

long-vacant buildings, and rejuvenate rather than despoil the seaside atmosphere of one of the best beaches in the Cape.

KALK BAY

From Muizenberg, the next port of call is Kalk Bay, one of Cape Town's most popular villages. Its name indicates that this was originally the location of a lime kiln, which produced much of the whitewash used to paint the famous Cape Dutch buildings of the colony. The kiln is no more, but the small business centre of Kalk Bay encourages many hours of happy browsing, with a row of restaurants, bakeries, antique shops, art galleries and ice-cream parlours (or gelateries, as I'm sure they would prefer to be called).

FISH HOEK

After Kalk Bay comes the larger town of Fish Hoek, with its built-up main street and expansive beach. At Fish Hoek, the mountains seem to falter before gathering steam for their final push to Cape Point. At various times in the past, when the sea-level was higher, this strip of low-lying land was actually submerged, and the Peninsula was effectively cut in half. Now, in drier times, the sandy channel functions as an access point to Sun Valley, Noordhoek and Kommetjie.

The interesting thing about Fish Hoek is that is still a 'dry' town – the only one in South Africa. This means that liquor stores and bars are not allowed to operate, under a by-law which dates back to 1818. At this time, the land was granted to Andries Bruins on condition that he did not sell any liquor to the thirsty sailors stationed at nearby Simon's Town. This clause was, quite wisely, incorporated into the town's charter when it was established in 1919, and so it remains today. Fish Hoek makes up for this lack of libation with a lovely beach walk, a museum and an important stone-age site called Peers Cave.

You see the kind of abuse that Joburgers have to put up with! Snotty café in Kalk Bay

Boulders Beach

In terms of beaches, Simon's Town has a beaut in the form of Boulders, just a few k's down the road towards Cape Point. Ideal for families, Boulders is a magical beach surrounded by large, round rocks, with a great view up the coast towards Muizenberg. It is also well protected from the wind and the sea is very calm. Plus, Boulders is the only beach in South Africa where humans and penguins share the same water.

In fact, it is the plucky penguins, who casually stroll between the beach towels and bob through the human flotsam, that are the main attraction of Boulders. Inevitably followed by a troop of wide-eyed kids, these little waterborne butlers seem quite unperturbed by their fellow bathers, and Boulders is a rare example of human beings actually sharing their environment with other creatures. The penguin colony extends to adjacent Foxy Beach, but this amenity is now closed for bathing, to give the penguins some privacy.

Admission is payable to enter Boulders and numbers are restricted as it is small. Additionally, when the sun starts to dip behind the tall rocks, the shadows creep quickly over the beach, so get there early. There are a couple of restaurants and small shops close by.

If Boulders is full, don't despair. There are other secluded beaches further down the road, like Seaforth, Rocklands and Millers Point, which all offer an excellent excuse to stop for a goef.

• *Boulders Beach: 021 786 2329*
  www.tmnp.co.za

SIMON'S TOWN

The main road from Muizenberg passes through Fish Hoek and arrives in Simon's Town which, for many years, marked the end of the line. Simon's Town has always been associated with shipping, and this natural harbour was first used in 1671 when a passing ship nipped into the bay to shelter from unfavourable winds.

As it was protected from the dangerous north-westerly winds of winter that tended to wreck the ships anchored in Table Bay, the ever-popular Dutch governor, Simon van der Stel, decreed that Simon's Town should become a seasonal mooring for the entire VOC fleet. The new harbour was opened in 1687, and

The penguins do some human-spotting on Boulders Beach

79

predictably named in Van der Stel's honour. The British Navy took over Simon's Town in 1814 and turned it into a maritime metropolis for the imperial fleet. It was finally handed over to the SA Navy in 1957.

With its long history of seafaring folk, a walk along the historical mile of Simon's Town has great appeal for historians and boat-nuts alike. Shoppers will also be happy to walk through the old terraces, filled with quaint shops and food vendors. Various memorials, monuments and museums cater for those with a nautical bent, and the statue of wartime doggy mascot 'Just Nuisance' holds pride of place in the middle of Jubilee Square.

The Legend of Adamastor

An ancient story tells of a family of giants who rose up and tried to overthrow the gods. This titanic revolt was eventually put down, and the angry gods punished the rebellious giants by banishing them to Earth and turning them into stone. Adamastor, one of these giants, was thus sent to the southern oceans and transformed into the rocks and mountains of the Cape Peninsula.

Adamastor then reappears in the literary record in 1572, when the Portuguese poet Luis de Camoes wrote his epic, 'The Luciads'. In this story, Camoes recounts the epic voyages of European discovery and, when telling of Da Gama's expedition around the Cape, he creates a memorable cameo for the menacing Adamastor.

According to Camoes, as Da Gama's ship neared the tip of the Cape, a dark cloud materialised and took the shape of an enormous human figure. It was Adamastor, guardian spirit of the Cape of Storms, and he had a menacing message for the explorers. "Beware", he intoned, "disaster will befall anyone who dares round the Cape". Sadly, his message did not deter Da Gama, and the Cape of Storms was repeatedly violated from that day forward.

CAPE POINT

The long, tapering finger of Cape Point may not

Cape Point Nature Reserve

Cape Point is a spectacular place to visit and the tourist facilities are well established. After paying your entrance fee, a gorgeous drive takes you to the parking lot, where you must disembark. From here, you can choose either to walk up the steep slope to the lookout point, or pay a bit more to ride the 'Flying Dutchman' funicular. Once at the top, a paved promenade leads to the tip of the headland and the most panoramic of views. An upmarket seafood restaurant and ritzy Curio Shop will complete the experience for those with cash to spend, but rest assured that the fresh air and wheeling sea birds are free.

Cape Point is surrounded by protected land, now united with Table Mountain under the banner 'Table Mountain National Park', and this delicate ecosystem can be explored on foot through the aegis of SAN Parks. There are also several side-roads in the Cape Point Nature Reserve, which lead down to secluded bays and open stretches of barren beach. Check at the gate about the condition of the roads, and ask which ones are open to the public at the time. If you have a valid Wild Card, entrance to the reserve is free.

- *Cape Point Nature Reserve: 021 780 9010/1*
- *Table Mountain National Park: 021 701 8692 www.tmnp.co.za*

be the southernmost tip of mainland Africa – that honour belongs to Cape Agulhas, about 170km due east – but why quibble? I think Cape Point is the most dramatic culmination of continent and sea in the world. And, despite the geographical realities of the situation, I see Cape Point as the metaphorical dot on which the entire question mark of Africa precariously balances.

With regard to the claim that this is the point where two oceans meet, once again, it's all in the eye of the beholder. While those with a cold, logical eye may stick to the cartographer's opinion that Cape Agulhas marks the divide between the Indian and the Atlantic, those with a bit of imagination usually put their money on Cape Point as the meeting place of the Oceans. Sadly, both of these propositions are somewhat spurious, as two great oceans don't meet in a neatly ordered line. They move and swirl and shift with the seasons.

A stronger claim is that Cape Point is the epicentre of South Africa's weather system. Our country's climate is largely driven by two ocean currents; the cold Benguela Current that slides up the west coast, and the warm Moçambique current that slips down the east. These currents advance and retreat with the season, but the Cape Point headland marks the one clear delineation between these two elemental engines.

We can also say, with growing confidence, that Cape Point forms the great continental divide between east and west. When the seafarers of old rounded Cape Point in their sailing ships, it was like turning the corner. Cape Point marked the end of the familiar old world of Europe, and the start of the brave new world of Asia, with all its associated adventure and drama.

So, even today, when you look out from the viewing deck right on the tip of Cape Point, it's easy to become a romantic. It's a grand promontory; a lonely pinnacle of rock thrusting out into the deep sea, defying Neptune to usurp its heights. Standing there on the edge of the Earth, with the deep seas breaking round, it's easy to imagine that the steep ridges and jagged rocks of the headland are actually the death throes of Adamastor, formed as the legendary giant petrified and sank into the icy waters.

Surrounded by thousands of miles of mighty, suffocating ocean, the hooked claw of Cape Point is a fitting summation to the African continent: wild, imposing and beautiful.

The finer things in life on Boulders Beach

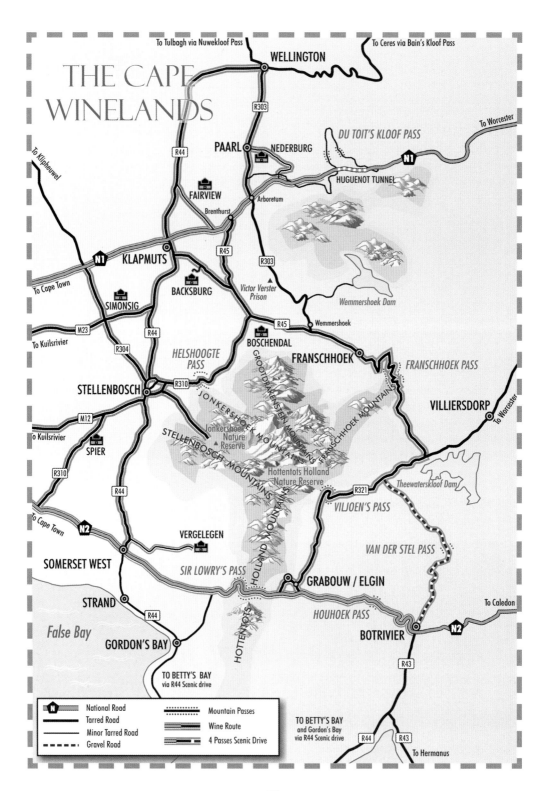

THE CAPE
WINELANDS

To Tulbagh via Nuwekloof Pass

To Ceres via Bain's Kloof Pass

WELLINGTON

To Worcester

R303

DU TOIT'S KLOOF PASS

PAARL

NEDERBURG

N1

R44

HUGUENOT TUNNEL

FAIRVIEW

Arboretum

Brenthurst

To Klipheuwel

KLAPMUTS

R45

R303

N1

To Cape Town

BACKSBURG

Victor Verster
Prison

Wemmershoek Dam

SIMONSIG

M23

R44

R304

To Kuilsrivier

HELSHOOGTE
PASS

R45

Wemmershoek

R310

BOSCHENDAL

FRANSCHHOEK

FRANSCHHOEK PASS

STELLENBOSCH

JONKERSHOEK MOUNTAINS

GROOTDRAKENSTEIN MOUNTAINS

FRANSCHHOEK MOUNTAIN

VILLIERSDORP

To Worcester

M12

Jonkershoek
Nature
Reserve

STELLENBOSCH MOUNTAINS

To Kuilsrivier

SPIER

Hottentots Holland
Nature Reserve

Theewaterskloof Dam

R310

R44

R321

VILJOEN'S PASS

N2

VERGELEGEN

HOLLAND MOUNTAINS

VAN DER STEL PASS

To Cape Town

SOMERSET WEST

SIR LOWRY'S PASS

GRABOUW / ELGIN

STRAND

R44

HOUHOEK PASS

To Caledon

False Bay

N2

GORDON'S BAY

HOTTENTOTS

BOTRIVIER

TO BETTY'S BAY
via R44 Scenic drive

R43

N	National Road
---	Tarred Road
---	Minor Tarred Road
---	Gravel Road

·········	Mountain Passes
---	Wine Route
---	4 Passes Scenic Drive

TO BETTY'S BAY
and Gordon's Bay
via R44 Scenic drive

R44   R43

To Hermanus

7. The Cape Winelands

ORIENTATION

From the city of Cape Town, the Cape Winelands spread out in a rough crescent, stretching from Gordon's Bay on the N2 to Paarl on the N1. The historical villages of Stellenbosch and Franschhoek are at the heart of the region.

Behind the Winelands, a wall of mountains is formed by the Hottentots Holland and Limietberg ranges. This creates a natural cup which catches the rain and waters the venerable vineyards below. On the other side of the mountains is the main deciduous fruit producing area of the country, the Greenlands Plateau. Both of these agricultural regions are sometimes grouped together under the vague but affectionate designation, 'The Boland'.

To get to Stellenbosch, take the N2 out of Cape Town. Once you are on the highway, you can either follow signs for the R300, which leads through residential areas, straight to Stellenbosch. Or, you can continue on the N2 towards Gordon's Bay, and follow signs for the R310. Either way, the drive is about 50km, and it should take you forty-five minutes to an hour to make the journey. An alternative route is to start in Muizenberg and follow the R310 from its beginnings as an obscure coastal road [see Chapter 14]. This intriguing route is 70km long, and should take around an hour.

From Stellenbosch, you can continue to Franschhoek by going up the Helshoogte Pass (R310), and then turning right onto the R45, which has come down from Paarl. Franschhoek is about 25 leisurely kilometres from Stellenbosch.

The Helshoogte Pass is also the first leg of the Four Passes Scenic Drive, which takes you around the circumference of the Hottentots Holland mountain range. The Four Passes Drive

The geometric quilt of farmlands and mountains that cover the Cape Winelands

Fynbos erupts in the Cape Winelands

is a round trip of around 250km from Cape Town, but allow the whole day (or even two) so that you have time to explore the wine estates and towns *en route*.

An interesting detour to the established Four Passes Scenic Drive is a gravel road that leads from the R321 to Botrivier, via the mild Van der Stel Pass. This little-used track takes in some wonderfully unspoilt country scenery, with sleepy farmsteads dotted along a rolling river valley. The gravel section is 30km long, and it took me just under an hour to drive. From Botrivier, you can head back to Cape Town on the N2, via Houhoek Pass, Grabouw and Sir Lowry's Pass. Alternatively, from this side of the Hottentots Holland mountains, you could drive on to Betty's Bay and take the spectacular R44 around the coast to Gordon's Bay, *[see Chapter 14]*.

To reach the Paarl side of the Winelands, take the N1 out of Cape Town. Paarl is 70km away from the centre of Cape Town, and the drive should take about fifty minutes (traffic permitting). From the N1, you can follow the R304 or the R44 to Stellenbosch. At Paarl, you can also take the R45 to Franschhoek. Paarl and the N1 will be detailed in an upcoming Back Roads guide, which will cover the journey from Cape Town to Johannesburg.

THE FREE BURGHERS

The Dutch did not thrive at the Cape. Not at first. The country was too wild, the natives were too restless, and the VOC was too strict in its policies. As a result, food was scarce, morale was low and Whitey was going hungry. Then someone in the Company had a brainwave.

In 1657, five years after the Dutch landed, the first freehold farms were granted to private farmers in an attempt to stimulate food production at the Cape. Initially, only nine 'free burghers' took up the Company's offer and moved into their new lands along the Liesbeek River.

The first title deeds were granted around a clump of thorn trees called 'Het ronde doornbosjen' – now simply called Rondebosch – but, over the years, the free burghers spread along the river and beyond. By the time Van Riebeeck left the Cape for his new post in Batavia, the official population stood at 134 Company officials, 35 free burghers, 15 women, 22 children and 180 slaves.

But it was a tough existence outside the aegis of the Castle. Khoikhoi raiders were a constant threat, there was no infrastructure, and knowledge of local farming conditions was severely limited. Yet, despite this inauspicious start, the flood gates had been irrevocably opened. The white occupation of South Africa had begun.

Even though this new class of aspirant entrepreneurs had completed their contracts with the Company and were technically 'free', the free burghers were still bound to obey the Company's rules and had to remain 'good and faithful' subjects of their *de facto* political authority. In return for their good behaviour, however, the free burghers' farms were 'granted in freehold' with 'as much land as [they] may desire for gardens'.

This was pretty generous stuff from the miserly VOC, but these were desperate times and the canny Company had made sure that its exposure to risk was limited. Firstly, the whole system was cheap to set up, since the fertile farm land along the river was settled without any

Stock up on fig jam and rusks at the farm stalls that line the Wine Route

permission from, or payment to, the local tribes. Secondly, the wily Company hedged its bets by maintaining a strict monopoly on the market for any goods produced by their free burghers.

This meant that free burghers were allowed to sell their produce only to the VOC, at whatever prices the VOC felt were appropriate. The VOC then whacked on a big mark-up and sold the goods to ships calling at the harbour. This may sound like standard business practice today, but remember that the cunning VOC could dictate the prices on both sides of the deal; paying a pittance for the farmer's harvest and ripping off the needy ships at anchor. Still, we shouldn't be surprised. This profit-at-all-cost attitude is actually specified in most corporate charters, and any well-run monopoly will eventually result in price gouging. Just look at Microsoft, or Telkom...

The free burghers soon became similarly disillusioned with the system, as it quickly became apparent that no one was going to get rich growing food for the Company. The VOC kept produce prices very low and, furthermore, instituted a covert system of kickbacks that made favoured farmers rich and left the poor ones with nothing. Many of these early farmers eventually gave up on their fields and drifted back into the towns, where they opened bars and eating places for the visiting sailors. This earned Cape Town the title 'Tavern of the Seas'.

Those farmers who didn't go into bartending often had to bend the law to make ends meet. Some started trading illegally with ships which snuck into False Bay. Others undertook surreptitious 'hunting' expeditions to supplement their income.

In time, illegal trade with the Khoikhoi also became a popular way of making a few extra guilders, despite the strict Company prohibition on fraternising with the locals. To make matters worse, many of these 'trading' parties were actually lightly veiled cattle raids, and the Khoikhoi forbearance of their European neighbours began to wear thinner than a politician's promises. Tempers started rising right across the Cape, and the whole region was becoming *vrot* with tension.

Worst of all, for the Company, it was becoming clear that their great agricultural experiment had failed. Ten years had passed since the first farmers started erecting their huts along the Liesbeek, and the Company men at the Castle were still eating rice imported from Batavia. Food production was low, the natives were on the verge of revolt, and the costs of running the Cape were mounting.

Ironically, by this time, the Company was in too deep. It couldn't change the current dispensation without causing major ructions with the free burghers and, despite tough working conditions and low profit margins, the inexorable movement of agricultural farmers across the land continued.

So, as they finished their contracts, more and more Company employees were choosing to remain at the Cape and take up the offer of free land. Even immigrants from Europe were coming to the Cape to avail themselves of the Company's uncharacteristic largesse. Farms were subsequently declared further and further afield, and all the Company's attempts to contain their presence at the Cape could not stop the farmers from extending the frontiers of the Company's authority every year. The tiny village around the Fort thus became the capital of an unwitting colony.

This initial expansion of European intent, however humble, caused a ripple of concern through the local tribes. And they were right to be afraid. Over the next 150 years, the white farmers spread out to the north, and along the south-east coast, taking over vast chunks of land without so much as a by-your-leave from the local tribes.

Many of these white farmers were not even interested in planting crops. They were quite happy to roam around like Hottentots, living in semi-permanent huts while raising and grazing their herds. But, as increasing numbers of cattle started competing for limited grazing pastures, the pressure on the land started to mount. Clashes with the native tribes became inevitable and, indirectly, we are still living with the consequences of this conflict today.

As for the Khoikhoi, they were reeling. From a silly little Fort, the Dutch colony had grown into a domineering force. Colonists raided local cattle kraals with impunity, and retaliatory attacks by the Khoikhoi on the European farms were revenged by ruthless Dutch commandos. Caught between the white Devil and the deep, blue sea, the indigenous Khoikhoi community was split into those who wanted to fight, and those who chose to join the enemy.

The VOC, for their part, did not want a war with the horrid Hottentots. Wars were expensive and messy. So, the Company tried to keep everyone in line, including the boisterous settlers. This was an impossible task, since the settlers were already resisting the Company's authority and, as far as the Khoikhoi were concerned, the Company had no right to tell the Khoikhoi chiefs what to do.

Always keen to observe the letter of the law, however, the VOC made several attempts to legitimise their tenancy of the Cape. Obviously, the Khoikhoi were unmoved until, finally, in 1672, after three major armed conflicts, the victorious VOC got the Khoikhoi to comply with a half-arsed ceremony of purchase, and formally bought the Cape from the Khoikhoi for a metaphorical box of beads and a couple of blankets. From the Company's point of view, they were now officially in charge, and it was time to consolidate their land grab.

STELLENBOSCH

In 1679, a new and energetic governor arrived at the Cape in the form of Simon van der Stel. He was an ambitious and determined man, who quickly set about expanding and entrenching his little realm at the Cape. Van der Stel's first territorial initiative was to break away from the Company's previous policy of keeping the free burghers within a day's ride of the Castle.

Unfettered from this constraint, Van der Stel rode out from Cape Town, scouting around for suitable new farmlands. He found them along the banks of a river, which he appropriately named the *Eerste Rivier* (First River), and subsequently granted land to farmers interested in settling there. He

Stellenbosch

Stellenbosch is a town best explored on foot. It is small and friendly and packed with interesting shops, restaurants and quaint cafés tucked away into old buildings. As befits a university town, it is great to while away the hours, knocking back coffee, as you watch the parade of crusty students and nubile young things. But don't be fooled by the languid pace of the lolloping students, Stellenbosch is a very desirable place to live and property prices are sky-high.

When you arrive in town, head to the info centre on Mark (Market) Street. It's just off the big green common in the centre of town called The Braak. Here you can pick up a walking-tour booklet to guide you through the city streets. The cunning linguists at Stellenbosch have translated this very thorough booklet into dozens of different languages, so there's no excuse for mistaking the Rhenish Missionary Church for the NG Moederkerk.

A stroll down Dorp Street is a particular highlight and should be tackled by anyone who visits town. This was the main thoroughfare in the old days, an extension of the wagon road which led to Cape Town, and it is blessed with a fine congregation of lovely homes and cottages that date back 300 years. Many of these buildings are national monuments, and several serve enticing teas on their open verandas. You can also check out the renowned Oom Samie se Winkel, an old-fashioned general dealer that has kept its prices right up to date.

There are other notable old buildings all over Stellenbosch, as detailed in the walking tour booklet, and one could spend a few hours strolling past the workers' cottages built by Herbert Baker for Cecil John Rhodes, or checking out Libertas Parva, the birthplace of Ouma Smuts – faithful wife of Jan. This is also the place where the eminent Jan Smuts married his wife, and the family home was so precious to Ouma that she named the President's residence in Pretoria 'Libertas' in its honour.

There are also several museums in Stellenbosch including the Burgerhuis House Museum (with magnificent period furniture), the Toy Museum (just behind the info centre) and the superb Village Museum. The latter is a living museum that is housed in four original buildings, each epitomising a different historical epoch. Staff dressed in period costume bustle around each house, giving the museum a special charm. Unfortunately, the well-stocked Rembrandt van Rijn Art Museum (named, surreptitiously, after the Rembrandt tobacco company) was closed the last time I visited, but should reopen in the near future.

The Jonkershoek and Assegaaibosch Nature Reserves are close to the town and offer trout fishing, bike trails and hikes.

Stellenbosch, in short, is a delightful place to visit: Tall oak trees dapple the light that falls across the old streets. Immaculately restored Cape Dutch buildings seem to sigh with settled contentment from behind their whitewashed walls. Blithe young university students swish past on their bicycles. Storefront fashion shows, complete with coffee and beskuit, encourage the walker to linger, while pretty little B+Bs beckon from the nearby valleys, and dozens of Ye Olde Coffee Shoppes tempt you with promises of melktert and home-made rusks.

Stellenbosch is much more than just another stop on the Wine Route, it's a historical little town with an eye on the future.

Tea and fashion in Stellenbosch

- *Stellenbosch tourist info: 021 883 3584*
- *www.stellenboschtourism.co.za*
- *Oude Libertas Amphitheatre (check for events): 021 808 7474*
- *Stellenbosch Village Museum: 021 887 2902*
- *Stellenbosch Wine Route (over 100 members): 021 886 4310*
- *Butterfly World: 021 875 5628*
- *Drakenstein Lion Park: 021 863 3290*
- *Le Bonheur Crocodile Farm: 021 863 1142*
- *Wiesenhof Game Park: 021 875 5181*
- *Jonkershoek Nature Reserve: 021 483 2949*

Cape Dutch gables nestle under the Drakenstein Mountains

eponymously called the place 'Stellenbosch' (Van der Stel's forest).

The fertile land around the Eerste River quickly drew many farmers to the remote area. In 1682, it officially became a village and, in 1685, it became the country's second magistracy, with an arbitrary authority that extended over 25 000 square kilometres of largely unknown interior. Stellenbosch is therefore the second oldest European town in South Africa.

Thanks to the ready supply of fresh water, the village of Stellenbosch flourished and abundant crops began to spring out of the rich soil. The streets were lined with young oak trees, which grew stately along with the aspirations of the town's inhabitants. Solid Cape Dutch houses, with graceful gables, were built all over the valley, and irrigation furrows provided the town's folk with water for their ambitious gardens. Educational institutions were set up as early as 1683, and Stellenbosch is now home to one of the Cape's most important universities.

Despite several debilitating fires, Stellenbosch continued to thrive over the centuries and today it is one of the best preserved 18th-century towns in South Africa.

THE 'WINE ROUTE'

Despite its singular moniker, the 'Wine Route' is not a pre-determined route that you follow, but rather a series of well-established roads which lead through the main wine-producing regions of the South-Western Cape. If your tastes run to the viticultural, this excursion into the cellars of the country's foremost wine producers is not to be missed.

South Africa has a long history of wine-making that dates back to the arrival of the French Huguenots at Franschhoek, over 300 years ago. When they landed here, these Protestant expats realised that the south-western Cape has excellent conditions for the cultivation of grapes: it is in a winter rainfall area, the soil composition is rich and varied, and it contains a number of micro-climates, so each region (and even each estate) offers its own unique flavours and blends of wine.

The heart of the Wine Route is roughly delineated by the triangle formed by Stellenbosch, Paarl and Franschhoek. Drive

The Wine Route

Since I am (unashamedly) a wine philistine, I will not attempt to regale you with details of blend, cultivar, nose and colour. I'll leave that up to the well-informed writers who have already produced a number of excellent guides to this region instead. I'll just mention some of the better-known wine estates and leave the rest up to you:

- Vergelegen, near Gordon's Bay, is a lovely estate with a famous rose garden. The homestead was built in 1700 by Willem Adriaan van der Stel, a controversial Dutch governor and son of the rather more eminent Simon. Willem actually lost his job over Vergelegen, after he and his cronies started playing fast and loose with the Company regulations and tried to appropriate some of the best farmland in the area for themselves. Suitably aggrieved, a group of farmers wrote a letter of complaint to the VOC. Van der Stel tried to imprison the whistle-blowers but, in 1707, the VOC dismissed Van der Stel and his councillors instead. The old camphor trees in the main courtyard were planted by Van der Stel 300 years ago.
- Spier is a large complex that has a manor house, rose garden, restaurant, cheetah park and an open-air amphitheatre that is home to a prestigious annual cultural festival – oh yes, and they also make wine.
- Fairview is known for its good wines, a variety of excellent cheeses and their resident goats who live in a tower.
- Backsberg has an interesting self-guided cellar tour with interpretive video displays.
- Simonsig lets you picnic on the grounds and has a small playground for the kids.
- Boschendal is an old Huguenot estate dating back to 1685, with a homestead that was built in 1812. It was bought by Cecil John Rhodes in 1887, and the estate has been restored over the years by its subsequent owners. Buffet lunches, an upmarket café and the cloyingly-named 'le pique nique' are all available.

Just be warned, many of the more popular estates positively bustle with the crowds of summertime, and some patience may be required if you are visiting during the holiday season. Most wine estates are open to the public during normal trading hours. Some of the smaller ones are accessible by appointment only.

But what if you're like me and you think that wine tastes like sour water? Well, don't despair. There is still much to do while your partner sniffs their snifter. The wine estates usually boast a beautiful, antique Cape Dutch Homestead and lovely gardens through which you can wander. Most estates also offer a restaurant, a gift shop and a classy atmosphere for the non-drinking contingent. Some even have wine-making displays and museums for the academics. And, since most modern wine tasters don't spit, they swallow; at the end of the day, the teetotaller in the group can be the designated driver back to your hotel.

As for the kids, it might be a little frustrating to watch Mommy and Daddy chatting about rosé and bouquet with the knowledgeable sales staff. While some estates offer playgrounds and facilities to amuse the little ones, others have no facilities to occupy the rugrats. If you are travelling with kids and can't leave them alone, my advice would be to leaven the wine tasting with some alternative activities available in the area, like strawberry picking and candle making. There are also farm stalls, little restaurants, craft shops and coffee shops all over the region that could break the trip.

- Cape Winelands Tourist Info: 021 872 0686
- Backsberg: 021 875 5141 / www.backsberg.co.za
- Boschendal: 021 870 4272/3/4/5 / www.boschendal.co.za
- Fairview: 021 863 2450 / www.fairview.co.za
- Simonsig: 021 888 4900 / www.simonsig.co.za
- Spier: 021 809 1100 / www.spier.co.za
- Vergelegen: 021 847 1334 / www.vergelegen.co.za

Vineyards line the roadside

The proudly Protestant Huguenot Memorial, Franschhoek

along just about any road in this part of the world and it will be studded with well-marked turn-offs for the various wine estates *en route*. Avid epicures can therefore spend days winding through the countryside, nibbling on cheese platters and letting the multitude of fine South African wines play across their palates. Alternatively, you can just go out and drink as much as you can before getting cross-eyed and horny. Either way, the Wine Route is a good excuse to get away from the buzz of the beach and escape into the tranquil countryside.

THE FRENCH HUGUENOTS AND FRANSCHHOEK

In 1687, Simon van der Stel decided to consolidate his new town of Stellenbosch with a new batch of farms to be established in the lush Berg River Valley, north of the town. A rugged group of twenty-three pioneers leapt at the chance, and followed their governor over the slopes of Helshoogte Pass into their new lands around the conjunction of the Berg River and its tributary, the Dwars.

In the following year, a community of 176

Protestant French Huguenots applied to the like-minded Dutch for permission to settle at the Cape. The French King, Louis XIV, had outlawed Protestantism in 1685, and these religious dissenters were very unhappy living under the oppressive Catholic regime in France. The Huguenots decided that they would do anything to worship freely, even if it meant sailing halfway around the world to a wild new country.

Luckily, the Huguenots were skilled farmers and the VOC were happy to oblige their Protestant brethren. So, the Company graciously offered the Huguenots free passage (one way) and all the land they could farm, as long as they swore an oath of allegiance to the VOC and promised to stay for at least five years. The first Huguenots arrived in 1688, and brought with them an element of culture and sophistication that was sorely lacking at the ramshackle Company outpost. They also brought the fine art of winemaking to the Cape.

This small group of French people certainly left a lasting impression on the young colony. They helped establish the renowned Cape wine industry, which is now an important contributor to the economy of the region, and they were also prolific breeders who founded several family dynasties. The familiar Afrikaner family names: De Villiers, Le Roux, Du Plessis, Fouche, Joubert, Rossouw and many others were all spawned by the Huguenots and their numerous descendants. As one kid succinctly wrote in an exam paper, "The French Huguenots landed at the Cape, intermarried with the Dutch and produced grapes."

At first, the Huguenots were sent to farm alongside Van der Stel's latest flock of settlers in the Berg River Valley, around the slopes of the Drakenstein (Dragon Rock) mountains. But the Frenchmen were unhappy with the soil of their farms, and started scouting around for better land.

They found it in an isolated, dead-end valley called Olifantshoek, which was sealed off by mountains to the east. Over the millennia, this lovely declivity had been the seasonal breeding ground for herds of elephants who migrated over the peaks each year, only to return for the calving season. It was a well-watered valley with good soil, and the Huguenots asked Van der Stel if they could have it. In 1694, nine farms were allocated to the diligent French settlers, and the valley was renamed Franschhoek. The last wild elephant was killed in the 1830s.

THE FOUR PASSES SCENIC DRIVE

To the East of Cape Town, you will find a large, green area called the Hottentots Holland Nature Reserve. It is a star-shaped area, dominated by five mountain ranges that radiate out from a lofty centre, like the arms of a star-fish. These are the Stellenbosch, Jonkershoek and Groot Drakenstein mountains to the west, the Franschhoek mountains to the East, and the Hottentots Holland mountains which stretch South, all the way to the sea at Gordon's Bay.

The Four Passes Drive takes the traveller right around the broad circumference of this towering outcrop, and promises some remarkable scenery. It is a popular day-trip, which can be done by any reliable vehicle, as it is tarred throughout. It also gives you the excuse to spend some time in the attraction-packed towns of Stellenbosch and Franschhoek, but is never more than an hour or two away from the centre of Cape Town.

Helshoogte Pass

The Four Passes Drive starts in Stellenbosch and leads up the R310 before reaching the first pass, which goes by the fearsome name of Helshoogte (Hell's Heights). The pass used to be known by the even more forthright name of Banghoek (Scary Corner); a name earned

---

Franschhoek

Nowadays, Franschhoek (literally meaning 'French Corner') is a small town awash with rampant Francophilia. The road leading into town is dotted with estates named La-Petite-this or Plaisir-de-that, and the main street is predictably clotted with bistros, antique shops, chi-chi art galleries and even a Belgian chocolaterie. The resolutely continental village atmosphere may be cultivated, but it's charming nonetheless. If you want to spend the night, lots of lovely little country inns can be found tucked away in the surrounding countryside.

- *Franschhoek Tourist Info: 021 876 3603*
- *Franschhoek Wine Route (25 members): 021 876 3806*

View from the Franschhoek Pass

because wild animals used to roam the mountains, scaring the passing travellers.

Today, Helshoogte is a rather mild mountain pass which seems unworthy of its demonic appellation. The modern road smoothly crosses a low nek between the Papegaaiberg (Parrot Mountain) and the Jonkershoek mountains before taking you down into the Berg River Valley. As you continue along the R310, the Drakenstein mountains form a majestic wall of rock on your right, while bucolic fields alternate with thick fruit orchards on your left.

At the intersection with the R45, continue on to Franschhoek as the Drakenstein Mountains keep up their constant vigil on the right. At Franschhoek, the eastward thrust of the Franschhoek mountains cuts across the valley, forming an extended amphitheatre which seems to bar any further attempts of progress to the east. There is, however, one small snaking pass out of the towering cul-de-sac and over the mountains. This is the spectacular Franschhoek Pass.

Franschhoek Pass

This pass was originally built along a course that migrating elephants had trampled into the slopes of the mountain over many centuries. It was noted by early governors, like Simon van der Stel, as a potential timber route to the interior, but it was simply too rugged and narrow to be practical. The pass remained undeveloped for over 150 years.

By 1818, however, the local farmers had succeeded in getting the (now British) government to put some money towards building a pass over the mountains, and a contractor, S J Cats, was appointed to construct a road. His attempts were rough and ready, and the pass was so steep that only a half-laden wagon could make the ascent. The original *Cats' Pad* can still be walked as a hiking trail, and permits are available from the Tourism Bureau.

Four years later, in 1822, the British governor Charles Somerset, always a man of action, appointed a commission to investigate the best route from Cape Town to the Overberg region in the East. The committee, chaired by one Major Holloway of the Royal Engineers, found that Hottentots Holland Kloof (now called Sir Lowry's Pass) was more direct, but Franschhoek pass would be much cheaper to build. As the British administration in South Africa was always keen on saving a bob or two, the Franschhoek Pass was duly opened in 1825.

The construction of the pass was supervised by Holloway, and he used some rowdy surplus

A derelict farm house on the Van der Stel Pass

soldiers stationed in Cape Town as an impromptu labour force. The Franschhoek Pass was the first engineered road pass in South Africa, and it remained the main route to the Overberg until Sir Lowry's Pass over the Hottentots Holland mountains opened five years later. After the Sir Lowry's route was built, traffic over the Franschhoek Pass declined and the road fell into disrepair until it was declared unsafe and closed in the 1920s. During the depression a new pass was built as a poverty alleviation project, and this was upgraded in the 1950s to become the road that we follow today.

The pass begins by spooling up through the tree-lined foothills of the mountain face. As you rise, the view into the Franschhoek Valley deepens and the fields diminish to become red and green squares on an irregular chess board. Alongside the road, there are several large viewing areas where you can stop the car and gaze out over the near-sheer sides of the mountain, down to the small town below. Beyond the town, the deciduous fruit orchards glisten greenly in the sunlight, waiting to drop their load into the Cape's economic basket.

At the summit of the pass, the road hops over a high *nek* and releases you into a narrow river valley. From here, the road's gradient becomes less urgent as it leads down the northward slopes of the Franschhoek mountains, twisting along the undulating valley walls. In several places, the tarred road cuts through the jutting rocks, while vestiges of the old sand road can still be seen running around the outside edge of the spurs.

Another relic of the old road can be seen halfway down the pass as you cross a small bridge with a faded sign that says 'Jan Joubert's Gat'. This is the oldest stone bridge still in regular use anywhere in South Africa. It was built by Holloway in 1825 to cross a deep ravine that would otherwise have deflected the intended course of the road. Named after some guy who died in the gully, Jan Joubert's Gat Bridge is a national monument and, if you are interested, walk down the path to the overgrown river bank and take a look at the intact, old brickwork.

After Jan Joubert's Gat, the road slowly winds down the inner sleeve of the mountain until it reaches the brown waters of Theewaterskloof Dam. The dam is imaginatively named after the distinctive tea-coloured water that characterises many of the Cape's mountain rivers. This light-brown tincture is caused by the rotten plant matter that washes off the high slopes of the mountains and stains the water with its organic juices. Nice!

The huge Theewaterskloof Dam is quite dramatic when full, and even more so during times of thirst. When I was there, the water level was very low and thousands of dead tree trunks were poking up like black toothpicks from the exposed dam floor. As I drove along the edge of the dam, the wind whipped up the soft sand into a dance of dust, which played among the black needles of long dead trees.

Once across the dam, the road hits a T-junction with the R321. Turn right, towards Grabouw. This is where the fruit orchards start to take over, and trucks laden with crates of fresh fruit and vegetables remind you that this area is the commercial garden of South Africa.

Viljoen's Pass
After a few ks, Viljoen's Pass can be seen rising up a low ridge. As mountain passes go, it's not a biggie; just a simple hairpin bend up to a saddle in the mountains that brings you out into the Greenlands plateau. The Greenlands is another important fruit-growing area, centred around the towns of Elgin and Grabouw.

The Four Passes Drive continues from Grabouw, down Sir Lowry's Pass and back to Cape Town. For more information on Sir Lowry's Pass, refer to *Chapter 9*. If you have the time, you could also turn left towards Betty's Bay, and then take the gorgeous R44 coastal road around the mountains to Gordon's Bay *[see Chapter 14]*.

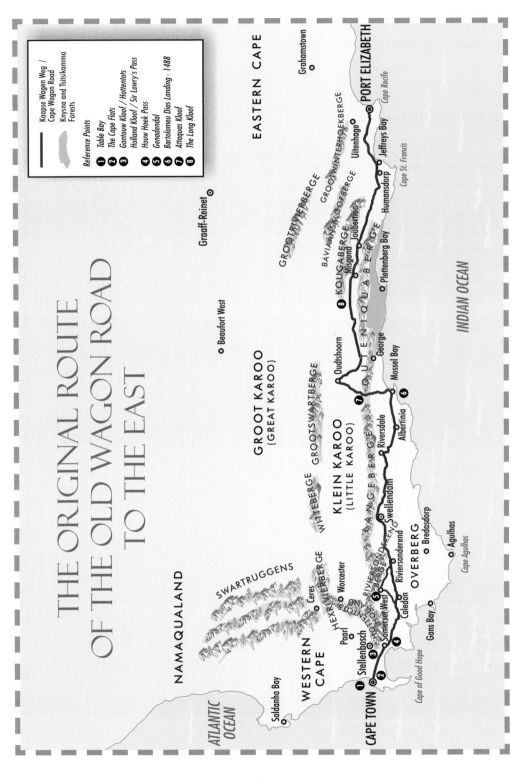

THE ORIGINAL ROUTE OF THE OLD WAGON ROAD TO THE EAST

Reference Points
1. Table Bay
2. The Cape Flats
3. Gantouw Kloof / Hottentots Holland Kloof / Sir Lowry's Pass
4. Houw Hoek Pass
5. Genadendal
6. Bartolomeu Dios Landing - 1488
7. Attaquas Kloof
8. The Long Kloof

Kaapse Wagen Weg / Cape Wagon Road

Knysna and Tsitsikamma Forests

94

CROSSING THE MOUNTAINS OF AFRICA

With the establishment of Stellenbosch and Franschhoek, farmers started spreading out across the flat lands that surrounded the Cape Peninsula. They would have gone farther afield but, beyond this deceptive strip of low-lying land, there suddenly rose a barrier of jagged mountains that cut off the Cape Peninsula from all further agricultural expansion. These mountains ran unbroken from the eastern seaboard at Gordon's Bay to Paarl, near the west coast. From there they ran north, through the Sandveld, for hundreds of miles before veering gently west to the coast again, thus closing the seal.

Van Riebeeck called them the 'Mountains of Africa', and they were an insurmountable obstacle to any form of wheeled transport. The Dutch governors all realised that these mountains would have to be breached if the European settlement at the Cape was going to keep growing, and various expeditions were sent out to find passable routes over the mountains. Eventually, several precarious egresses were uncovered from the jumble of peaks, but none of them was easy to negotiate.

The first mountain passes were usually game tracks, worn out of the rocks by endless generations of migrating animals, which crossed the mountains in their seasonal search for good grazing land. Eland, buffalo or elephant were thus the earliest trailblazers, instinctively finding the path of least resistance along the contour lines, until they had forged a track from one side of the mountain massif to the other.

After these animals came the Bushmen and the Khoikhoi. They followed the game and learnt their routes, adding their own footpaths when necessary. Later, when the white man arrived, these prehistoric tracks were often pointed out to the new settlers by helpful Khoikhoi, who had not yet come to distrust the white man's motives. Thus, by the late 17th century, *abelungu* had found their way over the mountains, and were able to gaze down upon the vast expanse of African interior for the first time. The wheels had begun to turn.

The first documented passage over the Mountains of Africa was found by Pieter Potter in 1658. It led from Paarl to the Roodezant Valley (now called Tulbagh) in the north-east. From Tulbagh, other passes were forged over the mountains further to the north, and this eventually gave access to the Ceres Valley and the Great Karoo beyond. Over the years, this network of road passes was extended and, for over a century, the 'Roodezant passes' were part of the main road to Joburg.

Next, a pass to the barren north was reported by Jan Dankaert in 1660. It was eventually named Piekenierskloof (Pikeman's Ravine), and it is still part of the modern N7 from Cape Town to Springbok. In the early years of the Dutch settlement, this was the most frequented pass of them all, as expedition after expedition penetrated through the Olifants River Valley into the wastes of Namaqualand. These explorers were spurred on by a silly map that vaguely indicated the location of Vigiti Magna, a glorious city of gold and supposed capital of the fabled empire of Monomatapa. They never did find any gold, and the rich mineral deposits found around the 'Copper Mountain' were too remote to be exploited by the expedient Company.

Then, in 1662, Hendrik Lacus documented his ascent of an old Eland's path over the Hottentots Holland mountains to the east. This game track eventually became Sir Lowry's Pass,

Thomas Bain's retaining wall still holds up the Swartberg Pass

and it offered access to a broad, fertile coastal plain over the mountains. This new region was appropriately named the Overberg.

And that was it: a pass to the north, a pass to the north-east, and a pass to the east. The mountains around the Cape Peninsula were so steep and rugged that only three access routes connected it to the rest of the country. In many respects, the situation hasn't changed. Geographically, the Cape still remains isolated from the rest of South Africa, and isolation is the first requirement for the creation of a new species. Perhaps that's why Joburgers like to joke about taking their passports when they travel to Cape Town. It's like another world, bru.

EXPLORERS, HUNTERS AND TRADERS

At first, the VOC were utterly uninterested in the land beyond the Cape of Good Hope. Their only concern was to turn a profit by selling stuff to the passing fleets that called at Table Bay. Like any modern company, the bottom line was paramount, and the VOC made no effort to invest in the country beyond its immediate operational needs. Besides, the 'Mountains of

Africa' seemed to cut off the Cape Peninsula from the wild interior of the country, and the VOC was in no hurry to build expensive roads over the formidable peaks.

The job of opening up the interior therefore fell on a motley crew of explorers, hunters, traders and cattle farmers (in that order). The first explorers were usually Company employees who were ordered to venture out into the wild unknown of the South African interior to gather intelligence about the local tribes. Men such as Jan Dankaert, Pieter Potter, Heironymus Cruse, Pieter van Meerhof, Ensign Buetler and Pieter Cruijthof were among the first to be sent out from the Fort, tasked with probing the mountains to the east and the north. Later, the occasional governor, like the conscientious Simon van der Stel or the intrepid Joachim Van Plettenberg, would also undertake a journey to the far-flung reaches of his realm, to check on the situation first-hand.

The next wave of explorers were botanists, ornithologists, scientists and adventurers; men of the Enlightenment who were eager to name new species and document natural wonders never before seen by western eyes. This group included learned people like Carl Thunberg and Anders Spaarman, both of whom sent samples of new plant species back to Carl Linnaeus (the Swedish botanist who developed the system of binomial nomenclature, which we still use to classify living things according to their genus and their species). These early scientific expeditions were often accompanied by surveyors and other Company employees, who constantly scanned the land to see if there was anything valuable to take.

The final wave of explorers were the gentlemen (and women) travellers who ventured out into the wild open spaces of Africa so that they could fill their journals with piquant observations and curious stories. These exotic tales, they hoped, would turn their books into best-sellers back in Europe, and were among the first examples of modern travel writing. Some of these literary adventurers were Lady Anne Barnard, William Burchell and John Barrow. From a modern perspective you could criticise these journeymen for being culturally specific or even condescending, but they did much to document the environmental and cultural condition of an untouched Africa.

In the footsteps of the explorers (and sometimes even ahead of them) came the hunters. They were a burly lot who hunted for the pot, for leather and for the hell of it. Much to the disgust of the indigenous people, the white hunter would often kill a noble beast, hack off a memento and leave the rest of the carcass to the vultures. This kind of waste was anathema to the natives, and it seemed to them that the Great White Hunter liked to shoot anything that moved, but didn't like to move anything they shot.

After the hunters came the cattle traders; first on behalf of the Company, then on behalf of themselves. These canny businessmen were always looking for a way to get ivory, gold, animal skins and fat cattle away from the local tribespeople. Sometimes they used beads, sometimes they used persuasion, sometimes they just used force. Many of their 'trading expeditions' were no more than poorly disguised cattle raids, and this made many of the natives understandably resentful.

As explorers, hunters and traders (sometimes in the guise of the same person) spread out over the tenuous mountain passes into the interior, the game and the local tribesfolk retreated before their thundering guns. Before long, the once great herds of buck, buffalo and elephant were depleted, and many of the indigenous people (the Bushmen, in particular) found their livelihood under threat. Things were looking bad for the locals, and the encroaching Trekboers were about to make the situation a whole lot worse.

THE TREKBOERS

At first, the VOC was absolute. They 'owned' all the land at the Cape and made all the rules. Settlers were merely company employees who received a salary and did as they were told. Punishment for insubordination was harsh and living conditions were pretty squalid. The meagre yield of food that was produced went straight to the Company for whatever purposes were most pressing. There was little incentive and even less enterprise.

Eventually, however, hunger got the better of the Dutch outpost and a new system was devised. From 1656, employees who had completed their contracts, and other 'free burghers' from Europe, were granted land on which to grow crops. These crops could then be sold back to the Company, at whatever rate the Company dictated. It was hardly an equitable situation, but it was the first time that the concepts of free enterprise and proprietary land ownership were exercised in South Africa.

At first, these free burghers were allowed to settle only on land demarcated by the Company, and these 'free hold' farms were inevitably located close to Cape Town so that the authorities could keep an eye on their new citizens. As the years passed, however, this new class of free burgher increased in number and became more powerful. Inevitably, they began

Bain's remote Baviaanskloof road slowly climbs up a valley

to bridle against the constricting policies of the Company, and started agitating for more rights and more space. Finally, after fifty years of rigid control, the VOC decided to change its policy entirely and in 1703 it was decreed that farmers could henceforth go where they liked and graze their herds on any 'unoccupied' land.

In 1717, this system was formalised by the granting of grazing permits, which allowed the farmer to secure his rights over a so-called loan place, or *leeningplaatsen*. These loan places were vast, about 6 000 acres each, and they were not allowed to be sub-divided. This meant that a father could not split his land between his progeny, and each scion had to go out and register a new loan place of their own. Luckily, this wasn't a problem as land was plentiful (if you ignored the irritating natives), and grazing permits were freely granted. Furthermore, the Company hardly ever collected the small 'quit-rent' revenues due from these new farms, so, basically, it was a free-for-all.

Unfettered from the Cape, each successive generation of farmers moved further and further away from the controlling influence of the Castle. These aspirant cattlemen (for most did not bother with the intricacies of agriculture) were of a rugged and individualistic stock. They resented the heavy hand of authority and preferred to make up their own rules. They were also loners. As Jose Burman puts it, 'they would pack up and move away if they could see the smoke from their neighbour's fire'.

Still, it was a tough life for Whitey out in the bush, far away from any form of Western civilisation. To survive, they had to adopt many of the native ways. They lived in rough mud huts built over a framework of sticks, they dressed in skins, and they moved with their herds from one seasonal grazing ground to another. Some also took Khoikhoi women as their lovers, but they were the exception rather than the rule. Even in these straitened circumstances, the God-fearing white Christians considered themselves a cut above the black heathens and, by virtue of their skin and their God, they were never really tempted to assimilate with the dark-skinned locals.

This ragged, iconoclastic group of farmers were called the Trekboers (travelling farmers), and they spread out over the country like a virus. By 1730, the Trekboers had reached as far as the Olifants River in the north and Mossel Bay in the east, a vast distance by the standards of the day. And they showed no signs of slowing down. It seemed that the anti-authoritarian Trekboers had an insatiable appetite for both land and freedom; although they weren't so concerned about the local population's claims to either of these ideals.

Much to the VOC's dismay, the restless journeying of the Trekboers kept extending the boundaries (and responsibilities) of the Cape Colony. The Company tried to keep up with them by establishing new magistracies at Swellendam in 1743 and Graaff-Reinet in 1786, but it was all to no avail. By the end of the 18th century, the VOC found itself saddled with a vast, troubled territory filled with uncooperative Trekboers and angry black tribes. This escalating atmosphere of conflict culminated in the numerous Xhosa Wars of Resistance, fought on the turbulent Eastern Frontier from the 1780s onwards.

It's ironic that the Trekboers caused so many headaches for the Company. Over the years, they had grown increasingly distant from the European heritage of the Cape. They ignored the Company's decrees, and railed against any attempts to halt their progress or criticise their behaviour. Gradually, as their isolation grew, they began to emerge as an entirely new species – The Afrikaner, hard and determined, the only white tribe native to Africa.

DIE KAAPSE WAGEN WEG / THE CAPE WAGON ROAD

While some farmers trekked to the north and entered the barren tracts of the Karoo, most of the Trekboers spread out along the great wagon road to the east. Also called the *Kaapse Wagen Weg*, this was a route established by various explorers who had taken it upon themselves to uncover the mysteries of the interior. For over one hundred

years, this great eastern highway carried horses and humans from the Cape to Uitenhage, near Algoa Bay (modern Port Elizabeth).

More specifically, the wagon road to the east started at Cape Town and traversed the sandy Cape Flats, heading towards Hottentot's Holland. In the early days of the Colony, crossing these sandy plains was quite a challenge. Stretching from coast to coast, this vast expanse of soft, sucking sand would drag at your horse's hooves and hold your wagon fast. It was a formidable barrier to wheeled traffic that effectively cut off the straggling settlement at Cape Town from the interior.

Building up a solid road on these shifting foundations proved a major undertaking for the early Dutch, and the first hard road was only completed by the British in 1845. This difficulty seems inconceivable today, now the Cape Flats have been covered by a morass of low-cost housing and bleak townships. But there is one remnant of the wild, old Flats still preserved in the Wolfgat Nature Reserve on the False Bay Coast, halfway between Muizenberg and Gordon's Bay.

Once the traveller had reached Hottentot's Holland, the road passed over the mountains via the Sir Lowry's and Houhoek passes, into the Overberg. From here, it ran over the rolling *ruggens* to Caledon, then through the Riviersonderend Valley and on to the regional capital of Swellendam. From this tiny cluster of homes, the road dropped slowly to the coast at Mossel Bay.

From Mossel Bay, the wagon road hit an impasse. To the north were the tall mountains of the Outeniquas, and to the east lay the impenetrable forests and deep ravines of Knysna and the Tsitsikamma. It seemed that this was the end of the line, but the momentum of the Trekboers had become an irresistible force and the mountains were just another immovable object.

It took some doing, but a ragged route over the mountains was finally developed along an old elephant track called 'Attaquas Kloof'. This wagon path crossed the Outeniquas above Mossel Bay, and brought the weary traveller out

A journey on the Old Eastern Highway

In the days of the ox wagon, there were no speed limits. A span of ten or twelve oxen could only pull a wagon at 4 to 6 kilometres an hour, and you could halve that if you were going over a mountain pass or crossing a river. This meant that there was no rushing from town to town, and the slow and steady amble of the oxen made for a deliciously leisurely pace of travel.

So, just to give you an idea of how it was done in the old days, we will now re-live a trip from Cape Town to Swellendam, circa 1805.

Two hundred years ago, it took about five days to journey from Cape Town to Swellendam. A day was taken as eight hours of travel, which equated to about 40 kilometres. One day was also called a 'schoft' – Dutch for 'rest'.

As the oxen trundled over the land, they were fed and watered at regular 'outspan' places, about 10 to 15km apart. These outspans were small pieces of government-controlled land that offered a fresh water supply and some shade for the ox-drivers. They were usually situated on land left over from the circular loan places, granted to farmers by the white government back in Cape Town. The facilities at the outspans were usually looked after by the local district.

The original route of the eastern highway went something like this:

From Cape Town, wagons hauled themselves over the sandy Cape Flats to the Helderberg, near present-day Somerset West. From here, wagons went over the Hottentots Holland mountains via the Gantouw Kloof (now called Sir Lowry's Pass). Once up on the Greenlands plateau, they forded the Palmiet River on the oldest bridge in South Africa (about 1,5km downstream from the current N2 bridge, near Grabouw). Then they passed the outspans of Knoflook's Kraal and Koffie Kraal before reaching the Houhoek Pass.

When the exhausted wagon train reached the bottom of the pass, they had to ford the Steenbras River at Grietjie's Gat, and then proceeded to Botrivier and Boontjie's Kraal. From here, the road headed over the ruggens (or ruëns) to Caledon, and then up to the populous mission station of Genadendal. The wagon road then wound down to the town of Riviersonderend, and from there it was a short distance to the regional capital of Swellendam.

into the narrow plain of the Klein Karoo, not far from Oudtshoorn.

From Oudtshoorn, the road east continued inland until it found the mouth of a long, fertile valley called the Langkloof (Long Kloof), which was sandwiched between the Tsitsikamma mountains to the south and the Kouga mountains to the north.

Driving their ox-wagons along the floor of the fertile Langkloof, travellers moved in a south-easterly direction until they once again hit the sea at Humansdorp. From here it was a short distance to Uitenhage, founded by the short-lived Batavian Republic at the turn of the nineteenth century. From this little town, it was 20km to the windswept shores of Algoa Bay, where Port Elizabeth was later established by the British. Here the wagon road to the east ended – albeit temporarily.

THE ROAD BUILDERS

When the British took over from the Dutch in 1806 [see Chapter 11], the administrators found the roads of their new colony in a horrible state. Soggy wagon tracks limped across the Cape Flats, and only a few suicidal passes crept over the mountains.

For the next twenty years, things stayed pretty much the same. The Cape Colony was taking on debt like Donald Trump, and the British Colonial authorities were being very austere with their latest acquisition. There was just no money for roads. Then, in 1828, Charles Michell arrived at the Cape.

Charles Michell

Michell (pronounced Mitchell) was your typical 19th-century renaissance man. By the time he was thirty-two, he had already fought in the

Peninsular Campaign against the French, run away to marry his fifteen-year-old sweetheart and become a 'Professor of Fortifications' at a well-known engineering school. That's when he got appointed to the joint posts of Surveyor-General, Civil Engineer, and Superintendent of Works at the Cape.

When he arrived, Michell and the governor, Sir Lowry Cole, made a tour of inspection around the Cape Colony. They were not pleased with what they found. There was no hard road across the Cape Flats and there was only one barely engineered pass, the Franschhoek Pass, over the mountains. The other road passes in the Cape were dismissed as 'uneffaced, rude tracks'.

Both men agreed that good roads were essential to grow the economy of the Cape and, in 1830, Cole and Michell's first big project was unveiled. It was Sir Lowry's Pass on the great eastern highway. The public were ecstatic with the new road, but then things got political. Cole had not asked head office for permission to spend money on the road, and the Colonial Secretary in London was pissed off. For the next twelve years, just about every subsequent request for road money was refused.

Michell was left spinning his wheels at the Cape. But he had plenty of other tasks to occupy his time. He scouted out a route for his proposed road over the mountains to the North, he served in the Frontier War of 1835, and he managed to build a hard road over the Cape Flats in the 1840s. Mitchell's Plain, by the way, is named after Charles Michell, but they misspelled his name. How annoying.

John Montagu

In 1843, John Montagu took over as Colonial Secretary at the Cape. He was an experienced administrator, and he took it upon himself to clear the colony's asphyxiating debt. He accomplished this feat in two years. Then, he turned his attention to the roads.

In short order, Montagu had two excellent ideas. First, he eschewed the road-building services of the local councils and set up a Central Road Board, under the capable Michell, with a mandate to plan and supervise the construction of all major roads within the colony. Then, to actually build the roads, he decided to use the standing pools of convict labour as a cheap and available work force. Both these innovations would become long-standing features of South African road construction.

The first pass built under the new regime was Montagu Pass, above George [see Chapter 11]. The fancy new Montagu Pass replaced the dreadful old Cradock Kloof, but it was not Michell's baby. Instead, Montagu imported the experienced engineer, Henry Fancourt White, to supervise the project, and Michell continued planning his road to the north through Mostert's Hoek to Tulbagh.

Sadly, by this time, Michell was growing a bit old for the tough life of a *padmaker* and he needed a proxy. Happily, that's when he met Andrew Geddes Bain.

Andrew Geddes Bain

Andrew Bain was a protean man of many talents. He was born in Scotland in 1797, emigrated to South Africa when he was twenty-five, and settled at Graaff-Reinet on the Eastern Frontier with his wife, in 1822. Once in South Africa, Bain embarked on a long and varied career that would take him from one side of the country to the other.

Bain started out working as a saddler. Then, after a few unprofitable years, he packed it in to become a wide-travelling trader who explored the country all the way up to the Limpopo. Unfortunately, in 1834, trader Bain was caught in the middle of a native conflict and lost everything, except his life. He returned to Graaff-Reinet, and decided to enlist in the Frontier War of 1935.

After the war, Bain chose to take a farm in the new province of Queen Adelaide, which was declared as a buffer-zone between the white settlers and the fractious Xhosa. A year later, this controversial new territory was abandoned by the authorities and the settlers were left destitute. For the second time, Bain was left with nothing. He had to find a new job.

Luckily, Bain had already gained some knowledge of road building. In the early 1830s, he had volunteered to help surveyor Charles Stretch build the Oudeberg Pass and the Van Ryneveld Pass, both near Graaff-Reinet. He even got a medal from the grateful citizens of Graaff-Reinet for his troubles. So, armed with a little experience and an eager mind, the pragmatic Bain took a job supervising the labour gangs who were busy building military roads through the Eastern Cape. He worked on these roads for nine years, building the lovely Queen's Highway from Grahamstown to Fort Beaufort via the Ecca Pass, and the Pluto Vale road to Breakfast Vlei.

In 1845, however, Bain's services were no longer required by the Royal Engineers and he was abruptly fired. Despondent but still needing work, Bain decided to take his fate into his own hands and applied to Charles Michell for a job as Inspector of Roads. His application was successful and, together, the triumvirate of Bain, Michell and Montagu would change the face of the colony's roads.

Bain immediately started working on several projects simultaneously: he began building the road through Mostert's Hoek, which would become Michell's Pass from Tulbagh to Ceres; he built the Gydo Pass, further to the north; and he also improved the Houhoek Pass and the road from Ceres through Karoo Poort into the interior.

After Michell retired in 1848, Bain went on to build his greatest road, Bain's Kloof Pass. This road was part of the great northern highway which carried traffic from Cape Town to Joburg for over one hundred years, and will be covered in more detail in another Back Roads book.

By 1851, Michell was dead and Montagu had retired to England, broken by the strain of keeping the Cape solvent. Bain, alone and aging, soldiered on to build one last road, the Katberg Pass, before dying in 1864.

When he died, Andrew Bain left behind a substantial legacy. Apart from the roads he built, he also published the first geological map of the Cape Province and wrote a pioneering monograph entitled *The Geology of South Africa*. It was the first major work of its kind in the subcontinent and it earned Bain the nickname, 'the father of South African geology'.

Apart from these material successes, Bain also managed to father eleven children. One of these offspring was a remarkable individual who went on to eclipse the achievements of Bain senior. His name was Thomas.

THOMAS BAIN – THE PASS-MASTER

Thomas Charles John Bain was born on the Eastern Cape frontier in 1830 and died, aged sixty-four, in 1893. Nevertheless, in his relatively short life, Bain the younger made an indelible mark on this country.

He was known by his peers as 'the man with the theodolite eye', a peculiar encomium that sounds more like a sci-fi movie title than an honorary nickname. But it was an attribute that summed up his amazing ability to determine the ideal routing for a road, using nothing more than his keen eyes and a pair of hiking boots.

Thomas Bain's accomplishments are legendary: he built twenty-three mountain passes, three major roads and several minor roads throughout the Cape colony; he discovered four new species of Stapelia, one of which (*Hoodia bainii*) is named after him; he helped discover the fossil of a previously unknown dinosaur, eponymously named *Bradysaurus bainii*; and he was consulted about the important mineralogical finds of gold at Millwood near Knysna, and diamonds at Kimberley.

Bain was also an excellent artist, surveyor and draughtsman, personally drawing beautiful relief maps for each of his major road works. But, despite his artistic proclivities, Thomas Bain the roadbuilder should not be confused with Thomas Baines the travelling artist, who created many memorable paintings of the South African landscape.

A rusty wagon crumbles into oblivion, Gamkaskloof

Nepotism notwithstanding, the young Bain's potential was soon recognised, and he was quickly promoted to take charge of one of the convict stations on the Bain's Kloof project.

Armed with his new-found experience, Bain was then sent to Paarl, where he built the Lady Grey Bridge over the Berg River and other roads in the area. Bain was later transferred and sent to build a new pass through Piekenier's Kloof, between Piketberg and Citrusdal. It opened as Grey's Pass in 1858.

Next, it was off to Knysna, where Bain planned the roads of the newly declared township around the lagoon. With this task out of the way, he began sizing up the mountains and forests that cut off Knysna from the rest of the world. Within a few years he had built Phantom Pass, which leads from Knysna to Rheenendal, and the epic Prince Alfred's Pass, through the tall trees, to Uniondale.

It was while he was building the Prince Alfred that Bain got word that his father was dying. Sadly, construction had just reached a critical stage, and he couldn't leave the site. Bain never saw his father again. But that was probably the way Andrew Bain would have wanted it. The calling of a *padmaker* is strenuous, and sacrifices have to be made for the sake of the job at hand.

Over the next forty years, Thomas Bain never neglected his duties and he never stopped working. He travelled incessantly, from one construction site to the next; scouting new routes over the mountains, while supervising the workers on others.

Bain also continued his studies and went on to qualify as an Associate Member of the British Institute of Civil Engineers, far outstripping his self-taught father's academic credentials. He was finally appointed Inspector of Roads, but only when his father retired from the post.

Happily, all this work didn't stop Thomas from falling in love. He married the well-connected Johanna de Smidt, daughter of the secretary of the Central Roads Board, and they had several children together. It was a happy

Thomas Bain began his eventful life on the eastern frontier, where his father was busy supervising the construction of military roads through the thick bush. At age sixteen, he joined the army and participated in the bloody and futile War of the Axe against the Xhosa. After he was demobbed, Bain decided to go into the family business and joined his estimable dad as an assistant. Together, they worked on Michell's Pass and Bain's Kloof, where Thomas learnt his craft at the feet of his father.

union, but the Bain family had to move around a lot, trying to keep up with the peripatetic Thomas. And even that didn't help. Thomas spent most of his time on the road, and Bain's children remember their father as a warm, pleasant but vague figure in their lives, more often absent than present.

His roads, however, speak for themselves and stand as a testament to a brilliant man. After completing Prince Alfred's Pass, Bain stayed on in Knysna to complete the road over Kaaimansgat, between George and the Wilderness. Then he moved over to Mossel Bay to build Robinson's Pass, a replacement for the crumbling Attaquas Kloof passage.

During the 1870s, Bain staked out and built a flurry of magnificent mountain passes: the Tradouw Pass from Swellendam to Barrydale; the railway pass through Tulbagh Kloof; Cogmans Kloof near Montagu; Garcia's Pass above Riversdale; Pakhuis Pass between Clanwilliam and Calvinia; Koo Pass between Matroosberg and Montagu; Molteno Pass and De Jager's Pass, both near Beaufort West; Van Rhyn's Pass in the far north; the Klein Swartberg pass from Ladismith to Laingsburg; the Oudeberg Pass from Wellington to Tulbagh; and Verlaten Kloof near Sutherland were all completed during this busy decade. In fact, it is recorded that Bain took a total of only one month's leave during his entire 46-year stint with the Public Works Department!

It's simply amazing that one man travelling by ox-wagon and Cape cart could complete so many major road works in such a short time. It's a feat made even more remarkable when you consider than Bain was working at a time when there was no earth-moving machinery, no modern explosives, no power drills and no aerial photography to help the road builder. Everything was done with pick-axes, gunpowder, sledgehammers and human sweat. But Bain was determined and inventive, always looking for new ways to conquer old problems. He even pioneered the practice of breaking up large boulders by heating them with fire until they became brittle

enough for a sledgehammer to crack.

But it was the 1880s that brought Bain his greatest challenges and his most enduring achievements. In 1879, Bain returned to the Garden Route and embarked on two mammoth projects: the Seven Passes Road from George to Knysna and the Tsitsikamma road from Plettenberg Bay to Humansdorp. He also tackled a couple of secondary access routes to the region, most notably the isolated and dramatic Baviaanskloof road.

In 1884, he was called away from his work on the Passes Road for yet another enormous undertaking. The time had come to build an all-weather road over the Groot Swartberg mountains, north of Oudtshoorn. This pass, which opened around 1888, was to become Bain's most impressive legacy. While he was in the area, Bain also improved the nearby Meiringspoort road, which was prone to flooding.

By this stage, Bain had poured his life-blood into the transport routes of the Cape colony, and he was running out of steam. He built only one more road, the glorious Victoria Drive from Sea Point to Hout Bay, and then slowed down substantially, spending some long-overdue time with his family and doing geological surveys for the government. He died at the family home in Rondebosch in 1893.

Thomas Bain is the unsung hero of South Africa's road network. He created more than two dozen invaluable roads, and he laid the foundations for a modern-day transportation infrastructure that is still the envy of the African continent. A hundred and fifty years later, many of Bain's passes are still in use, with little more than a tarmac surface and a minor re-alignment to bring them up to date. So, the next time you traverse the lofty heights on one of these picture-perfect passes, spare a thought for the lonely old *padmaker*, and give thanks to Thomas Bain.

THE NATIONAL ROADS PROGRAMME

By 1864, the Central Roads Board had been disbanded, and responsibility for the construction and maintenance of roads was handed over to the local Divisional Councils. In effect, this meant that quality of the roads varied greatly from region to region. No one seemed to mind, however, as the pace of the ox-wagon was slow and steady and, in those days, it took quite a lot to make a road impassable.

Then the motor car arrived on the scene, hooting and rushing around the countryside. These new-fangled vehicles were not suited to the old wagon roads; gradients were too steep, road surfaces were too uneven and the corners were too sharp to be taken by a motor car travelling at any kind of speed. The mountain passes were particularly problematic as they had been engineered for the nimble Cape cart, and were not suitable for 'horseless carriages'. Someone had to take charge of modernising the roads and, by 1919, the idea of creating a centralised structure was mooted once again.

But nothing came of the proposal until the number of cars grew to epidemic proportions and the road network really started showing its age. By the 1930s even the most blinkered politician realised that something had to be done and, in 1935, the first national roads programme was announced. The future was on the way.

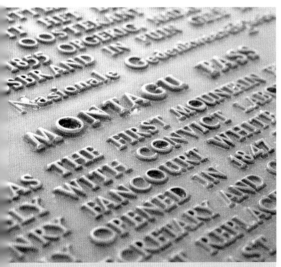

Memorial plaque at the foot of Montagu Pass

The idea was to build a modern road network that would link the country together through a series of well-built highways. A map of proposed routes was duly drawn up, but progress on the national road network was spasmodic. Plans were constantly being revised and abandoned, as local politics, international wars and lack of funds intervened. Nevertheless, one by one, new national roads were slowly laid down across the country.

Today, sixty-five years later, the national road programme is still not entirely complete. Many national roads are still interrupted by small towns and their traffic lights, and some sections of the national road network have been de-proclaimed, pending further investment. But we are getting there. We now have one real, honest-to-God, four-lane freeway (the N3 from Joburg to Durban), and other national roads are being improved all the time – with the help of the new toll fees.

THE N2

For all practical purposes, the current N2 is the closest thing we have to the old road to the east, and it is an extraordinary route.

The N2 starts at the Cape Town city centre and runs for 2 500km along the coast, through the Western Cape, the Eastern Cape, Kwa-Zulu-Natal and the southern tip of Mpumalanga before finally terminating in Joburg (as the N17). It is a long and beautiful carriageway that leads along the edge of South Africa's eastern seaboard, only curving away when deflected by Mozambique and Swaziland.

With thousands of k's of coastline spooling out along its flanks, the N2 is an excellent road for travellers. It takes in some of South Africa's most enticing tourist regions, including the Garden Route, the Wild Coast, the South Coast of Natal and the lush northern shores of Kwa-Zulu. It also takes in many of South Africa's premier cities: Cape Town, Port Elizabeth, East London, Durban, Joburg. If you have the time, a month or two spent driving along the N2 is a glorious way to see the country.

THE HELDERBERG / GORDON'S BAY

To Franschhoek

VILLIERSDORP

To Worcester

To Cape Town

R310

To Stellenbosch

To Stellenbosch

R44

Theewaterskloof Dam

N2

Hottentots Holland
Nature Reserve

Viljoen's Pass

Van Der Stel Pass

To Muizenberg

VERGELEGEN

SOMERSET WEST

SIR LOWRY'S PASS

GRABOUW

Greenlands
Plateau

To Caledon

Elgin

STRAND

R44

Houhoek Pass

GORDON'S BAY

BOTRIVIER

N2

False Bay

Koeël Bay

R43

Rooiels Bay

Kogelberg Biosphere Reserve

HOTTENTOTS HOLLAND MOUNTAINS

Rooiels Bay

R44

To Caledon

Kleinmond

Botrivier
Vlei

Pringle Bay

Harold Porter
Botanical Garden

Kleinmond Lagoon

R320

Pringle Bay

R44

Hangklip

BETTY'S BAY

To Gans Bay

African Penguin Colony

R43

HERMANUS

	National Road		Mountain Passes
	Tarred Road		R44 Scenic Drive / Clarence Drive
	Minor Tarred Road		Agulhas Coastal Route (see chapter14)
	Gravel Road		

9. The Helderberg Coast

ORIENTATION

From Cape Town, the road to the east crosses the Cape Flats to reach the foot of the Hottentots Holland Mountains near Gordon's Bay. To do this, you can either take the N2 from the City Bowl or you can try the R310, which starts in Muizenberg and runs right along the False Bay coast [see Chapter 14]. Either way, it's about 50 k's to Gordon's Bay, and the drive should take you about an hour.

At Gordon's Bay, the bulk of the Hottentots Holland mountains crowd all the way down to the sea. If you want to move forward, you have to cross them. In the old days, this was only possible by going up Sir Lowry's Pass and then down the Houhoek Pass. Now, you have the additional choice of taking the spectacular R44 (aka Clarence Drive) along the seaward cliffs to Betty's Bay [see Chapter 14]. A round trip from Cape Town, over Sir Lowry's and Houhoek to Betty's Bay, and then back to Cape Town via the R44 is highly recommended.

If you choose to go over Sir Lowry's Pass, you will find yourself on the Greenlands plateau, a fertile fruit-growing area. If you are doing the Four Passes Scenic Drive in an anti-clockwise direction [see Chapter 7], turn off to Grabouw and follow signs for the R321 towards Villiersdorp. After about 30 k's, you'll hit a T-junction with the R45. Turn left towards Franschhoek, over the Franschhoek Pass.

If you are following the Eastern Highway, continue on the N2, past the towns of Grabouw and Elgin, before descending to the Overberg coastal strip, via the Houhoek Pass. At the town of Botrivier, which was probably quite pretty once, you can take the turn-off to Betty's Bay and Hermanus if you want to explore the Overberg Coast, or if you want to drive back to Cape Town via the R44 [see Chapter 14].

Otherwise, stay on the N2, cross the pretty Steenbras River, and continue east into the Overberg towards Caledon [see Chapter 10].

GORDON'S BAY

The eastern end of False Bay is dominated by the urban developments of Somerset West, Strand and Gordon's Bay. This area and its coastline, dominated by the sublime Hottentots Holland mountains, is now known as the Helderberg Basin, and is a popular tourist destination in its own right. Gordon's Bay is a particularly nice town (especially when compared to the high-rise beachfront of Strand) and offers a quaint

A fishy deal at a Gordon's Bay take-away

harbour, good seafood restaurants and the beguiling Bikini Beach. Other beaches in the area include Main Beach, Macassar Beach, Melkbaai and The Strand, which has good facilities for the kids.

The popular Monkey Town primate sanctuary is right on the N2, and other nearby attractions include: the Helderbrau microbrewery, Lwandle Hostel Museum and Crafts Centre and the Vergelegen Wine Estate. If you are an outdoors person, you can take a charter cruise in False Bay, play a round of golf or hike one of the several trails in the area.

For the spiritually inclined, Sheik Yusuf, the founder of Islam in SA, is buried on the farm Zandvliet at Faure and his shrine (or *kramat*) is open to visitors. This kramat forms part of the holy Circle of Islam, which believers say protects the Peninsula from evil forces. Pilgrims will find the other sacred shrines at Signal Hill, Oudekraal, Robben Island, and in the suburb of Constantia.

There is a also good selection of restaurants in the Helderberg area, but if you want to try some real local fare, forsake the glitzy beachfront emporiums and sit on the pavement outside *Ooskus* take-away. They serve a great calamari and linefish combo, at a very reasonable price.

THE GANTOUW / HOTTENTOTS HOLLAND KLOOF / SIR LOWRY'S PASS

High in the mountains above Gordon's Bay is a narrow cleft in the rocks. The Khoikhoi called it the Gantouw (the Eland's Kloof) and, for generations, it served as a valuable footpath over the peaks to their brethren living along the Overberg coast.

Over the centuries, the Khoikhoi had carved out a very comfortable niche for themselves here, on the plains wedged between the mountains and the sea. But everything must change and their happy isolation ended when, one day, the Dutch found their way to the foot of this mountainous phalanx. Yet even these unwelcome guests couldn't ruffle the Khoikhoi's feathers, and the early Dutch expeditions to this area reported seeing large numbers of Khoikhoi, living happily in their family clans.

The natives' contentment was so evident, in fact, that the mountains were named the Hottentots Holland, as in 'Hottentot's homeland', and so they have remained. The Gantouw remained a secret, however, until some obliging Khoikhoi chap showed a Dutch Ensign, Hendrik Lacus, the path of the Eland over the mountains.

At first, the Gantouw route was used by Company officials who had business with the Khoikhoi chiefs on the other side of the mountains. Then, intrepid explorers, scientists and freebooters started climbing the Gantouw, looking for adventure and riches in the mysterious interior. By this time, the little cleft in the mountain peaks was called Hottentots Holland Kloof, and the pass was named accordingly.

Hottentots Holland Kloof Pass was a steep, narrow and rocky track that tacked along the mountain's face, before turning sharply left towards the final, bruising ascent to the Kloof itself. Many travellers left harrowing accounts of their passage over Hottentots Holland Kloof, and Captain Robert Percival seemed to sum it up when he said that the pass was 'sufficient to deter the timid from ever entering the interior of the country…wild, awful and steep'.

Nevertheless, it was such an important route that, by 1821, 4 500 wagons were using the pass each year. It should be noted, however, that 20% of these wagons were damaged by the journey.

The view from the summit of Sir Lowry's Pass

Then along came Sir Lowry Cole, British governor at the Cape from 1828 to 1833. Cole was an enlightened man who saw that the colony could not develop without proper access roads – an acute observation that still holds true to this day. Cole recognised the importance of the Hottentots Holland pass and ordered his chief engineer, Charles Michell, to improve the terrible track over the Kloof. After careful consideration, Michell decided not to route his new road over the original kloof. Instead, he found another crevice in the rocks, a little to the south, which could be crossed with less difficulty and on a more gentle line of approach. Funds were found and convicts were put to work. The brand, spanking new 'Sir Lowry's Pass' was opened in 1830.

Sir Lowry's was an instant success with the locals, but the road caused controversy with the Colonial authorities back in England. Evidently, the governor had given the go-ahead to build the pass without first asking permission from his masters in London. The Colonial Office responded with a sharp slap on the wrists, and Sir Lowry was censured for his insubordination. No further mountain passes were built by British authorities in the Cape for the next twelve years.

The well-engineered Sir Lowry's Pass remained open, however, and continued to ferry wagons over the mountains in relative comfort and safety for the next hundred years. In the 1930s, the original cutting became too congested for the mounting volume of traffic, and the pass was widened and tarred. In the 1950s, further improvements were made to the upper reaches of the pass.

By 1984, traffic had become so heavy that a narrow two-lane stretch, close to the summit, had to be expanded. This was easier said than done as there was simply no more rock on which to build. The solution was to construct a 'bridge over nothing' which transformed the pass into a grand four-lane highway. This is the distinctive Sir Lowry's Pass that we drive today.

The view from the top of the pass is outstanding, and it's worth stopping at the large viewing area for a quick look. Standing on the summit, buffeted by the wind, you can look out over the whole False Bay coast, from Gordon's Bay right across to the mountains at Cape Point. It's a gorgeous sight, especially when the sun hangs low in the sky, sending a slanting ray of silver light across the deceptively tranquil waters of the Bay. Just be prepared for a howling wind in summer, as the south-easter comes roaring around the Hottentots Holland mountains before gusting across the bay towards Cape Town.

As for the old Gantouw route, it can still be seen from the modern road we drive today. It is a faint brown track, barely visible on the green mountain slopes, which runs parallel to, and slightly above, the current N2. The original portal to the Overberg, Hottentots Holland Kloof, can also be seen from the main road. It is a low nek between two upright pillars of rock, and can be easily identified by the electricity pylons that still use the old route to carry power over the mountains. This old approach road to the Kloof, with well-defined ruts worn into the rocks by innumerable heavy wagon wheels, can be hiked as part of the Hottentots Holland hiking trail, administered by Cape Nature Conservation.

GRABOUW AND ELGIN

Once you are over Sir Lowry's Pass, you will find yourself up on a high-lying mountain plateau where the fruit orchards of Grabouw and Elgin flourish. This well-watered area, sometimes called the Greenlands, is an important fruit-growing region producing apples, pears, plums and nectarines for local use and for export.

Today, South Africa is renowned for the quality of its deciduous fruit, but this was not always the case. Wine farming was the Cape's big cash crop ever since the Huguenots arrived in 1688. So, by the late 1800s, few other fruits besides grapes were being grown anywhere on the Peninsula. Then, a deadly fungus called Phylloxera hit the Cape vineyards and wiped out the vines. Sammy Marks, the canny gold magnate, suggested to Cecil John Rhodes that this might be a good time to try and produce some alternative crops. Rhodes nodded sagely and quickly bought huge tracts of land from the bankrupt wine farmers around the Drakenstein mountains. The result was Rhodes Co-operative Farms, which was, for many years, a major player in South Africa's fresh fruit industry.

As you continue along the Greenlands Plateau, you will come to the Houw Hoek Inn. This was originally the last outspan before riders girded their loins and took their wagons over the Houhoek Pass, the next obstacle on the Eastern Highway.

THE HOUHOEK PASS

Houhoek is a close counterpart of Sir Lowry's Pass. Where Sir Lowry's lifts the traveller up onto the high mountain plateau, the Houhoek takes them down again to the coastal plain, and into the Overberg. That much is simple enough, but the history of the pass is quite complicated.

The name 'Houhoek' is of uncertain origin and varied spelling. Either transcribed as 'Hou' as in 'hold', 'Houw' as in 'rest' or even 'Hout' as in wood, this is a pass with many manifestations. The first route over the mountains at this end of the chain simply went straight up to the summit, and steeply down the other side. This was common practise in the days of the ox-wagon, as a span of oxen has more power when pulling in a straight line than when trying to negotiate a

---

Grabouw and the Elgin valley

Attractions in the Elgin Valley area include Fruit Farm Tours, the Apple Museum and the Elgin Rose Festival, which is held on the last weekend in October. There are also several wine estates to visit, and dozens of little lodges tucked away in the surrounding mountains. An annual New Year's Eve festival attracts many revellers to the orchards around Elgin for a weekend of camping, loud music and recreational intoxication.

- *Elgin Valley Tourist Info: 021 859 1398*
- *Apple Museum: 021 859 2042*
- *Paul Cluver Wines: 021 844 0605*

The Houw Hoek Inn

A nice place for a break is the historic Houw Hoek Inn on the far end of the plateau. It was founded on the site of an old toll booth, and the ground floor dates from 1779. An upper storey was added in 1860. Claiming to be SA's oldest operational coaching Inn, the hotel boasts a long guest list, including the feisty Lady Anne Barnard, who conducted an early tour of the region during the first British occupation in the 1790s.

The hotel offers a serene back garden for tea, and a well-worn bar which harbours a little secret. As you enter the bar, look up and check out the old money stuck to the roof. This is a tradition from an earlier time when travellers would leave a few coins glued to the ceiling so that they would have enough for a drink on their return visit, no matter how badly they fared on the unpredictable road ahead. Some of the money dates back a couple of centuries and is sure to appeal to numismatists.

- *The Houw Hoek Inn: 028 284 9646*

---

sharp bend in the road. Many of the old passes therefore eschewed all that gentle winding through the contour lines, and went for the straight up/straight down approach instead.

The first Houhoek pass proceeded in this manner, up from the Houw Hoek Inn and down to the Bot (Butter) River. It was, by all contemporary accounts, a hideous passage that was even more dangerous than the formidable Hottentots Holland Kloof. Various stories of runaway wagons careering down the steep pass have been recorded, and many early travellers were heard to say a prayer of thanks when the traverse was over.

Charles Michell, the engineer, tried to complete the work he had started with Sir Lowry's Pass by building a more sophisticated Houhoek road in 1831. But Michell and his governor, Sir Lowry Cole, were still smarting from the rebuke they had received from the Colonial office for the unapproved expense incurred by the building of Sir Lowry's Pass the previous year, and the new Houhoek road was a pretty makeshift affair.

Michell's road was eventually improved by Andrew Geddes Bain in 1846, and several other routes down the slopes seem to have been improvised over the years. None of these routes was entirely satisfactory, however, and each track was subsequently abandoned and swallowed up by the fynbos. Then, recently, a fire swept the Houhoek summit and revealed the fossils of no less than four different routes. This only added to the confusion, but road historians are having a ball, trying to put the pieces of the puzzle together again.

Around the time of the Anglo-Boer War, a different route across the mountains was added to the Houhoek passage. Rather than going over the mountains, this route went around them, following the path of the Poespas River valley. Poespas, by the way, means 'higgledy-piggledy' and does not, as I originally thought, refer to a tight fit.

The lower reaches of the Poespas River valley had already been used by the railway line, but this alternative road was cut into the slopes above the train tracks by British soldiers. This gravel 'Railway Pass' can still be followed by a car, if you are brave, but it is narrow, rocky and isolated; stuck halfway up the mountains, with the highway above and the railway below. The road is also unmarked, and you will have to find your own way into the pass, which starts at the small sign for Koffie Kraal.

Of course, I had to try it out for myself, and, as I was bouncing along the confined little road, I began wondering what would happen if I broke down. Help would be a long time coming and, with barely enough space between the rock and the retaining walls for the width of my car, there was little hope of getting a tow truck to pull me out of the cramped, intricate path. With these happy thoughts, I rounded a bend and almost drove into the bonnet of a low-slung Audi, incongruously inching its way up the pass towards me. It was being driven by the owners of a nearby stable who were looking for a runaway horse.

After discussing the whereabouts of the missing animal for a few moments, we turned to the more immediate problem of getting our cars out of the pass. There was absolutely no place for us to squeeze past one another, and even less chance of turning around. Eventually, the Audi had to reverse, painstakingly, back down the pass until we found a place where it could turn around.

In the 1930s this road was abandoned and a new road, the most recent Houhoek Pass, was built to modern specifications over the summit. In the 1970s–1980s this road was expanded into the current four-lane freeway that we drive today.

From the top of the pass, the view down into the Overberg is lovely, and the road quickly swoops along the contours, bringing us back to the coastal shelf on the other side of the Hottentots Holland mountains. The first major hurdle in the great eastern road has been surmounted.

Helderberg Coast Contacts:
- Helderberg Tourist Info (including Gordon's Bay, Somerset West and Strand): 021 851 4022 / www.helderbergtourism.co.za
- Helderbrau Brewery: 021 858 1309
- Lwandle Hostel Museum and Crafts Centre: 021 845 6119
- Monkey Town: 021 858 1060
- Vergelegen Wine Estate: 021 847 1334/46 www.vergelegen.co.za
- Hottentots Holland Nature Reserve: 021 483 2949/51 or 028 841 4826

The Audi I met unexpectedly on the Railway Pass

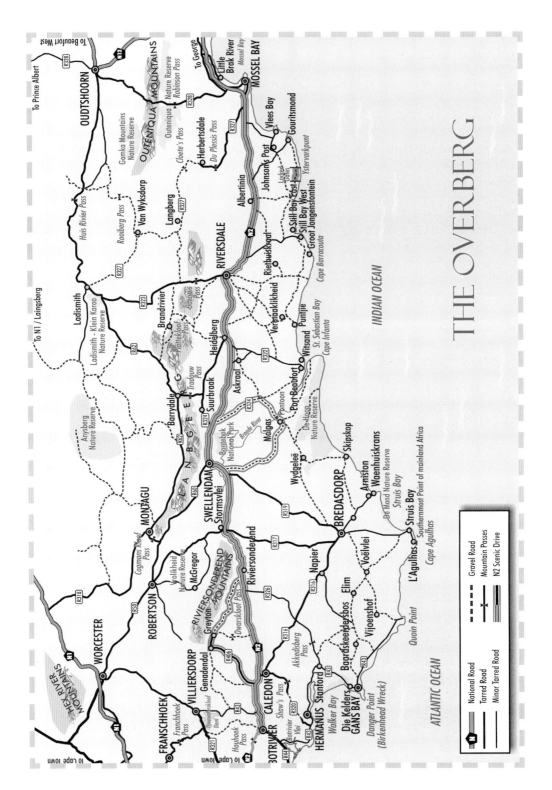

THE OVERBERG

Legend:
- National Road
- Tarred Road
- Minor Tarred Road
- Gravel Road
- Mountain Passes
- N2 Scenic Drive

ATLANTIC OCEAN

INDIAN OCEAN

10. The Overberg

ORIENTATION

After you descend Houhoek Pass on the N2, you will find yourself in the Overberg. This is a self-evident name for the broad coastal strip that lies across the mountains from Cape Town (Overberg/Over the Mountains – geddit?).

The Overberg region is large and rather vaguely defined. In the south, it is bounded by the Cape Agulhas coastline and, in the north, by a ridge of mountains which separates the Overberg from the Little Karoo. Laterally, it runs from the Hottentots Holland mountains in the west, to the mouth of the Breede River (near Mossel Bay) in the east.

This section of the book deals with the N2 from the bottom of the Houhoek Pass to Mossel Bay, a distance of 300 k's.

As you enter the Overberg from Houhoek, you will be driving along a line of mountains that emerge from the Hottentots Holland and run, unbroken, into the east. The first part of this wall of stone is called the Riviersonderend (River Without End) Mountains, and the undulating farmlands of the Overberg stretch out from its foothills, running south towards the sea.

The first town of any consequence is Caledon, a well-established *dorp* complete with hot springs and casino. At this point, the old Cape wagon road used to turn north towards the mission station of Genadendal, and then descended gently to Swellendam. The N2 has corrected this kink in the road's alignment, but you can still take the detour up to Genadendal by following the tarred R406. It's about 30 k's each way.

From Genadendal, you can continue following the old coach road on gravel (still marked R406) down to the town of Riviersonderend. This quiet back road leads through numerous farms and valleys and is a nice change from the hectic pace of the N2. Various gravel tributaries also lead off this part of the road back to the N2, if you wish to cut

A windmill spins in the russet soil of the Overberg

the detour short. If you aren't keen on a gravel excursion, turn around at Genadendal and follow the tar back to the N2 at Caledon.

From Caledon, you can:
➡ Follow the R320 over Shaw's Mountain Pass (some gravel driving required) to Hermanus *[see Chapter 14]*.
➡ Follow the R316 to Bredasdorp *[see Chapter 14]*.
➡ Or continue on the N2 to Riversonderend.

Riversonderend is a quiet town, which has been rudely cut in two by the national road. It

Farmlands roll from the feet of the Riviersonderend Mountains

looks like a typical *dorp* with a butchery, tyre fitment centre and café. But, as is often the case with these transit towns, the real quality of the place is found on the side roads leading off the main thoroughfare. Neat houses and nicely tended gardens look out at the picturesque mountains, and the local NG Kerk is very attractive in the soft light of sunset.

Beyond the town of Riviersonderend, the mountains change. The Riviersonderend range drops away, only to be immediately replaced by the line of the Langeberg, which sweeps down from the north. For the next few hundred k's, the Langeberg will be your constant companion while driving along the N2.

Undeterred by the change in mountainous taxonomy, the N2 continues impassively over the *ruggens* (a local word for undulating fields). At the town of Stormsvlei you can follow signs to Robertson *[see Chapter 15]*, follow signs to Bredasdorp *[see Chapter 14]*, or continue on the N2 to Swellendam.

From Swellendam:
➡ the R60 leads up to Robertson *[see Chapter 15]*.
➡ the R319 heads south-west to Bredasdorp *[see Chapter 14]*.
➡ If you want a fun dirt-road adventure, follow signs from the N2 to Malgas. This circular drive will take you through quiet farmlands to Malgas, where you can cross the Breede River on the last man-drawn pontoon in the country *[see Chapter 14]*.
➡ Alternatively, follow the N2 towards Mossel Bay.

Driving along this stretch of the N2 is pleasant but unexceptional. The farmlands rise and fall; the ploughed furrows make attractive geometric patterns in the red soil; the mountains drift upwards into the hazy blue sky. You know the kind of thing. During this part of the journey, the mountains also undergo another name change, from the Langeberg to the Outeniquas.

En route, there are a number of turn-offs:

➡ The R324 will take you to Suurbraak. From here you can travel over the Tradouw Pass *[see Chapter 16]* to Barrydale in the Little Karoo *[see Chapter 15]*.

➡ If you want to follow the Barry and Nephews story [see below], follow the gravel R324 or the tarred R322 to Port Beaufort and Witsand *[see Chapter 14]*.

➡ At Riversdale, you can take the R323 over Garcia's Pass *[see Chapter 16]* into the Little Karoo *[see Chapter 15]*.

➡ As you continue along the N2, turn-off's for the coastal towns of Stilbaai, Gouritsmond and Vleesbaai beckon *[see Chapter 14]*.

If you have resisted all these tempting deviations, you will soon arrive at the often-ignored town of Mossel Bay.

From Mossel Bay, you have a choice:

➡ You can follow the line of the old wagon road over the Outeniquas to Oudtshoorn in the Little Karoo *[see Chapter 15]*. Originally, this route went over Attaquaskloof Pass, but this is now a private 4x4 trail. Instead, the modern traveller should follow signs for the R328 to Robinson Pass *[see Chapter 17]*.

➡ If you want to continue onto George, you can either take the N2 highway, or follow the old main road (the R102), which amiably rises and falls along the Brak River Heights *[see Chapter 11]*.

CALEDON

This historic town was once the health spa of the VOC, and the hot, mineral-rich water which burbles out of the ground attracted stressed Company employees and their delicate constitutions for many years. The settlement itself began in 1710, when a Mr Ferdinand Appel got the rights to control the springs, as long as he built accommodation to house the visitors. A town was finally established by the

British in 1813 and, as always, named after the current governor at the Cape, the Earl of Caledon.

At first, the Spa itself was little more than a warm, muddy pit surrounded by several unassuming hostelries. Then, in the Victorian Era, a rather splendid bath house was constructed, and the accommodation was upgraded to the standards of the day. Today, the Caledon Spa has been incorporated into the new Caledon Casino and Hotel, and it offers a comprehensive range of beauty therapies.

Lovin' the sugar rush

Unfortunately, at time of writing, the old Victorian bath house had become structurally unsafe and was closed, pending restoration. In the meantime, you can still bathe in the hot water, which has been channelled into a series of attractive modern pools, nicely arranged on terraces down the hillside.

Caledon town centre is the usual blend of shops and churches, and it may not look like much to the passing motorist. Stop the car, however, and the place comes alive. There is an interesting historical walk around town, which takes in most of the important old buildings that are squeezed between the modern, low-rise office blocks. You can pick up the walking guide from the old city hall, which now does double duty as the local museum, art gallery and tourist info centre. The museum also sells lots of local crafts, baked goods and books. Farm tours can be arranged, and Caledon also boasts a well-established wild flower garden, just outside town.

GENADENDAL AND GREYTON

A few kilometres before you reach the town of Caledon, there is the opportunity for a detour to the lovely mission station of Genadendal and the perfect little village of Greyton. If you choose to take the detour, follow the R406 (tarred) which leads through rolling farmlands, towards the face of the mountains.

Genadendal

Cradled in a small nook of the Riviersonderend Mountains is the mission station of Genadendal (the Valley of Peace). It was founded by the Moravian Church in 1793 and, at one time, was the second largest town in the Cape, after Cape Town.

The Moravians are an interesting sect of Protestants who established many mission stations across the Cape. Originally from Bohemia (now part of the Czech Republic), they left their homeland in the eighteenth century to escape religious persecution. After much travelling, they eventually found sanctuary near Berlin, under the patronage of Count Van Zizendorf.

Safely ensconced in Germany, the Moravians proceeded to send out missionaries to spread the good word to the world. They established several thriving mission stations in the Cape, set up schools and taught the locals useful crafts like thatching and needlepoint.

By the 1960s, however, the Moravian Church had peaked, and the head church in Germany handed over their various South African mission stations to the local congregations, who were largely coloured. Today, Genadendal and Elim are the best-preserved examples of Moravian communities in the Western Cape, and these little enclaves are a wonderful throwback to an earlier age of religious autonomy. You can read more about Elim in Chapter 14.

Today, as you drive into Genadendal, it

A dusty sunset on the gravel roads around Greyton

looks much like any other country *dorp*. Crumbling houses and dirt streets lead off the main road, while wrinkly old folk watch the passing parade from their peeling *stoeps*. It is only when you reach Church Square in the centre of the town that the unique appeal of Genadendal becomes apparent. This serene square, bordered with grand old oak trees, is like something out of a story book.

Dominated by the double-storey bulk of the old church itself, Church Square also offers a museum, a coffee shop selling home-made bread, a craft shop and a soon-to-be completed accommodation block; all housed in old cottages that are declared National Monuments. At the back of the square is the fruit orchard and the old cemetery, full of priests. The whole complex has a restful, tranquil atmosphere, and the wind ruffles the leaves in the tall oaks, as horses wander freely through this placid precinct. All in all, it is an enchanting place to sit and relax.

Outside of the Church Square, though, Genadendal is looking rather the worse for wear. In the early days, the Moravians owned all the land around the village and acted as both the municipal and spiritual authorities for its congregation. As with all the Moravian mission stations, the church granted houses to its parishioners as part of their church membership fees. The church also looked after all the rates, taxes and other residential expenses. Today, however, the local municipality has reclaimed the town, and the Moravian Church holds onto only Church Square and its immediate surrounds. One wonders whether the locals would not have been better off as tenants of the Church.

Greyton

A few k's away from Genadendal is the little village of Greyton. This attractive cluster of whitewashed houses is a popular weekend getaway for well-heeled Capetonians, and property prices are very high, despite the remote location. The main street offers a country store, several appealing coffee shops and a post office.

However, the humble High Street of Greyton can't hide the wealth hidden away in the sandy lanes that lead off the main thoroughfare. The roads are dripping with trees, the houses are confidently quaint, and the little country gardens are bursting with flowers. All this makes Greyton a delightful place, glowing with the healthy sheen of rural prosperity. I would not be surprised if wellness and healing centres start springing up here. It's that kind of place.

For walkers, Greyton has a lovely location right under the peaks of the Riviersonderend Mountains, and the well known Boesmanskloof walking trail runs from Greyton, over the peaks, to the village of McGregor on the other side of the range.

SWELLENDAM

Swellendam is a major historical pit-stop on the great wagon road to the East. It was the first real settlement to be established in the Overberg and, in 1743, it became the third magisterial district in the Cape (after Cape Town and Stellenbosch). The town was named jointly after the Dutch Governor, Hendrik Swellengrebel and his wife, Helena Ten Damme.

Breakfast at the Old Gaol Museum, Swellendam

Sending a Landdrost out into the wilds of the Overberg may have been a feeble attempt to keep the ever-irascible trekboers in check, but Swellendam nevertheless became an important administrative centre. However, things got off to a slow start. thirty years after it was established, there were still only four permanent houses, and life in Swellendam was rather quiet.

Proceedings were livened up somewhat in 1795, when a group of disgruntled farmers threw off the shackles of VOC misrule and declared themselves a Republic. This short-lived 'democracy' lasted all of six months, but then the British arrived for their first tour of occupation. Deprived of their Dutch nemesis, the fractious members of the Republic couldn't hold things together and the town soon fell back into its comfortable country torpor.

BARRY AND NEPHEWS

The lucrative South African wool industry had its start in the Overberg, and Swellendam was its centre. But the town still only had one store, and most of its supplies were brought over the mountains by travelling salesmen. Then, an enterprising man named Joseph Barry visited

Swellendam

In light of its long local history, it comes as no surprise that Swellendam has an excellent museum complex. Based around the old Drostdy and the Old Gaol, the museum complex is a great place to visit even if you aren't a history buff. The Drostdy is the old Landdrost's house, built in 1747 and substantially expanded in 1813. It is a wonderful example of the classic 'H-shaped' Cape Dutch houses that the VOC built for its officials, and it is furnished with exquisite period pieces. The outbuildings are all original, and each contains an assortment of old wagons and other transport-related paraphernalia. The grounds of the Drostdy are very atmospheric, surrounded by herb gardens, green lawns, tall trees, rose bushes, aloes and flowering hedgerows.

The Old Gaol Museum is just across the road from the Drostdy, and it is a fantastic installation. Built at the same time as the Landdrost's house and expanded over the years, the Old Gaol houses an excellent gift shop which sells local crafts and a good range of hard-to-get books on the area. Out in the sunny prison courtyard, a restaurant serves great breakfasts and, in between courses, you can venture into the darkness of the original jail cells to cool off.

The Ambagswerf (trades yard) is just behind the prison courtyard. This is a superb open-air museum that re-creates many aspects of old village life. A threshing floor, smithy, kitchen, tannery, mill, cooperage and wagon shed are all arranged around a lovely green commonage, where you can picnic or relax while the others in your party pop in and out of the little cottages that house the exhibits. The mill is still in working condition, and you can buy the stone-ground flour that they produce on-site. The staff are well informed and very engaging, and the tame goat who lives on the property will delight the kids.

The Swellendam Museum complex is supplemented by the Mayville House Museum, depicting a typical late Victorian household, and the Zanddrift farmhouse, which houses a restaurant. The eccentric Swellendam city hall is also an interesting building worth checking out, and the well-stocked tourist info centre is across the road. A booklet outlining a walking tour of Swellendam is available from the info centre.

Across the road from the Old Gaol is a small shopping centre with a Belgian chocolaterie, coffee shop and a travel centre where you can book for one of the more adventurous Overberg outings. Horse rides, river rafting on the Breede, abseiling, aeroplane flips and mountain bike trails are all on offer. The Marloth Nature Reserve is close by, and this rugged terrain offers many challenging walks and overnight trails.

- *Swellendam Tourism: 028 514 2770 / www.swellendamtourism.co.za*
- *Old Gaol Complex: 028 514 3 847*
- *Drostdy Museum: 028 514 1138*
- *Marloth Nature Reserve: 028 425 5020 / 028 514 1410*

There's no place like gnome, Sulina Fairy Sanctuary

the region in 1819, and he quickly fell in love with both the land and a local farmer's daughter. He resolved to return when the time was right, and settled down in Cape Town to wait for a good business opportunity to present itself.

It came in the unlikely form of a drought that left the Swellendam district destitute and hungry. The government promised to help the struggling farmers, and asked for tenders to carry supplies of rice and grain from the Cape to Swellendam. Since the passage over the Hottentots Holland mountains was difficult (Sir Lowry's Pass had not yet been built), Barry had the bright idea of shipping the stuff along the coast to the mouth of the Breede River. From here he arranged ox-wagons to carry the load to Swellendam.

Things went so well for Barry that he soon established a little depot at the river mouth, which he called Port Beaufort. The local farmers were thrilled with this new development, as they could now get their goods to market without having to undertake the gruelling two-month trek to Cape Town. The merchants of Cape Town were similarly delighted because they could now get their merchandise into the interior. Barry made a packet with his trading venture, and moved to Swellendam in 1824.

For ten years, Joseph Barry had his ups and downs, but by 1834 he had entered into a partnership with his nephews, Thomas and John, and a trading empire was born. By the 1850s, there were branches of *Barry se Winkel* all over the Overberg, as well as in Cape Town and London. The Overberg farmers stepped up production in light of their new access to markets, and the whole region prospered with 'Barry and Nephews' at its heart. Things were going so well that in 1859 Barry and Nephews ordered a brand-new screw-steamer from Scotland and, soon enough, the SS *Kadie* started making regular trips from Cape Town to Port Beaufort. From there, the little steamer chugged up the Breede River to the Barry's newly established inland depot at Malgas.

This was the golden age of Swellendam, and it seemed as if it would last forever. But in 1865, things took a turn for the worse. First, a fire destroyed much of Swellendam. Then, the brave little *Kadie* sank when it hit a sandbar at the Breede River mouth. Finally, to top it all off, old man Barry died. In terms of their original agreement, the partnership had to be dissolved and one-third of the company assets paid out to Barry's heirs. It was all too much for the business to bear, and the whole enterprise collapsed. Malgas and Port Beaufort became virtual ghost towns, and Swellendam's fortunes went into terminal decline.

The Barrys, however, lived on and today there are hundreds of Barrys living in SA, Germany, Australia, France, Argentina, the UK, the US, Zimbabwe and Namibia. In fact, there are so many descendants that they hold an International Barry Festival every few years, so that the family can stay in touch. The old 'Barry and Nephews' store can still be seen on Swellendam's main road, and the Drostdy Museum has a fascinating exhibit on their local dynasty. Check out that crazy family tree!

BONTEBOK NATIONAL PARK

Just outside Swellendam is the Bontebok National Park. This reserve was established in 1931 to protect the once-plentiful Bontebok, which used to roam the southern coast of Africa

A morning's work for a spider at Bontebok National Park

in great numbers. They are called Bontebok, meaning colourful buck, because of the bold markings that make them so distinctive. Unfortunately, these white stripes were also a great help to the hunters, who had a field day gunning down thousands of these placid animals. By the 1930s, there were only twenty-two Bontebok left.

Urged on by a small group of right-minded farmers, the National Parks Board granted the Bontebok a sanctuary near Bredasdorp in 1931. But the buck did not take to the rocks and sand of their new home, and were relocated to their present enclosure in 1960. Today, there is a healthy population of over 300 Bontebok in the park, and there are plans to extend the boundaries of the reserve to make room for a larger population. The park has also been stocked with many other kinds of buck, as well as the rare Cape Mountain Zebra.

While Bontebok National Park is small, the scenery is pretty and a lovely walk has been marked out along the Breede River, which winds through the reserve. The Bontebok themselves are quite forthcoming, as there are no large predators in the park. The camping facilities are very good and the campsite is green and thickly wooded.

The city streets look out on the calm expanse of Mossel Bay

MOSSEL BAY

Historically, Mossel Bay is a very important town. It was where Bartolomeu Dias first landed on South African soil, and it has popped up in the annals of our history over and over again. The present-day settlement began in 1787, with the establishment of a granary and a port to service the Southern Cape.

However, like me, you may not be very familiar with Mossel Bay. This is because the N2 national road gives the centre of town a wide berth. This bypass was initially seen as a disaster for the town, but now it's seen as a blessing. With no thundering traffic ploughing through the streets, Mossel Bay is peaceful, clean and unpolluted. So, while it has never been as cool as nearby Knysna, it is a great place to visit.

THE BARTOLOMEU DIAS MUSEUM COMPLEX

Mossel Bay is the place where Bartolomeu Dias first planted his European-shod feet on naked African soil. He took this giant leap to access a stream of fresh water, which he spied springing out of the slopes facing the bay. Luckily, the natives were friendly enough and, over the years, Mossel Bay became a regular stop-over for the early seafarers. It was so popular, in fact, that it became an unofficial maritime post office.

It worked like this: sailors passing from Europe to the East would pop their notes, missives or epistles inside an old boot or bottle. They would then tie the container to a large Milkwood tree close to the freshwater spring. The next ship that came sailing down from the

Mossel Bay

One of the big attractions of Mossel Bay is the safe, extensive swimming beaches around the town. These are well established, with good tourist facilities, and can get quite busy during the summer holidays. If the beach is a little bit crowded, take a walk down the long, grassy promenade which runs along the hooked finger of the bay. Two large caravan parks (Die Bakke and Hartenbos) are right on the sea's edge, and this keeps the views open and pleasant. Unfortunately, I am told that these open spaces have been sold, and the plan is to build highrises where the caravan parks once stood. I hope I am misinformed. It would be a crime to cut off the bay views to all but a handful of condominium cronies.

The main road of the town (George Street) runs along the narrow coastal shelf, hemmed in by the sea-facing cliffs and the waters of the bay. Dozens of restaurants, shops, B+B's and a backpacker's line the street, while charming old homes populate the slopes leading up from the shore. At the intersection of George and Church, you will find the town's main shopping centre, the harbour and the Bartolomeu Dias Museum complex.

From this intersection, George incongruously becomes Bland and runs along the beachfront to The Point, at the very edge of town. The Point is a jutting headland which separates the sheltered waters of the Bay from the wide, open sea. More accurately called Cape St. Blaise, The Point is a good place to start (or end) your exploration of Mossel Bay. There are several restaurants, a noisy bar with a great view out to sea, and a natural swimming hole which has been established in-between the serrated ridges of rock that run perpendicular to the open ocean.

The locals call this impromptu tidal pool the 'Champagne Baths' because of the thousands of bubbles that are created as waves push in and out of the narrow channel. It looks a little dangerous, but I am assured that it's quite safe and chains have been extended along the rocks to help people get in and out of the water.

Next to the Point is the Mossel Bay Lighthouse, built on top of an adjacent cliff face. Beneath the lighthouse is a large, open overhang, called Bat Cave. The short walk up the cliffs to Bat Cave offers good views and some interesting interpretive boards on the natural history of the grotto. Human artefacts dating back over 80 000 years have been found in the cave, and the piles of mussel shells scattered over the cave's floor gave the town its name.

Mossel Bay has lots of attractions: there is a guided historical walk that takes you through the museum complex and around town; you can take a cruise out to Seal Island; dive with the sharks; or test your nerves on the Gouritz River Bungy jump, twenty minutes out of town. Mossel Bay is also a large industrial centre with a busy harbour and the colossal Mossgas power plant, which squats outside town like a sci-fi nightmare.

- *Mossel Bay Tourist Info: 044 691 2202*
- *Bartolomeu Dias Museum Complex: 044 691 1067*
- *Gourits River Bungy Jumping: 044 697 7001*
- *Shark Africa Cage Diving: 044 691 3796*
- *Seal Island Trips / Whale Watching / Sunset Cruises: 044 690 3101*

East, on its way back to Europe, would then collect the mail from the tree and deliver it to the recipients back home. It was an effective, symbiotic system, and it's a pity that modern postal communication is no longer seen as a collaborative effort.

The Post Office Tree still stands in the grounds of the Dias Museum Complex and, at the foot of the tree, there is a special post box shaped like a boot, where you can post your modern letters and postcards. Any mail posted in the boot gets a special franking mark, but the speed with which the mail is delivered doesn't seem to have improved much over the last few centuries.

The Post Office Tree is only one of the attractions that makes the Bartolomeu Dias Museum Complex a very worthwhile stop. The museum consists of several buildings which collectively house South Africa's largest shell museum, a re-creation of the old Mossel Bay

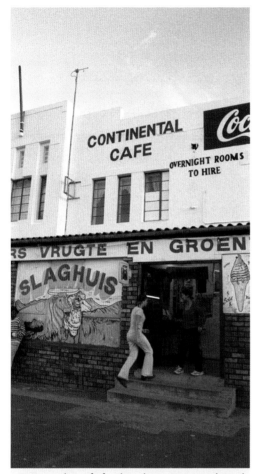
Going to the cafe for slap chips, Riviersonderend

shoebox-with-sails could have taken Dias from the Algarve all the way to Mossel Bay.

It's even more remarkable to think that the current replica in the museum completed the same sea journey in the 1980s. The old-fashioned caravel now on display was actually built from scratch by a Portuguese shipyard to celebrate the 300th anniversary of Dias' landing. The ship was completed using traditional implements and materials, and then sailed to its current location by an intrepid crew.

When the shallow-draft vessel finally reached Mossel Bay in 1988, it was greeted by an ecstatic crowd, and a whole brigade of proud Nationalists (including *onse eie* PW Botha) waved their old '*oranje, blanje, blou*' flags in commemoration of the white man's first toe-hold in South Africa. The caravel was then plucked from the sea and installed in its new museum dry-dock, with all due *pomp* and ceremony.

Overberg contacts:
- Overberg Tourist Info: 028 214 1466
- www.capeoverberg.org
  www.capeoverbergmeander.org
- Caledon Tourist Info: 028 212 1511
- Caledon Casino and Spa: 028 214 5100
- Caledon Wild Flower Garden:
- Genadendal Church Square: 028 251 8291
- Greyton Tourist Info: 028 254 9414
- Riviersonderend Tourist Info:
  028 261 1511
- Bontebok National Park (SAN Parks):
  012 428 9111

granary (which contains a cultural history exhibit of life in the old town), and an 'ethno-botanical' garden with a Braille trail for the visually impaired. Several important Malay graves, a collection of old houses in Munro Bay and an excellent maritime museum are also located within the large museum grounds.

The Maritime Museum has interesting exhibits on the early Portuguese explorers, and a life-size replica of the ship that Dias used to sail around the tip of Africa. It's worth paying the small premium that will grant you access to this boat, so that you can walk around its tiny deck and creep below to see the cramped living quarters. It seems impossible that this little

Power lines sweep through the Overberg

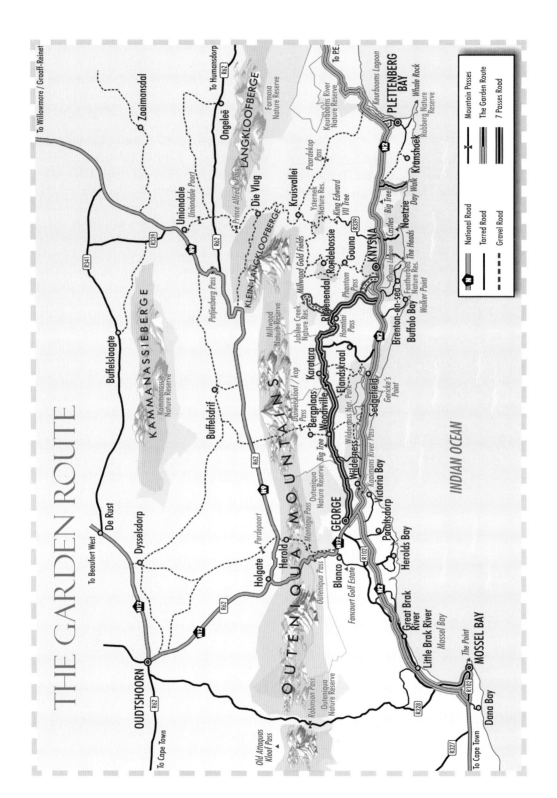

THE GARDEN ROUTE

11. The Garden Route

ORIENTATION

The Garden Route region extends from Mossel Bay to the eastern edge of the Tsitsikamma Mountains, near Humansdorp. It is a narrow coastal strip, about 300 k's long, hemmed in by sea to the south, and mountains to the north.

This region was once covered with impenetrable forests, cutting off all access from the west and, for 150 years, the magical forests remained inviolate. These thick agglomerations of trees and ferns are actually the 'gardens' of the Garden Route, as they reminded early travellers of the Garden of Eden. Many of the old forests are now gone but, despite the great fire of 1869 and years of reckless logging, the Garden Route still contains about 65 000 hectares of indigenous forest, the largest expanse in South Africa.

The N2 leads from Mossel Bay to George, gateway to the Garden Route. From George, you must choose your trajectory: either go over the Outeniqua Mountains towards Oudtshoorn in the Klein Karoo [see Chapter 15], or continue east along the coast towards Knysna.

If you want to cross the Outeniquas from George, you can either take the modern, tarred Outeniqua Pass, or you can trundle up the old, untarred Montagu Pass [see Chapter 17].

Once you are in the Klein Karoo, you can return to Cape Town via Oudtshoorn and the fascinating R62 inland route [see Chapter 15]. If you want to do a round trip from Cape Town to the Garden Route, try taking the coastal N2 in one direction and then return on the R62 – that way you get the best of both worlds.

If you want to continue on to Knysna from George, you can either take Thomas Bain's old semi-tarred Seven Passes Road, or continue on the beautiful stretch of the N2 through The Wilderness and Sedgefield.

Once you arrive in Knysna, your road options diminish rapidly. There is only one main road between Knysna and Plett: the N2. All the other roads leading out of town eventually turn into enticing sand routes through the hills, or lead down cul-de-sacs to the sea.

When you are ready to move on from Knysna, follow the N2 out of town. Then, either follow the R339 through the indigenous forests and up the gravel surface of Prince Alfred's Pass to the head of the Long Kloof [see Chapter 17], or continue on the N2 to Plettenberg Bay.

THE BRITISH ARE COMING!

The VOC had been running the Cape as its own private fiefdom for close on 150 years. In that time the Company had become bloated, corrupt and inefficient (as big companies are wont to do), and a degree of ennui had settled over the whole enterprise. By the last decade of the 1700s, the once-mighty Dutch East India Company was tottering on the edge of bankruptcy.

It was a bad time for corporate weakness. The trekboers were becoming increasingly obstreperous, the wild eastern frontier of the colony was up in arms, and even the little town of Swellendam had declared itself an independent republic.

To make matters worse, public tastes had turned away from Batavian tea to Caribbean coffee and the company was losing revenue. Just to top everything off, Europe also happened to be in a state of major political upheaval, again.

This time round, it was Napoleon causing all the trouble. He was at the height of his power, and wreaking havoc across the mainland. The Peninsular War was in the offing. Britain had already established itself as Napoleon's main adversary, and they were determined to stop the half-pint dictator from taking over Europe. In the throes of the titanic struggle that was to follow, many of the smaller European powers would suffer collateral damage.

Fighting with France is something of a hobby for the British. They had fought against the Bourbon royal house in the 1780s and, after a brief lull, the old animosity was rekindled when a post-revolutionary Napoleon declared war on Britain and Holland in 1793.

At first the war went in Napoleon's favour and, by 1795, the French armies were steadily advancing on Amsterdam. The once-popular Dutch royal House of Orange was about to topple, but William V, Duke of Orange, kept his head and fled to Britain to seek asylum with his new allies. The British were happy to oblige and slyly suggested that they send out some troops, just to help protect Dutch foreign territories from a perceived French invasion.

The Duke reluctantly signed the order, on condition that all Holland's possessions were to be handed back when peace was restored. The British said 'sure' and quickly despatched a small armada of ships to the Cape, to prevent that Corsican upstart from taking control of Table Bay and the sea route to the East.

A few months later, the British fleet ceremoniously landed at Simon's Town, and handed their writ of occupation to the Company officials. It was greeted with great suspicion. In those days, mail took three to six months to get from Europe to South Africa, and news of the Duke's flight had not yet reached the Cape. Besides, local loyalties were already split between the Dutch royalists and the Dutch republicans, and the British were known for pulling sneaky stunts to suit their own inscrutable motives. All in all, the arrival of the British threw the Cape into a state of great confusion and mistrust.

Then a passing American ship brought some important news. Holland had fallen and become a puppet state of France. The Dutch homeland was henceforth to be known as the Batavian Republic of the Netherlands. This was great news for the Republican contingent at the Cape, who rallied at the news and declared themselves French allies. The crippled VOC, for its part, was in no condition to resist and went along with popular opinion.

Accordingly, a ragged force of Cape soldiers was called out against the British invaders, and a brief but decisive battle was fought on the shores of Muizenberg on 7th August 1795. The British navy bombarded the coast, whereupon many of the Dutch infantry ran away. The British troops then disembarked and, after several weeks of skirmishing and the arrival of a second English fleet, the Dutch surrendered and the triumphant British marched into Cape Town to begin their first tour of occupation. It lasted seven years, from 1795 to 1802.

The new British authorities did their best to appease the Dutch inhabitants of their new demesne. They guaranteed religious freedom, they upheld the existing legal and monetary systems (including the rickety rix-dollar) and they even included many of the old officials in their new government. Most importantly, they reduced the heavy taxation that the VOC had levied on its subjects, and abolished the much-hated system of monopolies that the corrupt Company had nurtured with its favoured suppliers. This won the British many fans who supported any new administration that could bring free trade and a degree of solvency to the dwindling fortunes of the Cape of Good Hope.

THE BATAVIAN REPUBLIC TAKE OVER AND THE VOC IS DISSOLVED

Despite their successful occupation of the Cape, the British considered themselves as nothing more than caretakers. English imperialism was still incipient, and the British already had a trading post on the little island of St Helena in mid-Atlantic, which gave their ships secure access to the East. South Africa just didn't seem worth the effort, and there were many politicians back in Britain who felt that there was no profit to be had from the troublesome Cape Colony.

So, when the diplomats patched together a rough European peace in 1802, the British went along with the Treaty of Amiens and handed the Cape back to the new masters of Holland. The Batavian Republic also officially took control of all the VOC's remaining assets and foreign territories, and folded them into the national treasury. The once-great Dutch East India Company had ceased to be.

However, peace between Britain and France did not last long. About six months after the new Batavian administrators arrived at the Cape, Napoleon and John Bull were at loggerheads again. Britain did not want to give up Malta, and the French army didn't want to withdraw from the Low Countries of Holland and Belgium. As the Batavian Republic was now a definite ally of France, it was obliged to join in the fun.

The new administrators at the Cape, meanwhile, had many ambitious plans for the colony. But they had barely cleared their throats before political uncertainty in Europe put paid to their efforts.

At first, the new war between France and England was fought in the Mediterranean and in the Atlantic, leaving the Cape relatively untouched. However, intelligence soon reached the Admiralty in Britain that Napoleon intended occupying the Cape. Once again fearful that Frenchy would take control of the strategically important port in Table Bay, the British became offensive. The days of Batavian rule at the Cape were numbered.

THE BRITISH ARE BACK!
Fearful that their route to the riches of India would be compromised by Napoleon's imperialist impulse, the British took action and, for the second time, sent a fleet to seize the Cape. They anchored at Table Bay in January 1806, and quickly scattered the Batavian force of mercenaries at the Battle of Blouberg.

After the battle, the Batavian administrators gallantly conceded defeat, got into their ships and sailed away, waving goodbye to the Cape after just three short years. The British took over the Cape for the second time and, this time round, they went on to make a century, not out.

To complete this part of the story it will suffice to say that Napoleon met his Waterloo in 1815 at the hands of the Iron Duke, Lord Wellington. He was banished to the British-controlled island of St Helena, where he ended his days drinking bottles of sweet Constantia wine and mourning his lost empire. The British took formal control of the Cape under the Treaty of Paris, and many of the officers who took part in the mighty campaigns against Bonaparte went on to serve as governors and administrators of the new British colony.

George

Although, technically, the Garden Route region starts at Mossel Bay, George is commonly acknowledged as the gateway to the Garden Route.

George is also the region's industrial and shopping headquarters. All the major retail chains are represented in one of the bland commercial developments, and George is a good place to stock up on those hard-to-get supplies before plunging into the smaller towns ahead.

If you are a steam-train enthusiast, visit the steam train museum, and don't miss a trip on the Outeniqua Choo-Tjoe. This excursion goes from George to Knysna and takes in some glorious coastal scenery. It runs daily from Monday to Saturday and is an excellent family outing.

- *Outeniqua Choo-Tjoe: 044 801 8288*
- *George Tourist Info: 044 801 9295*
- *www.georgetourism.co.za*
- *Fancourt Golf Estate: 044 804 0000*
  www.fancourt.co.za
- *George Airport: 044 876 9310*

George was the first town founded by the British after their second invasion of the Cape in 1806. Prior to this, the Dutch had already shown interest in establishing a new administrative district further east from Swellendam, and the first British governor of the Cape, the Earl of Caledon, concurred. The town was established in 1811, and named after the ruling British king, George III – he of the porphyria and madness fame.

George isn't a particularly beautiful town. It's situated about 10 k's inland and, if you want to swim in the sea, the closest bathing spots are the tidal pool of Herold's Bay, or the stunning beach of Victoria Bay. Still, George has a nice setting at the foot of the Outeniqua Mountains, and it is a historical town with its fair share of attractions.

The old town centre of George is dominated by a huge oak tree. This is where the British used to hold the slave auctions, and an old iron chain is still embedded in the tree's gnarled trunk. The tourism office is opposite the slave tree, and the museum (housed in the old Drostdy) is across the road. The holy trinity (Anglican, Catholic and NG Kerk) all have excellent architectural representation, and the tiny Anglican cathedral of St Mark is the cornerstone of George's city status.

Fancourt and the Curse of the Golf Estate

George is a thriving commercial centre, but it is golf that has put the town on the modern tourist map. There are a number of courses in the area and more are being built all the time. In fact, all over the Garden Route, plantations and forests are slowly being eroded by the smooth greens of the common golfer. And this pest is spreading. Already golf courses have been seen eating up the coastal thicket on the South Coast of Natal, and there are rumours that golfing estates are breeding near Ballito.

The current mania for an upmarket golfing experience had one of its earliest progenitors in the form of Fancourt, a gracious golf estate near George. Fancourt is built around a beautifully restored Victorian manor house, now a national monument, and therein lies a funny story.

Fancourt was originally the home of one Henry Fancourt White. He was the engineer who had supervised the building of nearby Montagu Pass over the Outeniqua Mountains. Grateful for his work on the new pass, the people of George helped White build a country house at Blanco; a small village that had grown around the base camp for the pass labourers, and subtly named after the shy engineer. The original manor house was built in the late 1850s but, sadly, ten years later, White lost both his money and his lovely estate. He died shortly afterwards.

Deprived of his inheritance, White's son went to the gold fields of the Transvaal to make his fortune. The estate, meanwhile, passed through several hands until White Jnr returned to Blanco in 1903. He had made a packet on the Highveld, apparently helped by some dubious dealings with President Paul Kruger, and bought back his family farm at a public auction. Earnest Montagu White then renamed the estate 'Fancourt', after his father, and enjoyed spending the English winters in the warmth of the Garden Route, sipping Pimm's on the patio and walking through the woods. Things seemed to be looking up for the Whites, but fate had a nasty trick in store.

In 1916, Montagu threw a lavish dinner party. The main course was topped off with wild mushrooms picked by White himself. Unfortunately, he was not clued up on his fungi and, by the end of the evening, he, his sister and a friend were dead from food poisoning. To this day, guests and former owners tell of White ghosts wandering through the dark corridors.

The Fancourt estate subsequently stood empty for many years, slowly falling into disrepair. In 1960 the house was bought and restored by a Dr Krynauw. It was then sold several more times, finally opening as a golf estate and hotel in 1989. In 1993, the current owners bought the estate out of liquidation and built the place up to its present glory; golfer's shorts and short golfers notwithstanding.

An emphatic sign gives dog-owners pause for thought, Victoria Bay

FORESTS AND FIRE

Way back when, the Garden Route was a terrifying section of the South African coast. The raging sea thrashed against jagged rocks. Deep, steep river gorges slashed through the cliffs to the ocean. A dark line of mountains trapped the clouds and squeezed them for rain, which grew into tall forests that cut out the light and gave succour to a menagerie of dangerous wild animals.

From ancient times to about 150 years ago, the entire coast from George to Plettenberg Bay was one long, impenetrable rain forest. Over the centuries, tall indigenous giants, like the Yellowwood and the Stinkwood, grew to great heights. Moist ferns and lichens spread along the ground, and the black smell of soil was everywhere. Today, some pockets of these indigenous forests still stand, but most have been taken out by fire, logging or pine plantations.

I suppose it's inevitable. A forest full of valuable wood wouldn't just be left to stand there and look beautiful, and logging began as soon as the white man reached the Knysna coast. But it took a while for technology to catch up with human avarice. First, roads had to be built to carry the heavy timber out of the forests, and sawmills had to be established before the industry could really take off. The rugged landscape, however, made this very difficult to accomplish.

Nevertheless by the middle of the 1800s several access routes had been hacked into the Garden Route, and lumberjacks were happily chopping down the ancient indigenous hardwoods in the most unsustainable manner imaginable. In fact, the forests were disappearing so quickly that a conservator was appointed to control access and supervise loggers. A few years later, unfortunately, logging restrictions were lifted because there was a growing timber shortage in the country. The trees just couldn't win.

Then, in 1869, a carelessly tended campfire got whipped up by the wind, and there was a forest fire. But this was no ordinary forest fire. This was the Great Fire that swept through the trees in a huge conflagration that ran from Riversdale to Humansdorp, a distance of about

350km. Millions of trees went up in flames, and the forests were substantially thinned out. Only the thickest parts were saved, because of the lack of oxygen under the dense canopy. The rest turned to ashes.

The Great Fire of 1869 had two significant after-effects. Firstly, it enabled road builders to forge new wagon paths through the attenuated underbrush. Secondly, and more disturbingly, a well-meaning French botanist tried to undo some of the fire's damage by planting new trees across the region. His actions would change the course of South Africa's forests forever.

You see, this helpful chap, who went by the grand title of Comte de Vasselot de Regne, was suffering from the common colonial malaise of pig-headed superiority, and he chose to plant such fast-growing, exotic species as Pine, Port Jackson, Eucalyptus and Wattle where the noble indigenous giants had once stood. This was the start of the bland softwood forestry plantations that blight the slopes of South Africa, from the Cape to the Kruger Park.

Now, I shouldn't hate plantations. They serve an important economic purpose and they are a valuable, well-managed natural resource. But plantations (pine or otherwise) are so relentlessly monotonous, with their rigid ranks of identical trees, that I despise their regimented aloofness and their mass-produced anonymity.

I mean, plantations are so ugly, so man-made, so industrial. I just hate them! I hate plantations when they are saplings. I hate them when they are fully grown. And I especially hate them when the trees have just been felled, and the thin trunks lie strewn across a brown patch of scarred earth.

But it's the resources they consume that make plantations so odious. Apart from the land they occupy, these exotic tree species grow quickly, spread like a pestilence and push out the milder, indigenous vegetation. They also poison the soil with acid, drink up all the ground water and reduce the run-off into our rivers and dams. This is a big problem for a dry country with an expanding human population.

The Australian trees (wattles, gums and acacias) are particularly thirsty (just like the Australian people), and there is now a large-scale movement towards removing all exotic trees from the water-catchment areas of our rivers. This 'Working for Water' campaign is being handled by the Forestry Department, and it employs the people from poor communities to help eradicate the foreign interlopers. So far, the project has had much success in alleviating poverty and in restoring our river systems to their previous vitality. It is a countrywide programme and one well worth supporting.

Interestingly, some of the forestry plantations in the southern Cape are now being actively decommissioned. I was told by one ranger that it has become cheaper to import pine than it is to grow it in the Cape. I was told by another ranger that the demand for pine has decreased because, with the advent of cell phones we no longer need new telephone poles.

Perhaps the forestry department has just realised that tourists can be harvested more profitably than pine trees, and the land is better used for recreational purposes. I don't really care why they have fallen out of favour. I'm just glad the horribly homogenous plantations are getting chopped down, and the native fynbos is being allowed to take over.

But plantations or no plantations, the Garden Route is still very beautiful and it is one of the highlights of our coastline. Verdant mountains crowd down to the sea, orange rocks burst out from the golden beaches and lambent sunsets bathe the region in a warm yellow glow. While it is certainly true that some parts of the Garden Route have become over-developed in recent years, the region still has abundant charms which will never grow tired.

KAAIMANSGAT AND TREK-AAN-TOUW

From George, the smaller, coastal towns of Wilderness, Sedgefield, Knysna and Plettenberg Bay beckon, each with its own history, identity and appeal. But, before you can plunge into the

Garden Route proper, there is a fearsome obstacle that must first be tackled: the Kaaimans River.

In the early days of the ox-wagon, the only way to progress from George into the thick forests of the Garden Route was as follows: First, you had to go from the high-ground around George, down a dizzying descent, to the Kaaiman's River. Once the black river had been forded, wagon drivers faced a near-vertical haul up the other side onto a high, flat piece of ground, cut off from the sea by a sheer rock face to the South.

But the ordeal wasn't over yet. After trekking a couple of kilometres across the top of this high ground, the wagon had to tackle another awful incline at the nicely named Trek-Aan-Touw (Pull-on-rope). After this gruesome descent, relieved travellers found themselves back on the coastal shelf, where the mountains retreated from the sea and offered rough and ready access to the Knysna district beyond.

The Kaaimans River (literally meaning Crocodile or Cayman, but more likely referring to a leguaan or monitor lizard) was originally called the Keerom (Turn around) River. This indicates just what a formidable barrier it presented to the early explorers. The first person to get wagons across this fearsome gorge was the indefatigable Cape Governor, Joachim van Plettenberg, who wouldn't be dissuaded from completing his tour of inspection in 1778. Once he broke the seal of the *Keerom* with his courageous crossing, other's were bound to follow.

At the time, the only other way into the Wilderness Lakes area was from the other side of the Outeniquas, via the difficult Duiwelskop Pass. This route was never very popular, however, as it was a strenuous journey that required an extensive detour. So, for the next ninety years, the coastal route to the east included the treacherous Kaaimansgat and Trek-Aan-Touw passes.

It was such a challenging passage that twenty-eight oxen were needed to pull each wagon up the steep slopes and, on the way down, wooden *rem-skoene* (brake shoes) cut deep ruts into the rocks.

As usual, it was Thomas Bain to the rescue. The ever-astute Bain realised that it was impossible to tame Kaaimansgat with the technology of the day, so he scouted out an alternative route that crossed the troublesome river about four kilometres inland, where the ravine wasn't so deep. The road Bain subsequently built in the 1880s was called the Passes Road, and it became the main coastal highway from George to Knysna until the 1950s. After the Passes Road came into service, access roads (such as White's Road) were built down from Bain's in-land thoroughfare, and the Wilderness Lakes area was slowly opened up for settlement.

Finally, in the 1920s, a Wilderness local got tired of driving the long way round to nearby George, and took it upon himself to make his own road over Kaaimansgat. This enterprising chap, Owen White, repaired the old causeway across the river, and hacked out a private road that ran low along the river valley. This is more or less the line used by the current national road.

The elephants of the Garden Route

Many years ago, the Garden Route was a home to the elephants, great herds of them, roaming through the woody plains and green forests. When the white settlers arrived, however, the shy elephants were forced into the dense, dripping foliage by the human onslaught. Their self-imposed exile didn't help matters, sadly, and their numbers were decimated over the years by hunters and deforestation. Today, there is only one small group of wild Knysna elephants still roaming the deep forest. Sometimes, this little family group of between three and five pachyderms can be glimpsed around Jubilee Creek, and the latest news is that one of them has calved. Otherwise, the Knysna elephants have become yet another part of our natural history.

• *Knysna Elephant Sanctuary: 044 532 7732*

By the 1950s Bain's 'Passes' Road had become too small for the large numbers of cars shuttling from George to PE. An alternative route had to be found, and the new national road was re-directed over the Kaaimans River. A smart new curving bridge (one of the first of its kind) was built to replace the old causeway and, to the local's delight, a smooth tarmac surface was laid down. This road was upgraded in 1986 and remains in use today. Sadly, a large chunk of the original Kaaimansgat wagon track was destroyed by the national road works, but such is the price of progress.

Yet even today, the Kaaimans River Pass is not to be taken lightly. The curves are very sharp, and the low speed limit is both advisable and strictly enforced by means of a permanent traffic camera installed at the bottom of the gorge. Nevertheless, Kaaimansgat is one of the highlights of any road trip through the Garden Route. The ravine is dramatic, full of dark recesses, black water and exposed rock; and the little houses on the other side of the river (accessible only by boat) are picture perfect.

Driving from George, the modern pass swoops down to the curving bridge, crosses the dark river, and then gently climbs up the opposite bank. Just before the end of the ravine,

Remskoene and Wagon Ruts

The Wilderness Heritage Walking Trail is full of scenic delights. Part of the trail takes you around the Kaaimans River Mouth and up a section of the original Kaaimansgat Wagon Pass. First thing you will notice, as you tramp up the slope, is just how steep it is. It seems inconceivable that this incline was tackled by anything with wheels. Going down must have been even worse, especially since ox-wagons didn't have very good brakes.

The only thing that could stop the wagon (and oxen) from careering down a precipitous descent were remskoene. Remskoene (or brake-shoes) were simply wooden blocks with a slot cut into the top. Each wagon wheel was fitted into a remskoen and a rope was then tied to the back of each 'skoen. As the wagon crested the slope, the people standing above would hold onto the ropes to try and moderate its progress downhill. In this manner, the wagon slid down the mountain slopes in its wooden shoes. Over the years, thousands of wagons used this precarious method of traversing the near-vertical slopes of mountain passes all over the Cape Colony. You can still see the parallel scars left in the rocks on an extant section of the old Kaaimansgat River Pass, and in the original Hottentots Holland Kloof.

Gazing into the Wilderness from Dolphin Point lookout

where the Kaaimans River reaches the sea, the road hangs a sharp left, cuts through a spur and suddenly opens out to reveal an exquisite vista over the Wilderness coastline. This viewsite is called Dolphin Point, and it's worth stopping at the parking area for a long, lingering look at the romantic interplay of yellow beach, sandy ocean and shaggy green mountains. It's the view that made me fall in love with the Wilderness.

WILDERNESS

This is one of my favourite places in South Africa. I can't really say why, although the excellent beach, lagoons, lakes and towering mountains are all good reasons. Perhaps it's the laid-back village atmosphere, which hasn't yet been ruined by dozens of shopping centres and a golf course. Or maybe it's the guilty thrill of knowing that this is the last refuge of ex-president P W Botha, and there's a slim chance that you will catch a glimpse of *die ou krokodil*, rocking himself to sleep on the *stoep* of his house.

In any event, Wilderness is a dozy little holiday village, with lovely homes built along the lagoon and up the green slopes of the mountain. It has a petrol station, a convenience store, a couple of restaurants, several estate agents and one or two clothing stores. And that's it. Wilderness is the one place on the Garden Route that has not been ripped up and re-developed.

But that may be changing. A retirement village is being punted from billboards opposite the petrol station, and a Joburg big shot is trying to get planning permission to turn the entire north shore of the main lake into an upmarket housing complex for rich Euro-trash, complete with polo field and golf course.

It would be an environmental crime of the first order if this development went ahead. The developer is boasting that his little project will create jobs, but one can only imagine how quickly the workers will be locked out of the ritzy complex once they have finished building it. Thankfully, the Wilderness locals are trying to fight the property baron, but litigation is an expensive business and guess which side has more money in the bank…

The government is still sitting on the fence in this matter, but they are sure to be open to talk of investment and employment, no matter how spurious. Hugo Leggett, a local writer, acutely summed up the situation by pointing out that "in South Africa, 'Eco' stands for economic, not ecological". As far as I'm concerned, development is great, but we don't need any more holiday homes for wealthy absentee landlords. We need to concentrate on housing the nation and, in the Garden Route, it appears as if there's only room for the rich.

Thankfully, an extensive 'Garden Route National Park' has recently been proposed. This ambitious conservation initiative aims to open up natural corridors from the Outeniqua mountains to the sea, and protect land from the Kaaimans River to the Tsitsikamma. One hopes that this will finally defeat those avaricious property developers with more money than sense.

THE SEVEN PASSES ROAD

The new district of George had a tricky problem. The coast to the East was filled with the most gorgeous, the most noble and the most

View from the log cabins over the lake, Wilderness National Park

The Wilderness Lakes National Park

There are dozens of places to stay in the Wilderness but one of the best is Wilderness National Park. There are several accommodation options: you can camp, rent bungalows overlooking the lagoon, or relax in one of the spacious log cabins, built on stilts, that peer out over the magnificent lakes and wetlands of the reserve.

Birdwatchers will be paralytic with joy at the ornithological smorgasbord succoured by the Lakes and, if your interests are a little more robust, the adjacent Eden Adventures offers all kinds of adrenaline-flavoured outings. Families will enjoy renting canoes and paddling along the miles of entrancing waterways that thread through the countryside, and walkers will love the overnight hike through the park.

* Wilderness Lakes National Park: 044 877 1197
* Eden Adventures: 044 877 0179

Wilderness

The Wilderness is wonderful. The beach is spectacular, whether you like swimming or sunning or sleeping. The adjacent lagoon offers safe bathing and a large grassy area for braais and ball games. And there's a lake for bird-watching or canoeing. But, a word to the wise: the lagoon can be very busy on holidays and weekends and you might want to have a back-up plan, in case the crowds are too claustrophobic.

If you are looking for alternative outings, there are a number of hikes, day walks and drives in the area. One of the best short walks is the Wilderness Heritage Trail, maintained by the local eco-tourism association. The three to four hour trail starts and ends at the tourism bureau where you will get your informative trail map and a permit.

* Wilderness Tourist Info: 044 877 0045
  www.wildernessinfo.co.za

Some idiot goes rock jumping, Wilderness

valuable trees in the whole country. It was a natural bounty of hardwood that Britain was keen to harvest, but the landscape was so forbidding that no proper road could be built to access the wooden wealth.

The dreaded Kaaimansgat River Pass and the equally unpopular Duiwelskloof Mountain Pass were the only two ways to get into the Knysna forests, and all attempts to alleviate the suicidal slopes of these passes were unsuccessful. So, they called in Mr T Bain!

Good old Tom looked at the realities of the situation and wisely decided to take a different approach. He headed inland, towards the main face of the Outeniquas and, high up on the foothills of the range, he discovered that the fearsome Kaaimans River valley was much less formidable in its early stages. The same principle applied to the other rivers that started in the mountains and flowed down to the coast, slicing increasingly steep gorges into the high plateau.

Thomas Bain was already familiar with the area. He had moved to Knysna in 1860, and built many of the original roads for the straggling little settlement. Then, in 1863, Bain and his brother-in-law, Adam de Smidt, heeded the call from the local community and started working on a road that would connect Knysna and George. The first leg of the road, the Phantom Pass from Knysna to Rheenendal, was soon completed, but here the road faltered. Bain was called away to other projects, and additional sections of the road were completed in a somewhat haphazard manner.

Clearly, this was a very tough road to build. The forests were thick, the ravines were jagged, and on-going arguments over the routing of the road destroyed the relationship between Bain and his brother-in-law. After one particularly big blow-up, they fell out permanently and never spoke personally to one another again. Yet, for all the problems they encountered, the Seven Passes Road was finally opened to traffic in 1883, twenty years after work had first begun.

The houses across the dark water of the Kaaimans River

It was called the Seven Passes Road because the thoroughfare had to cross several major river valleys in the course of its lateral passage from George to Knysna. They are the Swart, Kaaimans, Silver, Touws, Diep, Hoogekraal, Karatara and Goukamma rivers. Building each one of these seven passes was a fully fledged epic, and it required the consummate skill of an experienced *padmaker* to bring the route to completion. As soon as it opened, the Passes Road proved a popular success, and it remained part of the main eastern highway for over seventy years.

Driving the Passes Road today is an interesting experience. The road zig-zags constantly; down one valley, across the river, and up the other side, only to descend again to the next valley, and so on. Even though progress along the twisting road is quite slow by modern standards, it is very well engineered, gently beating the contours by running in and out of every little crevice in the ravines, and the leisurely pace is part of its charm. After all, this route was built in the days when the line of the road was dictated by the landscape, and not the other way around.

Over the years, sections of the Passes Road have received a tarred surface, and some sections were still getting an asphalt top as late as 2004. Nevertheless, the course of the road remains relatively unchanged from the narrow, winding route built by Bain and his captive labour force. And it is a beautiful journey. The stands of indigenous forests, hidden in the depths of each ravine, are ravishing, and the view from the open plateau ain't too shabby neither, with the sea on one side and mountain peaks on the other. Several small towns, such as Karatara (pronounced Ka-rat-ra) and Rheenendal can be visited *en route*, and a detour to the old Millwood Gold Fields is quite rewarding.

A word of warning, though, don't take this road if you are in a rush. You can't drive too fast around the tight corners, and there are few opportunities for overtaking. In particular, the final stretch to Knysna, called Phantom Pass, is still untarred and the road was badly corrugated when I drove it. A tarred access road from Rheenedal down to the N2 can be taken instead.

THE MILLWOOD GOLD FIELDS AND JUBILEE CREEK

From the town of Rheenendal there is a very rewarding detour into the Goudveld Forests. Hikers and mountain bikers will love this large reserve, filled with alternating clumps of pine plantations and indigenous wilds. Motorists will get less of a thrill from the corrugated, bumpy gravel road through the trees, but two unusual destinations hidden in the depths of the forest make the effort worthwhile.

First, you can visit the Millwood Gold Fields. In 1876, the first nuggets were found in this remote stretch of forest and fortune seekers started arriving soon afterwards. Ten years later, a gold field was officially proclaimed and hundreds of new diggers transformed the makeshift tent town into a bustling boom town. Drinking saloons, hotels, three digger's newspapers, a bank and a music hall quickly sprang up, eager to cater to the hundreds of men who had flocked here in the hope of finding their fortune.

At first, things looked promising. Several significant alluvial deposits were found and some gold-bearing reefs were uncovered. The gold fever was whipped up into a frenzy and by 1888 the town had about 400 permanent residents working on over 1 400 claims on behalf of 40 different syndicates and companies. A stamping battery was dragged up through the forest to the goldfields, and shafts were dug into the mountainside.

Then it all went bust. The gold coming out of the mines was not materialising in viable quantities, and all the alluvial deposits had dried up. Bankrupt diggers left the town in droves and, as quickly as it had grown, the town of Millwood sank back into the soil. The pre-fab houses that lined the dusty streets were packed up, and sent off to other towns in the colony. The bank

A glittering dragonfly welcomes visitors to the Millwood Gold Fields

closed its doors and the saloon packed up its prostitutes. Millwood became a ghost town.

Today, there are only two corrugated iron shacks still standing on the abandoned gold field. One houses the museum and coffee shop, while the other has been furnished in humble period style, and is rented out as inexpensive self-catering accommodation. The rest of the town is a distant memory, smothered by the fynbos and scattered by the fresh, cool mountain air.

And yet, amid the blissful stillness of abandoned dreams, there is still some life left in Millwood. The Millwood Goldfields Society has taken it upon itself to reclaim the town and restore some of its character. They have already erected signs naming the old streets and pointing out the location of buildings that defined the town during its brief, halcyon days. Happily, the offensive plantations around the town have been cleared, and fynbos covers the slopes.

Additionally, some of the old mining equipment has been reclaimed from the underbrush, and is proudly displayed next to the old Bendigo mine shaft. The mine shaft itself has been cleared out, and guided tours into the black depths of the diggings can be arranged. The eerie old graveyard has also been cleaned up, and a walking trail has been laid out through the ethereal village.

All in all, Millwood is a strange, melancholy, brooding place to visit. It is a ghost town without the ghosts, a gold field without the gold. Yet it is also peaceful and calming. Peter, an amiable expat who lives in Millwood and shows people around, has been there for over two years and, last I heard, he was considering his wife's ultimatum to come back home to England or else. I'm guessing that Peter's still at Millwood, sitting on the *stoep* of the coffee shop, smoking his pipe and patting the two fat daschunds who keep him company.

After the solitude of Millwood, head back into the forest and follow signs to Jubilee Creek. This is a cheery little picnic ground laid out along the green banks of a crystal clear stream. The indigenous forest is lush and thick in this part of the reserve, and dappled light plays across the sparkling water, which rushes over the rocks with a throaty gurgle. Short walks lead through the trees to picturesque little waterfalls, and an afternoon spent at Jubilee Creek is an utter delight.

KNYSNA

Everybody loves Knysna. It's been declared South Africa's favourite town two years in a row, and there is certainly much to enjoy. The main street is lined with interesting boutiques, craft shops, restaurants and attractive shopping centres that are refreshingly free of the predictable litany of chain stores. The Knysna lagoon is a wonderfully tranquil expanse of flat water, and the famous Knysna Heads are very dramatic.

The history of Knysna begins with a handful of Dutch settlers who hacked their way through the forests and established farms in the region. The farm *Melkhoutkraal*, which included the entire Knysna lagoon basin and the Heads, was first granted to Stephanus Terblans in 1770. But it was George Rex who really put Knysna on the map.

This larger-than-life personality bought the *Melkhoutkraal* farm in 1804. He had arrived in the Cape during the first British occupation, married a widow with several kids and went on

The tranquil Knysna Lagoon mirrors the distant Heads

to hold a number of impressive, but minor, administrative posts with the British government. When the Batavian regime took over in 1803, Rex decided to ignore the change in the country's ownership and stayed on in South Africa.

By all accounts, George Rex was a moody man, although he was certainly well-educated and articulate. He could also be a right bastard, as some of his colleagues would testify, but his humour and hospitality were legendary. His personal history, however, was what made him the stuff of legend.

Soon after he arrived at the Cape, rumours began to circulate that Rex was actually British royalty – the illegitimate son of King George III and Hannah Lightfoot. It is unclear whether Rex himself was the source of these rumours, but he certainly knew how to play on the public's perceptions. He maintained a large retinue of servants, and was often seen riding around Cape Town in a large coach plastered with heraldic arms.

As he approached middle age, however, George Rex tired of the Cape Town high-life, and he relocated to *Melkhoutkraal* where he built a homestead fit for the illegitimate son of a king. After his wife died, he married one of her daughters (from a previous marriage, thankfully) and went on to father eleven children. From his huge estate, Rex and his progeny kept themselves busy by farming, hunting and cutting down trees. Rex also started agitating for the government (by now British again) to establish a harbour inside the Knysna lagoon. This would get around the logistical difficulties of building a road through the thick forests that swaddled the coast, and help Knysna become economically viable.

The problem with the harbour idea was that the currents which roared through the Knysna Heads were very fierce (and they still are). This narrow channel, flanked by the two tall sandstone sentinels of the Heads, separates the placid waters of the lagoon from the wild, open sea. So, any boats that wanted to anchor in the calm, expansive estuary first had to run the formidable gauntlet of the Knysna Heads.

In 1817, after endless nagging by George Rex, the British navy sent a ship to try to navigate the passage through the heads. The experiment was not a success as the vessel hit a submerged reef and had to be run aground. A second ship was sent to salvage the first ship, and this one did manage to get through the Heads safely. Rex was delighted, and he donated some land for a shipbuilding yard. He also built a slipway, in expectation of all the boats that would be launched into the lagoon, but the shipbuilding enterprise failed.

Eventually, Knysna did get its port, and it was declared a village in 1825. For a change, the town wasn't named after the ruling British governor. Instead, it retained its original Khoikhoi name, which is thought to translate as 'place of wood'. In 1928, a standard gauge railway line from Knysna to George was completed, and this helped precipitate the closure of the Knysna port in 1954.

After presiding over the growth of his town from farmlands to thriving village, George Rex died in 1839 and was buried in the ground of his beloved *Melkhoutkraal*. His grave can still be visited, and is signposted from the main road, just outside of town. It is a humble grave for such a preposterous figure, but it is pretty, surrounded by trees and thick foliage. However, the air of quiet solemnity is somewhat spoiled by a bloody great power sub-station which has been erected about ten metres away. George Rex is probably fulminating in his grave at this final indignity.

And he isn't alone. The once-abundant natural beauty of Knysna has actually been heavily compromised by the rampant development of the town. Every time I go to Knysna I see that houses are being built further and further up the mountain slopes, and the vast township keeps getting bigger (without any attempt at organisation). One of the Knysna Heads is thoroughly pockmarked with over 100 large holiday homes, and this has destroyed much of its wild beauty.

Knysna

Visitors in Knysna are spoiled for choice.

The Knysna Quays Waterfront shopping and residential development on the lagoon is nice enough, with lots of shops and restaurants. For less mainstream retail therapy, walk along the high street which has several intimate shopping complexes and lots of individualistic stores, restaurants and flea markets.

Knysna is also known for its timber, and there are many manufacturers and retailers selling indigenous wooden furniture. Then, if all the shopping is making you thirsty, take a trip around Mitchell's Brewery, which offers tours through its yeasty facilities.

Featherbed Nature Reserve has lots of offer the visitor including beautiful walks over the pristine cliffs, a trailer ride to the top of the Western Head, cave trails, a floating restaurant and a catamaran journey into the mouth of the Heads. The reserve can be accessed only by ferries, which depart from the Waterfront and the Municipal Jetty.

Historically speaking, the Knysna museum is housed in an old, prefab house that used to stand on the abandoned Millwood Gold Fields. It has interesting displays on the early days of the town. The nearby Old Gaol Complex contains a maritime museum, angling exhibit, art gallery and restaurant. If you want an altogether more irie cultural experience, book a tour through Judah Square, the largest Rastafarian community in South Africa.

Fishing is a popular local pastime and there are several companies offering deep-sea charters. Alternatively, rent a canoe and paddle out into the waters of the lagoon, which teem with more than 200 kinds of fish. The lagoon also supports a variety of swimmers, scuba divers, boaters, canoeists and snorkelers. Outdoor enthusiasts can sign up for abseiling, paragliding, windsurfing, kayaking and a suicidal drift dive in the fast-moving currents through the Heads.

If you feel like something more sedate, there is a company offering relaxing old-fashioned wagon trails through the forests between Knysna and Plett.

Walkers will have a field day in Knysna, as there are dozens of day walks and overnight trails through the surrounding countryside. One of the most rewarding trails is the Kranshoek Coastal Day Walk through the Harkerville indigenous forest reserve. This circular 9km hike is quite strenuous but the scenery is gorgeous, especially on the rocky beach, which rumbles when the white waves wash over the rounded pebbles. Shorter walks through the forest can also be tackled.

Cyclists and off-road motorists may also enjoy a journey along Salt River Road, which takes you on a high circuit through the plantations that cover the mountain-tops around town, and back to Knysna via the bustling township. Avid readers may enjoy also following the characters of Dalene Matthee's Kringe in 'n Bos by taking the circle in the forest from the Old Cape Road to Gouna-se-kant.

While you can swim in the lagoon, Knysna does not have an ocean beach. For that you have to drive out of town to Noetzie, Brenton-on-Sea or Buffalo Bay. The beach that stretches from Brenton to Buffalo Bay is particularly beautiful and quite vast, so that it never gets overcrowded. The cliffs above Brenton Beach used to house the attractive Brenton Hotel, which recently burnt down.

When in town, it's always good to go local. Taste the home-grown Knysna oysters, and keep an eye out for the elusive and lucky Knysna Loerie (now officially called the Turaco). In terms of wildlife, Knysna has several unique species, including the Brenton Blue Butterfly and the Knysna Seahorse. Both of these are under threat of extinction as their habitat is being polluted by holiday homes and motorboats.

- Knysna Tourist Info: 044 382 5510
- www.visitknysna.com / www.knysna.org
- Featherbed Nature Reserve: 044 382 1693/7
- Forestry Knysna: 044 382 5466
- Harkerville Forestry Station: 044 532 7770

The thick, green Knysna forests are full of leafy secrets

Thankfully, the Western Head is part of the Featherbed Nature Reserve and is still blissfully undeveloped. The interesting thing about this nature reserve is that it is the private property of William Smith, the well-known television educator and scientist. Smith's family has a long association with Knysna and, back in 1938, his father was the first western scientist to identify the Coelacanth, a fish long thought extinct and in fact previously known only from fossil remains.

No doubt, the international fame that followed J L B Smith's stunning classification of 'Old Four Legs' helped feather the family nest, and enabled them to buy a rather nice little piece of real estate on the Western side of the lagoon. One only hopes that Mr Smith has enough money to fight off the circling property developers, and will keep Featherbed Nature Reserve in the public domain for years to come.

PLETTENBERG BAY (PLETT)

The Portuguese seafarers who first landed on the shores of Plett called the place *Bahia Formosa*, meaning Beautiful Bay. And how right they were. It is a magnificent cove with wide, soft beaches and dreamy mountains wherever you look.

The town's name changed after the redoubtable Dutch governor, Joachim Van Plettenberg, toured the region in 1778, and decided that it would be much better to re-christen the place after himself. Initially, the Dutch had high hopes for Plettenberg Bay, but attempts to develop a harbour in the bay were unsuccessful.

Instead, it was left to the British to develop the town, and one of George Rex's descendants opened the first inn in the 1820s. This is now called the Formosa Inn, and some of the original buildings have been incorporated into the new structure.

On the south side of the bay is Beacon Island, so-named because the Dutch had installed a navigational beacon there in 1772. This piece of land was initially used as a whaling station, until a low-key hotel was built there in the 1940s. In the early 1970s, Sol Kerzner's Southern Sun group bought the land and built a new hotel on the site, called the Beacon Isle. This evergreen resort put Plett on the map, as far as aspirational Vaalies were concerned, and the town has been growing ever since.

So, once upon a time, Plett was a little town with a few holiday homes, one fancy hotel, the Piesang River caravan park and a magnificent beach. Today, the caravan park is gone, the beach is crowded, and the hills of Plett are awash with pink palaces and ghastly apartment complexes. I think that the person in charge of Plett's town planning has either been visually impaired by all the dollar signs, or is just an idiot.

Thankfully, the beaches are still beautiful, and the Robberg Nature Reserve is a stirring reminder of how things used to look before people with more money than taste despoiled the area. Central Beach and Lookout Beach are the two main swimming beaches in Plett, and they are heart-wrenchingly lovely. Don't miss out on a sunset walk along the sand, when the warm, diffuse light bathes the sea and drenches the bobbing fishing boats with a pink glow.

Garden Route Contacts:
- Garden Route Regional Travel Info: 044 873 6314
- www.capegardenroute.org
  www.gardenroute.co.za
- Sedgefield Tourist Info: 044 343 2658
- Plettenberg Bay Tourist Info: 044 533 4065
  www.plettenbergbay.co.za
- Robberg Nature Reserve: 044 533 2125/85
- Keurbooms Lagoon and canoe trail: 044 802 5300

Sunset over Central Beach, Plettenberg Bay

ROADS THROUGH THE TSITSIKAMMA

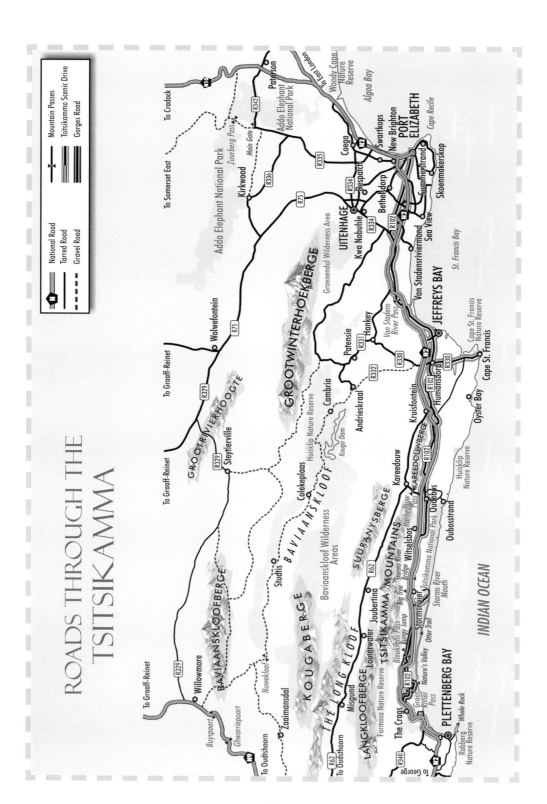

Legend:
- National Road
- Tarred Road
- Gravel Road
- Mountain Passes
- Tsitsikamma Scenic Drive
- Gorges Road

12. Roads through the Tsitsikamma

ORIENTATION

From the luxury of Plettenberg Bay, the N2 continues through the Tsitsikamma forests towards Humansdorp. This used to be easier said than done, as the Tsitsikamma was the wildest and most fearsome stretch of coast in the old Cape Colony. Today, several tarred roads twist through the forests, but the scenery remains as powerful and stirring as ever.

As you proceed east from Plett on the N2, the mountains keep up their constant vigil to the north, but change their name from the Outeniquas to the Tsitsikamma. The name is derived from the Khoikhoi phrase meaning 'where the waters begin' or 'place of abundant waters'. This is a reference to the high rainfall, which causes many rivers to run down from the mountain slopes.

After the tiny town called The Crags, you have a choice. You can either travel via the R102, Thomas Bain's beautiful Gorges Road which takes in Nature's Valley, or you can take the N2 toll road which boasts a succession of large-span bridges. These two roads join up again, just before the turn off to the little village of Storms River. At this junction, you can either turn off to Storms River Village and the Tsitsikamma National Park, or you can continue on towards Humansdorp.

From Humansdorp, the N2 evens out and the terrain becomes less challenging. This is the Kouga region, incorporating Jeffreys Bay, Cape St Francis, the Long Kloof, Baviaanskloof and the Gamtoos River valley.

There are a number of ways that you can now proceed:
⇒ Turn-off the N2 and follow the old main road, the R102, as it winds through the countryside all the way to PE. This will take you past the Van Stadens Wild Flower Reserve, and down the old Van Stadens River Pass. This tarred road through an attractive river gorge was made redundant when the Van Stadens Bridge opened in 1971.
⇒ Follow signs to Kareedouw. This will take you up to the Long Kloof [see Chapter 17]. From here you can head into the Klein Karoo on the R62 [see Chapter 15].
⇒ Detour to the beach resort of Cape St Francis on the R330. St Francis Bay is well known to surfers, thanks to Bruce Brown's seminal surfer flick 'Endless Summer'. This film, shot in the 60s, documented Brown's quest to find the perfect wave. After searching the world, the sunburnt pilgrim finally found his holy rollers off the beaches of Cape St Francis. Unfortunately, the property developers followed in Brown's footsteps and subsequently destroyed 'Bruce's Beauties' by meddling with the submerged sand banks. Surfing is nevertheless a popular activity at Cape St Francis, and shell collectors also rate the beach very highly.
⇒ Detour to the surfing mecca of Jeffrey's Bay. With its innumerable surf shops and world-renowned breaks (each with dramatic names like Boneyards and Super Tubes), Jay Bay is the surfing mecca of South Africa. It is also popular with shell collectors, and has a museum dedicated to these fragile jewels of the sea.
⇒ For the more adventurous, follow signs to Hankey off the N2. This leads to the magnificent Baviaanskloof road to Willowmore [see Chapter 16]. Baviaanskloof is a rough gravel road,

recommended for 4x4s and 4x2s only, and leads you into the Klein Karoo [see Chapter 15].

➡Otherwise, continue along the N2 towards Port Elizabeth.

THE GORGES ROAD

The Tsitsikamma Forests, lying between Plettenberg Bay and Humansdorp, were the thickest and the most forbidding in the entire Cape Colony. And, despite many attempts, the dense forests deflected any human attempts to penetrate their verdant violence.

For years, the tangled roots, dark ravines, mighty rivers, towering trunks and clinging underbrush of the region stumped even the most determined of explorers. In 1839, Charles Michell, chief engineer of the Cape Colony, went so far as to write 'There is no practical way – not even a foot path – [to get from] Plettenberg Bay to the Zitzikamma country'.

But fate intervened when the Great Fire of 1869 thinned out the trees. This gave ambitious roadmakers a small window of opportunity to blaze a new trail through the thicket. Accordingly, after planning his Passes Road from George to Knysna, Thomas Bain

Nature's Valley

Nature's Valley is an unpretentious holiday resort located within De Vasselot Nature Reserve. It contains several small shops, a couple of restaurants and fast-food stalls of the ilk that sells soft-serve and stale marshmallow fish. Built on the shores of a large lagoon with uninhibited access to the adjacent coastline, it's a perfect vacation destination. The beach is excellent, the lagoon is warm, the pace is leisurely and no buildings higher than two storeys may be built. My kind of place!

• *De Vasselot Nature Reserve: 042 281 160*

proceeded to scout out a path through the wooded wilderness from Knysna to Humansdorp.

With many of the trees gone, he did not have to worry so much about clearing the path, but he was faced with another problem – conquering the steep river gorges that cleave through the land. Undeterred, Bain plotted a winding course down to the river and up again, down to the next and up, just as with the Passes Road. It would be tortuous, tedious and slow work, but it could be done.

Concrete bridges have replaced Bain's old causeways at the bottom of each gorge

The Bloukrans River Bridge, home of the world's highest bungy jump

Bain was a busy man, however, and he was simultaneously building, planning and supervising roads all over the country. So, what with one thing and another, construction on the Tsitsikamma Road began only in 1879. It was finally completed six years later, in 1885. With three major gorges, the Groot River, Bloukrans and Storms River, to be crossed, it was a mammoth undertaking. But Bain accomplished it all with his customary aplomb and, after years of hard work, it must have been more than a little annoying to hear the Chief Inspector's dismissive description of his new road as "a somewhat shorter and more cheerful route than that through Long Kloof".

With the Seven Passes Road and the Tsitsikamma Gorges Road in place, the eastern highway along the coast was finally complete. The old route from Mossel Bay, over the mountains to Oudtshoorn and down the Long Kloof to PE, had been supplanted by Bain's new roads, which connected George directly to Port Elizabeth along the coastal shelf.

Accordingly, Bain's gravel Gorges Road was included in South Africa's first national road scheme of 1936 and, after the Second World War, work began on improving and tarring the road through the Tsitsikamma. This work was on-going through the 1950s.

Meanwhile, the national road programme was continuing, and engineers were trying to work out how to expand the convoluted course of the Gorges Road to conform to modern specifications. They eventually abandoned the idea of improving the old road and instead decided to build bridges over the troubled waters instead.

Accordingly, in the 1980s, an ambitious programme of bridge building was initiated to span the remaining gorges. When complete, these bridges would enable the new N2 freeway to run straight and flat along the plateau, cutting out all those time-consuming twists and turns.

As a result, the old Gorges Road became a little-used byway, often forgotten or ignored by modern motorists. This is a pity, because Bain's beautiful old road is still there, tarred and ready to use, and it's toll-free. So, next time you are driving from Plett to PE, give yourself a couple of extra hours and take the Gorges Road, now labelled the R102, to Nature's Valley. It's wiggly and it's slow, but it is lovely.

THE BRIDGES OF THE N2

It's strange to think that the current N2 between Plett and Storms River Village opened only in the 1980s. Before that, the single route through the intricate Tsitsikamma Forests was Thomas Bain's Gorges Road, now the R102. The reason it took so long to build a modern freeway through this part of the world is not because of the thick forests, but because the high-lying plateau is gouged by several sheer-sided gorges, cut into the rock by eager rivers desperate to reach the sea.

So, when Bain's road couldn't be widened to accommodate the specifications of a modern highway, an alternative had to be found. The only solution was to build a new road along the flat coastal plateau, with a series of large bridges to leapfrog over the impassable ravines.

Small bridges over the Storms River, Gourits River and Van Stadens River had already been built in the preceding decades, but the real challenge remained: spanning the mighty gorges of the Bloukrans, the Groot and the Bobbejaans. Finally, in the 1980s, a graceful series of single-span bridges was designed to accomplish this feat, and the work was farmed out to three different construction companies. It was one of the biggest construction projects in South Africa at the time. The grand, new N2 toll route was opened to the public in 1983.

Of all the N2's bridges, Bloukrans is the

The Big Tree

On the N2, just before the turn-off to Storms River Village, there is a sign to the Big Tree. This is one of several indigenous giants that still stand, towering over the surrounding forest canopy. While it cannot compare with the almighty California Redwoods of America's west coast, the short walk through the glistening forests to the Big Tree is glorious. There are several other big trees in the Knysna/Plettenberg Bay area which can be visited; one is on the Passes Road and another is along the access road to Prince Alfred's Pass. One can only imagine what it must have looked like when the forest was full of these dendritic monsters.

• Tsitsikamma Big Tree: 042 541 1157

most impressive. This used to be the largest single-span bridge in the Southern Hemisphere, and it took three years to build. At the time, it cost a massive eleven million rand. Nowadays, eleven bar won't get you a condo in Clifton.

Construction on the 272 metre arch of the Bloukrans Bridge was started simultaneously from both ends of the gorge and, when they met in the middle, an adjustment of only 10mm was required to match the levels. Not bad, considering that each section weighs 7 500 tons. In recent years, the Bloukrans Bridge has become better known as the home of the

A dark river mouth on the Tsitsikamma Coast

highest Bungy Jump in the world, a 216 metre leap of faith.

After the excitement of Bloukrans, the next big bridge is the Storm's River Bridge. More properly called the Paul Sauer Bridge, this bridge was built in 1954 and named after some forgotten footsoldier of apartheid. It has a nice pedestrian walkway, so you can stroll across the ramparts to take in the views, and the nearby petrol station is worth checking out for the interesting photographic display inside the restaurant. This informal exhibit, which hangs incongruously over the heads of diners, details the construction of the various N2 bridges, and boasts an extensive gallery of famous bridges from around the world.

Tsitsikamma Contacts:
- Tsitsikamma Tourist Info: 042 280 3561
  www.tsitsikamma.info
- Bloukrans Bungy Jump: 042 281 1458
  083 231 3528

The waterfall that greets day-walkers in the Tsitsikamma National Park

Stormsriver Village

Five kilometres before the Storms River Bridge, there is a sign pointing off the N2 towards Storms River Village, Storms River Mouth and the Tsitsikamma National Park. This is a great detour if you have the time.

Storms River Village is just a short distance off the N2. It is a small cluster of country shops, a few houses and the idiosyncratic Tsitsikamma Village Inn. The inn is built around an old hunting lodge that used to belong to the well-to-do Duthie family of Knysna. The reception rooms and the bar have several original features from the 1860s, and the original fireplace with its huge mahogany mantelpiece is marvellous.

Next door to the inn is Stormsriver Adventures. This is a dynamic company that offers blackwater tubing, abseiling, scuba diving, mountain biking and cruises along the chiaroscuro depths of the Storms River gorge. They also operate the exhilarating Tree-Top canopy tours, on which people are harnessed up and made to slide along thick wires suspended from tree to tree.

They also offer an enjoyable tractor excursion along the old Storms River Pass, which includes a picnic at the river. This is a little-seen but entrancing road through the Plaatbos State Forest that winds past misty indigenous forests, down to a low-level causeway over the brown-black Storms River. It was originally part of Thomas Bain's Gorges road, but was cut out of the route in the 1950s when the Storms River Bridge was built overhead. The road is now closed to the public, but mountain bikers can still ride over the pass by filling in a free, self-issuing permit at the gate.

- *Stormsriver Adventures: 042 281 1836*
- *Tsitsikamma Village Inn: 042 281 1711*
- *Horse Rides and Quad Bike trails:*
  042 281 1398
- *Plaatbos Forestry Station / Tsitsikamma State Forest: 042 281 1557*

Tsitsikamma National Park

Suspension bridge over Storms River Mouth

Storms River Mouth

If you continue past Storms River Village for another nine kilometres, you will come to the gates of the Tsitsikamma National Park. This gem is one of the best coastal reserves in the country, and is just begging to be explored. The park is situated right on the coastal shelf, hemmed in by the lush mountains and the ragged red rocks of the shoreline. Accommodation is in rustic (but well-appointed) log cabins or in a sloping block of apartments, built right at the edge of the ocean. A large camping ground is also available, and all the sites have a staggering view of the unfettered ocean. The rest camp also has a swimming pool, shop and a restaurant.

While there is only one rest camp in the reserve, the protected area is quite large, and the park stretches out over a long, narrow piece of land that runs along the coast from Nature's Valley to Oubosstrand, a distance of about 60km. The protected area also extends for a few kilometres out into the sea. The park was (thankfully) established in 1964, and it is South Africa's oldest marine reserve. If you want to get an idea of how the Garden Route used to look before the human onslaught, this is the place. It is a staggeringly beautiful reserve, thronged with deep, primeval forests and grand river gorges.

There are a number of walks through the reserve. Families will enjoy the easy stroll along the wooden boardwalk to an exciting suspension bridge over the Storms River Mouth. Day walkers can also trek to the nearby waterfall, for a swim in its dark, inviting pools. For the more ambitious hiker, there are no less than three multi-day trails through the Tsitsikamma National Park. The guided Dolphin Trail is the expensive, luxury option,

which includes freshly prepared meals and porters to carry your baggage. The Tsitsikamma Trail is a six-day, inland trail that runs through the forests from Nature's Valley to the Storms River Bridge. Then, there is the world-famous Otter Trail.

• Storms River Mouth Rest Camp: 042 281 1607

The Otter Trail

King of the Tsitsikamma hiking routes is the superlative Otter Trail. This five-day hike is easily the most famous hiking trail in the country, and is usually booked up a year in advance. And for good reason. The trail is challenging but not gruelling, organised but pristine, and beautiful beyond words. To put it in a personal perspective, the Otter Trail quite literally changed my life.

I never used to be a walker. If I had to get to get up off the couch to fetch the remote, it was a big day. But one afternoon I got a call from a friend in Cape Town. He had mates going on the Otter Trail and there were some last-minute cancellations. Did I want to come? In an untypical moment, I said yes and then sat back to contemplate what I had just agreed to.

Unsurpassable views precede a steep descent to the river

With my head full of trepidation, I distracted myself by borrowing a backpack and spending a fortune on other hiking gear. Then, a week later, I suddenly found myself at the Storms River Mouth rest camp, ready to tackle the Otter Trail. I didn't know what to expect. I didn't know if I had brought enough food. I didn't even know if I would make it. But I needn't have worried. The experience was utterly, miraculously, entirely fantastic.

For five whole days, I was in paradise. There were no electric lights, no cars, no sirens. Only the roaring sea, the squealing gulls and the crackle of the campfire filled my ears. The trail takes in the best of the coastal finery as it rises and falls, from the beach, through the forests, up to the plateau blanketed with fynbos, and down again. While the constant ups and downs might make your knees a little wobbly, the visual panoramas keep you going, and the exciting river crossings keep you cool. Drinking water is plentiful along the route, and the hike is broken down into short but strenuous sections, with the longest stretch being only 13km, so the walk never becomes overwhelming.

Yoga and muesli for breakfast

The overnight huts all have exquisite locations, and it is a rare pleasure to peel off your socks after a hard day's hiking, while you sit on the wooden stoep and gaze out over the rampant waves. And when it's time to answer the call of nature, you're in for a treat because the toilets have all been fitted with one-way glass which lets you look out while you let off. This is one place where the view from the throne is fit for a king.

When we finally emerged from the forests onto the white sands of Nature's Valley holiday resort, I wanted to turn around and start all over again. I had become a hiker and I've never looked back.

• Otter Trail bookings: 042 281 1607

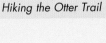

Hiking the Otter Trail

Relaxing after a hard day's walk

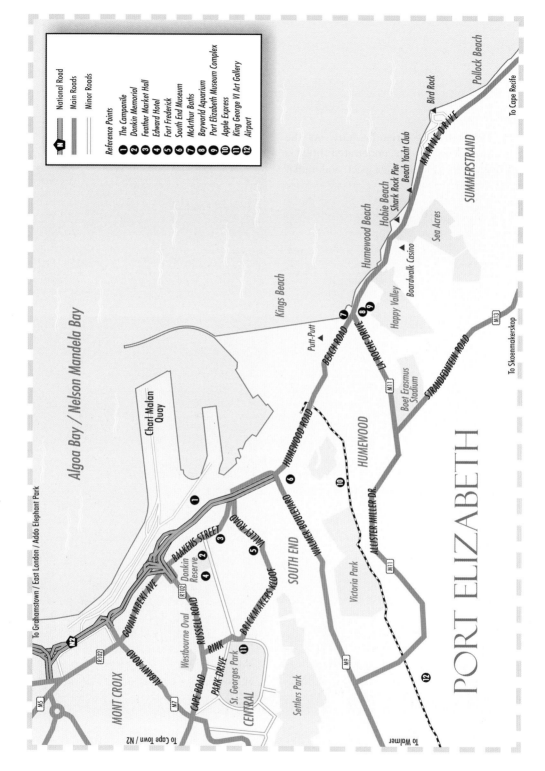

PORT ELIZABETH

Algoa Bay / Nelson Mandela Bay

National Road
Main Roads
Minor Roads

Reference Points
1 The Campanile
2 Donkin Memorial
3 Feather Market Hall
4 Edward Hotel
5 Fort Frederick
6 South End Museum
7 McArthur Baths
8 Bayworld Aquarium
9 Port Elizabeth Museum Complex
10 Apple Express
11 King George VI Art Gallery
12 Airport

To Grahamstown / East London / Addo Elephant Park
To Cape Town / N2
To Cape Town / N2
To Walmer
To Skoenmakerskop
To Cape Recife

Chart Malan Quay

Pollock Beach
Bird Rock
MARINE DRIVE
SUMMERSTRAND
Beach Yacht Club
Shark Rock Pier
Hobie Beach
Sea Acres
Humewood Beach
Boardwalk Casino
Happy Valley
Kings Beach
Putt-Putt
BEACH ROAD
LA ROCHE DRIVE
Boet Erasmus Stadium
HUMEWOOD
STRANDFONTEIN ROAD
M13
M11
HUMEWOOD ROAD
MARINE BOULEVARD
ALLISTER MILLER DR.
Victoria Park
M11
SOUTH END
Settlers Park
M9
St. Georges Park
CENTRAL
RINK
PARK DRIVE
CAPE ROAD
ALBANY ROAD
M7
Westbourne Oval
Donkin Reserve
R102
RUSSELL ROAD
BRICKMAKERS KLOOF
BAAKENS STREET
VALLEY ROAD
GOVAN MBEKI AVE
MONT CROIX
M5

13. Port Elizabeth

ORIENTATION

Port Elizabeth, the Friendly City on the Sunshine Coast, is an underrated holiday destination. It is clean, compact and rather pretty city, but it is often left off the holiday itinerary. One of the reasons for this is that the N2 by-passes the centre of PE, so you have to leave the highway to get into town. It's worth the detour, however, and if in doubt about which turn-off to take, just follow signs to the beaches of Summerstrand.

Port Elizabeth is built around the Cape Recife headland, the tip of which is now a beautiful nature reserve. From this point, the main face of the city extends up the eastern shores of Algoa Bay, through the suburbs of Summerstrand, Humewood and South End, to the City Centre.

The city itself is built along a narrow coastal shelf which rises steeply to a plateau, along which the inland suburbs sprawl. The CBD looks onto the harbour and the docks but, sadly, the city centre seems cordoned off from the sea by a knot of highways, railway lines and over-passes. The main commercial thoroughfares of the city run parallel to the coastline, on a narrow strip of low-lying land. The ground then rises steeply above the city, to the suburb of Central – not the most imaginative name, perhaps, but accurate! The other residential suburbs of PE extend westwards from Central, all the way to the N2.

The main swimming beaches, the casino, the shops and most of the tourist attractions are draped along Marine Drive in Summerstrand. This road, which starts below the harbour mouth, is lined with apartment blocks and retail complexes on the one side while, on the other, grassy dunes and a brick-paved promenade run adjacent to the warm sea.

The holiday fun-fair on the PE beachfront

Within a 100km of PE, there are several impressive game parks, including the ever-increasing Addo Elephant National Park and luxury lodges such as Shamwari, which also takes day visitors. The smaller nature reserve of Schoenmaker's Kop can be found on the far side of Cape Recife.

If you want to go to Addo, head east on the N2 towards East London. Alongside the road you will see a concrete jumble of white *dolos*, those strange anchor-like constructions that line the sea-front. These curious objects were developed by a local tech student to break the power of the waves that pound the shoreline. They proved so effective that they have subsequently been used all over the world to protect harbours and other sensitive seaside developments. From the N2, follow signs to the

Addo Elephant National Park on the R335.

For the purposes of this book, the great wagon road to the east ends at PE, as there were no European settlements further up the coast until the British intrusion of 1820. But that is a story for another day!

From PE, you can return to Cape Town via the N2, or you can head up the Long Kloof (R62) to Oudtshoorn and the Klein Karoo [see Chapter 15].

PORT ELIZABETH

Port Elizabeth – The Friendly City. The Windy City. The city on the Bay. The Nelson Mandela Metropolitan Area. Whatever you call it, PE is a *lekker* place. It's not humid like Durban. It isn't stuck up like Cape Town. The beaches are great. The locals are friendly. The sea's warm. So why don't more people go there? Well, I'm not sure. PE just has a bad rep.

Historically, PE goes back a long way. Bartolomeu Dias saw the bay on his momentous journey around the Cape, and named it *Bahia de Lagoa*, or Lagoon Bay. This was soon corrupted to Algoa Bay, which it remained for a few hundred years, until it was recently renamed Nelson Mandela Bay, for no apparent reason other than to curry favour with the tourists. Maybe they should just call South Africa 'Madiba-land', and get it over with.

Algoa Bay, by the way, should not be confused with Delagoa Bay, which is the old Maputo, which the Portuguese renamed Lourenco Marques, which has now again become Maputo, the capital of Mozambique, a country that used to be called Portuguese East Africa. I tell you, nomenclature is a tricky business in this part of the world.

Anyhoo, the Dutch did little to develop the potential of Algoa Bay because the strong summer winds had a habit of driving ships onto the rocks. Nevertheless, in time, the eastern districts of the colony needed a harbour, and Algoa Bay was the only one around. In 1799, the first British administration built a small outpost (called Fort Frederick) on the banks of the Baakens River mouth, and a small town began to develop. The subsequent Batavian administration then founded a town quite close to Fort Frederick that they called Uitenhage.

Once the second British Administration had found its feet, they began to appreciate the

The friendly façade of the Edward Hotel

Port Elizabeth

The main road along the beachfront links the main hotels, the Boardwalk casino and shopping centre, dozens of restaurants, kids' playgrounds and the Bayworld aquarium complex, which includes a snake park and the local museum.

Other attractions along this strip (variously called Humewood Road, Beach Road or Marine Drive) include the Cape Recife Nature Reserve and lighthouse, Brooke's Pavilion Entertainment Complex and the newly refurbished McArthur Baths complex, which offers several clean swimming pools set in an attractive wooden deck. McArthur Baths also has two restaurants with great views out over the bay and the harbour. I ate at 'Up The Khyber' restaurant, and that's exactly where the food hit me.

Surfers should check out Hobie Beach, next to the Red Windmill restaurant and the pier. Windsurfing and other watersports can be enjoyed in the area. Hobie Beach, incidentally, has been transformed from a rocky shingle into a reclaimed sandy oasis, thanks to the calming effects of the nearby pier.

Walkers will enjoy a stroll through Cape Recife Nature Reserve, the Maitland Nature Reserve, Schoenmakerskop-Sardinia Nature Reserve or Settler's Park, a wonderfully wooded retreat in the centre of the city. Schoenies and Sard's, as the area beyond Cape Recife is known, also has quiet beaches.

Inland from the coast, the city flattens out into a sea of suburbia which has grown to include Walmer, which once had its own municipality. While the older suburbs, such as Central, are off the beaten tourist track, they do offer some interesting shops and out-of-the-way restaurants in a beguiling semi-urban environment. Several nightclubs and bars can also be found in Central, and these should be checked out if the beachfront hotspots are too mainstream for your tastes.

Out of all the residential suburbs, Central is considered the melting pot of PE, with odd little restaurants, coffee shops and antique dealers spilling out of crumbling Victorian homes. Local eccentrics are a feature of the Central coffee scene, and this was once the stomping ground of Joshua Abraham Naughton, the self-proclaimed Emperor of PE! If you are a cricket fan, St George's Stadium and the adjacent green park can also be found in Central.

For train enthusiasts, don't miss a ride on the Apple Express. Operational since 1903, this charming steam train goes on regular excursions over the highest narrow gauge bridge in the world, across the Van Stadens River. Trips run on most weekends and during the holidays. Phone for a timetable.

- *Port Elizabeth Tourist Info: 041 585 8884*
- *www.ibhayi.com / www.nmbt.co.za*
- *www.pe.org.za / www.nelsonmandelabay.co.za*
- *The Boardwalk Casino and Shopping Centre: 041 507 7777*
- *Bayworld (aquarium, museum, snake park): 041 584 0650*
- *South End Museum: 041 582 3325*
- *Apple Express: 041 583 2030*
- *Port Elizabeth International Airport: 041 507 7319*

The MacArthur Baths

value of the little harbour at Algoa Bay, but they were troubled with the on-going friction between white settlers and the native Xhosa tribes living in the vicinity. The Brits, in their ineffable wisdom, decided that the solution was to build up a buffer zone of European settlers, which would neutralise the threat of any independent tribal authorities. Undeterred by any thoughts that they may actually be making the problem worse, a campaign of sponsored immigration was launched to attract new settlers from England, Scotland and the other parts of the empire.

When this first wave of organised

An eclectic mix of buildings in downtown Port Elizabeth

immigration arrived at Algoa Bay in the motley form of the 1820 settlers, the British governor travelled from the Cape to welcome the new arrivals. This melancholy man, named Sir Rufane Donkin, gave the settlers a rousing speech, welcoming them to their new home. He also decided to rename the town around Fort Frederick after his dear departed wife, Elizabeth, who had died of fever two years earlier while the couple were stationed in India. Port Elizabeth became a magistracy in 1825 and, a hundred years later, an artificial harbour was built to give the ships an anchorage that was safe from the wind.

Now, PE is the fifth largest town in SA, and the centre of our motor manufacturing industry. It is also the financial capital of the Eastern Cape, and a hotbed of industrial development. In fact, the jewel in the crown of South Africa's current public works programme is the ambitious, multi-billion-rand industrial complex being developed around the nearby port of Coega.

But PE is more than a big business centre. It is also a major tourist centre. Yes, the main bathing beach might look out over the huge cranes of the harbour, and the shoreline might be littered with thousands of ugly, concrete *dolos*. But so what? The wide beaches, well-stocked aquarium, flashy casino, beachfront shopping centres and a long, grassy promenade all work together to create the ideal holiday vibe.

Most of the beachside attractions of PE are spread out along Summerstrand but, if you are interested in history, you have to start your explorations in the city centre. Once you get past the network of ugly overpasses that screen the centre of town from the speeding traffic, the PE CBD is quite attractive.

The main roads through 'lower' town are Baakens Street and Govan Mbeki Avenue, named after the ANC stalwart and father of our current president, Thabo. These roads are lined with a strange collection of old churches, art deco office blocks, and monolithic slabs of concrete with repetitive stylistic motifs from the 70s. The pedestrians buzz along the pavements and the stores are thronged with people buying clothes, shoes, phone cards and vetkoek.

If you're interested in architecture, head to Market Square for a historical overview of the town. This is the location of the City Hall, the Old Post Office, the Library Building and the Feather Market Hall. The Campanile watch tower, built in the 1920s to commemorate the arrival of the 1820 settlers, can also be reached from the square. These gorgeous old buildings are a charming assortment of Victorian, Gothic, Edwardian and Art Nouveau styling, and a typically dour statue of Queen Victoria casts her benediction over the whole *piazza*. Nearby, you'll also find the world's only memorial to Prester John.

Prester John is a mythological figure, dating back more than 500 years. He was reputedly a white Christian emperor who improbably ruled a powerful and wealthy tribe, somewhere in

Africa. Making contact with Prester John was actually the ostensible reason many European nations propounded for exploring Africa in the first place. But no trace of the elusive Emperor ever materialised. The existence of Prester John seems to have been conjured up by generations of Europeans, who just could not conceive of a black civilisation that was advanced enough to account for the inexplicable supplies of gold that had been coming out of the dark continent for the past 1 000 years.

From Baakens Street, you can turn up towards the Donkin Reserve. This is a large green common on the top of a hill, which looks down on the harbour and city centre below. The reserve is dominated by an old lighthouse (which can be visited), and the large, grey concrete pyramid that functions as the Elizabeth Donkin Memorial. If you don't mind the wind, this is a good place to pull up a park bench for a few moments of R&R. The main tourist bureau is at the foot of the lighthouse.

Around the park are a number of interesting old buildings. The Edward Hotel is a particularly fine example of late-Victorian–early Edwardian architecture. Built about one hundred years ago, the hotel has a wonderful façade lined with lattice-work balconies and domed windows. The interior of the Edward is fantastically old fashioned, and tea in the faded Palm Court is a treat for lovers of retro-dining.

At the other end of the Donkin Reserve there stands a row of restored terrace houses, built between 1860 and 1880. This whole street has been declared a national monument. An African restaurant, with incongruous orange-coloured walls, and the Victorian bulk of a Presbyterian church also hold court around the green. An excellent walking tour (The Donkin Heritage Trail) will guide you through the historical heart of the city centre, and an interpretative booklet can be bought from the tourist bureau.

For more modern history, visit the South End Museum on the outskirts of the CBD, and pick up a walking tour booklet that will lead you through PE's apartheid past. The South End area is akin to District Six in Cape Town, or Sophiatown in Joburg, as it was the scene of many bitterly contested forced removals in the 1960s.

ADDO ELEPHANT NATIONAL PARK

About 50km outside of PE is the Addo Elephant National Park. The history of this park is a little bit ignominious, but it has subsequently grown to become one of the foremost conservation areas in the country.

Once upon a time, this area was all open

Elephant parade outside the chalets at the Addo Elephant National Park

bush – the last refuge of many wild animals, driven away from their traditional grazing lands by the humans creeping up from the Cape. Then, when the Sundays River Valley was developed in the early 1900s, local farmers started nagging the government to get rid of the destructive elephantine nuisance that was getting in the way of their agricultural activities.

In 1919, a professional hunter was called in and he went on to kill 120 elephants in 12 months of concentrated slaughter. Only 15 elephants survived. The farmers were delighted, and encouraged the final extermination of the remaining elephants from the region.

Thankfully, by this time, public opinion had changed, and a tiny little reserve was set up on

Addo Elephant National Park

Accommodation at Addo is a bit of a mixed bag. The main rest camp is large, and there are some old chalets and some new ones. The old chalets are a little bit grotty, but the new ones are spic and span. The real beauty, however, is found outside the bungalow walls, and you should try and get a chalet on the outer perimeter of the camp. There's no better way to enjoy a sundowner than sitting on your stoep and watching, as an afternoon procession of elephants strolls casually past.

The rest camp also offers a swimming pool, a well-stocked shop selling gifts and supplies, and a restaurant which serves pretty good food. The restaurant is also notable as the final resting place of 'Hapoor'. This famously grumpy bull elephant used to rule the park in the 1950s. As he grew older, however, he grew increasingly curmudgeonly, until he finally became a danger to visitors and had to be put down.

His colossal head is now stuffed and mounted above the fireplace in the restaurant, and his giant trunk arches over the diners, making him an unavoidable talking point during dinner. He got his name, by the way, because a local farmer once tried to shoot him, but only managed to take a chunk (hap) out of his ear (oor). It is reported that Hapoor never forgot this act of violence, and it did not endear him to humans once the park was proclaimed.

Besides the obligatory game drives, there are several other activities you can do in the park, like guided walks, bird watching and horse rides. The horse rides are particularly memorable as they give you an opportunity to get really close to the elephants. There are two out-rides each day: inexperienced riders go out in the morning, keeping close to the fence to avoid trouble; and more capable riders go out in the afternoon, plunging into the bush to look for elephants. I would strongly advise riders to be realistic about their abilities.

Since I've done a couple of out-rides, I chose the afternoon excursion and went trotting off to check out the wildlife. Our expert guide, whose name is Story, spotted a herd of elephants in the distance and we walked slowly up to them, staring in well-deserved awe. Then, a nervous mother elephant decided she didn't like our horses so close to her calf, and started flapping her ears. At first, our guide thought this was just for show, but the elephant soon indicated that she wasn't joking and charged us. Story shouted 'Go!' and led the horses off in an unrestrained gallop. As we ran away, I could hear the heavy, thumping footsteps and loud trumpeting of the angry mamma at my back. It was fantastic.

After a short gallop, we stopped and turned around to get another look. The mother still wasn't happy, however, and charged us again. This time, we skedaddled, hearts pumping, over the grassy plains. I couldn't help shouting 'Yeee-hah', just once. When we were safely away, I asked Story if the elephants often charge like that. He said, 'Occasionally'. I then asked what would happen if one of us had fallen off. He looked at me for a moment, shrugged and said that he would go back to help. 'Help scoop up the pieces', I thought, as I kicked my horse into a canter and rode off into the sunset.

- Addo Elephant National Park: 042 233 0556/7 / www.addoelephantpark.com
- Zuurberg Mountain Inn: 042 233 0583
- Addo Area Tourist Info: 042 233 0040 / www.addopark.com

a sympathetic farmer's land to protect the critically endangered native elephant population. This reserve was declared a national park in 1931, so that the fragile elephant herd could be permanently protected from those local farmers who still wanted them gone.

So, for once, right prevailed over might and the elephants stayed put, restoring their numbers to become a sustainable breeding population once again. Today, Addo has grown in both hectares and stature to become one of South Africa's most important national parks.

Buoyed by its proximity to the Garden Route, and its malaria-free location, Addo has big plans to take on the supremacy of the Kruger Park in international travel itineraries. Recently, lions were reintroduced to Addo, after a 150-year absence from the region, and the World Wildlife Fund has granted the reserve $5 million to help buy up and rehabilitate adjoining farms. In the next few years, Addo plans to extend its boundaries all the way down to the sea, which will make it the second largest game reserve in the country.

It all sounds good to me. The more land we have set aside for conservation, the better. And besides, Addo is an excellent place to end your journey along the south-eastern seaboard of South Africa. It is a scenically diverse park, boasting the Big Five and a well-established tourist infrastructure. In addition to the lions, fresh elephant breeding stock has been introduced to revive the stagnant gene pool of the native Addo elephants, which have become so inbred that female elephants are inexplicably born without tusks. These new elephant herds are slowly being introduced into the vast new tracts of land that have recently been incorporated into the park's boundaries, and many exciting environmental developments are taking place on a daily basis.

DETOUR TO ZUURBERG MOUNTAIN PASS

If you feel like a drive outside the Addo National Park, exit the reserve gates and follow signs to the old gravel road up the Zuurberg Pass. This is a little-used mountain road with great views out over the countryside.

At the summit of the pass, you can enjoy a spot of tea at the historic Zuurberg Mountain Inn. This is a delightful old boarding house, with much of its colonial charm intact, despite its many incarnations. Once down the other side of the Zuurberg, you can continue on gravel to Somerset East, or you can head back to Addo by turning right onto a beautiful back road through the aloes, to rejoin the tarred N10 above the town of Paterson.

The Zuurberg Pass has a long history, and its dusty course bears testimony to the controversial ambush of Andries Stockenstrom during the Anglo-Xhosa Frontier Wars. It was also a main highway to the interior during the days of the Kimberley diamond rush.

Port Elizabeth Contacts:
- Shamwari Game Reserve: 042 203 1111
- Volkswagen Factory Tours – Uitenhage (by appointment): 041 994 4607

Cheerful art-deco decay in PE city centre

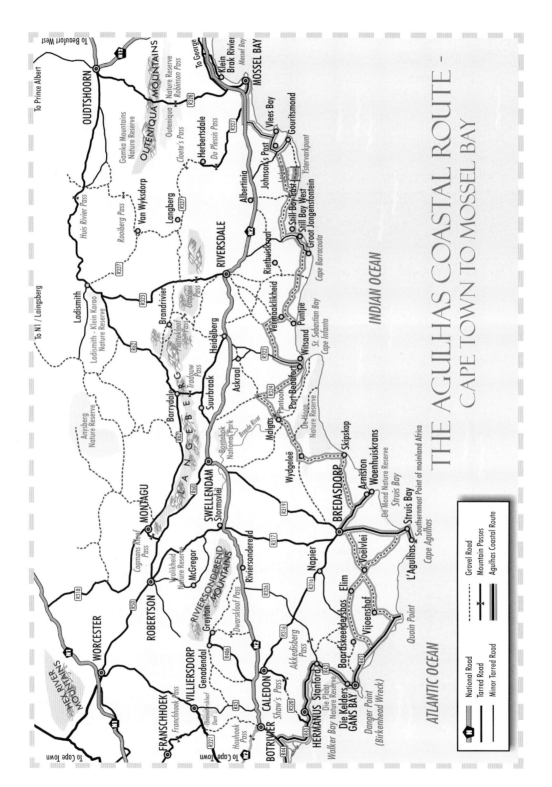

THE AGULHAS COASTAL ROUTE - CAPE TOWN TO MOSSEL BAY

Legend:
- National Road
- Tarred Road
- Minor Tarred Road
- Gravel Road
- Mountain Passes
- Agulhas Coastal Route

ATLANTIC OCEAN

INDIAN OCEAN

14. The Agulhas Coastal Route

ORIENTATION

The Agulhas Coastal Route is my unofficial designation for a very lovely, very lonely and very wild road that takes in the dramatic scenery around the southernmost tip of Africa. It does not boast the tremendous green mountains and lush farmlands of the N2, but it does contain some remarkable landscapes, fascinating little towns and isolated beaches.

Sections of this road are still untarred and this makes the route quite slow, but that is all part of its charm. So, if you are in a rush, stick to the N2. If, however, a leisurely road trip along dusty country lanes sounds appealing, this

A sand road slices through the Agulhas Coast

is a great route to follow. But, I would advise you to do this drive before it's too late. The government seems to be planning an all-asphalt link from Hermanus to Mossel Bay, along the coast.

I'm not sure whether this new road would be a good thing or a bad thing. A tarred road will certainly improve access to the region, and will also encourage more tourists to visit. However, everything in life comes at a cost and I'm afraid that a tarmac thoroughfare will destroy the character of this remote peninsula with its idiosyncratic towns. Still, *que sera sera* and, for the moment, the Agulhas Coastal Route is an entrancing journey through one of the less explored regions in SA.

As I was compiling this route from Cape Town to Mossel Bay, my self-imposed brief was to keep as close to the sea as the road would allow. This directive forced me to start my trip from Muizenberg, just outside Cape Town. From here, I took the R310, which runs between the top of False Bay and the bottom of the Cape Flats, towards Gordon's Bay *[see map in Chapter 6]*.

Alternatively, you can skip out this first bit and take the N2 straight to Gordon's Bay, where the Agulhas Route begins in earnest.

From Gordon's Bay, take the breathtaking R44, otherwise known as Clarence Drive. The R44 runs along the seaward cliffs from Gordon's Bay to Betty's Bay *[see map in Chapter 9]*.

From Betty's Bay, the R44 leads through the larger town of Kleinmond and continues along the Botriver Vlei, an attractive wetland that has been spoilt by the large golfing resort, which squats on the water's edge. At the head of the vlei, the R44 joins the R43 coming down from the N2.

If you are doing the circular 'R44/Houhoek/ Sir Lowry's' day drive from Cape Town, continue straight to rejoin the N2 [see Chapter 9]. Otherwise, turn right onto the R43 and drive on to Hermanus.

From Hermanus, follow the R43 around Die Plaat Nature Reserve and back to the sea at Gansbaai. From here, the road continues close to the coast, until it terminates at Quoin Bay. This latter part of the R43 is unexceptional, as the road runs between trees and sand dunes, which cut out any view of the sea. Turn-offs for a number of holiday resorts and caravan parks beckon from along this road, and each one bears a promising name, such as Pearly Beach, Uilenkraalsmond and Buffelsjagrivier.

So far, the Agulhas Coastal Route has been tarred, but to continue eastwards, you now have to leave the coast and hit one of the gravel roads which lead towards Bredasdorp. If you have the time, a detour to the nearby Moravian mission station of Elim is highly recommended.

From Bredasdorp, you have a number of choices. You can:
➡ Head north on the tarred R319 to the N2 and Swellendam [see Chapter 10].
➡ head north-west on the tarred R316 to Napier and Caledon [see Chapter 10].
➡ Head south on the R319 towards Struisbaai and the atmospheric Cape Agulhas. This road is a dead end, and you will have to return to Bredasdorp.
➡ Or take the rewarding detour to Arniston.

When you want to continue east along the Coastal Road, follow the gravel from Bredasdorp, past the De Hoop Nature Reserve, to Malgas. At Malgas, you have to cross the Breede River on the last man-drawn pont in the country.

Once you have crossed the Breede, the road splits. Keep right until you meet the R324. At this junction, the coastal road gets a little bit vague. If you've had enough, head back to the N2 by going left or straight; or turn right and return to the coast to check out Port Beaufort and Witsand.

From Witsand/Port Beaufort take the tarred R322 to the North. This road leads up to the N2, but there are a number of gravel roads to the right, which wind over the rocky coastal plains to Still Bay. If this sounds too tricky, turn right when you hit the N2, and then take the R305 down to Still Bay.

From Still Bay, follow the gravel road to the town of Gouritsmond. From here, you can return to the N2 on tar, or head towards the unfriendly, fenced and boomed town of Vleesbaai. This is the last stop before my Agulhas Coastal Route meets up with the N2 and terminates, just before Mossel Bay.

R310 FROM MUIZENBERG TO GORDON'S BAY

The Agulhas Coastal Route from Cape Town to Mossel Bay starts at Muizenberg, on the western shores of False Bay. When I was growing up, the whites-only beach stopped a few hundred meters outside of Muizenberg, and we weren't really encouraged to venture any further east on the coastal road through the fringes of the Cape Flats. Now, such petty distinctions have been removed, and the R310 is once again open to all.

But the R310 is still a wild road. Large white sand dunes, held together by creeping vegetation, pile up on either side of the road, threatening to swamp the little strip of tar. The wind blows. The seagulls shriek. The sun shines brightly on the muddy waves of the ocean. Great stuff!

On the landward side of the dunes, the road runs along the southern edge of the Cape Flats. The tightly packed housing complexes of Mitchell's Plain can be seen reaching down towards the sea, and substantial road works are proof that these residential developments are moving ever closer to the coast. It seems inevitable that, one day, the dunes will be covered in concrete.

As you drive along the R310, you will see several Eastern-themed beach pavilions leading onto the sands of False Bay. With their minarets, onion domes and garish canopies, these bits of Oriental whimsy were all built in the days when this was the non-white bathing area of Cape Town. Those days have blessedly come to an end, and today the pavilions offer visitors of all persuasions the requisite ice-creams and hot dogs that a beach visit demands.

After a while, the housing developments disappear, and the wind-swept sands of the Wolfgat Nature Reserve rear up out of the road. This reserve was set up to protect the fragile Strandveld eco-system, and it is the largest protected area in the Cape Metropole. This is a particularly dramatic stretch, as the road runs along low cliffs, which tumble down to the empty beach below. From here, the R310 veers inland to join the N2 to Gordon's Bay.

R44 / CLARENCE DRIVE
Once you arrive at Gordon's Bay, you have a choice: you can either go over the Hottentots Holland mountains via Sir Lowry's Pass, or you go around the side of mountains by taking the outstanding marine drive which clings to the sea-facing mountain slopes. This gorgeous scenic road is the R44, also known as Clarence Drive.

The road is named after 'Jack' Clarence 'whose vision, faith and determination helped to bring the road into being', or so sayeth the commemorative plaque at the side of the road. In reality, Clarence's motives were a little less philanthropic.

Jack Clarence was a real estate speculator, and his Cape Hangklip Beach Estate Company had big plans to develop the coast around Betty's Bay. Eager to make his little scheme more appealing to the people of Cape Town, he pushed the government to build a road along the coast so that the driving distance from Cape Town to his proposed development would be reduced. Luckily, the housing development never materialised, but the road did. And, for that, I am absurdly grateful.

Words can hardly do justice to Clarence Drive. It is a superlative trip along silver-green mountain sides that plunge down to a roiling

Koeël Bay on the R44 Scenic Drive

sea. The road is scenically thrilling throughout and the vista over Koeël Baai (Bullet or Cannonball Bay), with the dark sea under a soaring, boulder-strewn mountain amphitheatre, is unforgettable. Thoughtfully, the road builders constructed many parking areas along the road where you can pull over for a better look.

After you round Koeël Bay, the lopsided bulk of the Hangklip (Hanging Rock) becomes apparent. This is the geographical feature that gives this section of the coast its name. From here, the road moves inland and leads on, towards Hermanus.

Despite all the praise I may lavish on Clarence Drive, I also have two words of warning. First, Clarence Drive is a very popular day trip for Capetonians and tourists alike. On weekends and public holidays, you might find the route very busy. If it is, a degree of patience will be required. It is not a road built for overtaking, nor is it a road to be rushed. My advice would be to pack a picnic and get into the spirit of things. If you can't beat them, join them.

Secondly, while the beaches along Clarence Drive look inviting, heavy currents make bathing a little bit unpredictable. Fisherman, who are very fond this section of the Hangklip coast, should also be careful as rogue waves have been known to sweep anglers off the rocks. If you are especially keen on getting wet, however, the wild water off the coast contains some coral reefs, and several scuba diving sites have been established.

CAPE HANGKLIP – ROOIELS BAY – PRINGLE BAY

Once you round the headland of Spark's Bay, the visual pyrotechnics of Clarence Drive start to subside. From this point, the road levels out and leads through a number of scattered holiday villages. This land was once part of the Cape Hangklip Beach Estate Company's holdings, and one can only praise the gods of nature that this development concern went bust before it could louse up the coastline.

As it is, the holiday homes and retirement villas are already starting to dominate the bushy fynbos, and the once dusty side roads are starting to sprout coffee shops and other tourist amenities. But it's all good, as long as a degree of restraint is exercised and massive housing developments are curtailed.

A fisherman strides across the beach at Pringle Bay

After you drive through the quiet village of Rooiels, you can take a short detour down to Pringle Bay. This blossoming town has a spectacular location in a small bay wedged between mountains, sky and the silver sea. New holiday homes are growing at an alarming rate in Pringle Bay, but visitors will enjoy the small shopping centres that are taking root between the beach and the main road.

At one time, you could follow a sand road from Pringle Bay to the lighthouse at Cape Hangklip, and round the peninsula to rejoin the R44 just below Betty's Bay. You can still drive down to the lighthouse, which is situated on a lovely strip of deserted beach, but the road has been closed beyond this point, for no discernible reason, and you will have to turn around and return to Pringle Bay.

BETTY'S BAY – KLEINMOND

Betty's Bay is another collection of beach cottages that is slowly growing into a town. It has two good attractions, though, and both give the traveller ample opportunities to stop the car and stretch their legs.

First up is the African Penguin colony at Stony Point. This is one of two penguin breeding colonies on the Cape mainland – the other is at Boulders Beach, near Simon's Town – and it is fun for kids to walk around, spotting the penguins.

Formerly known as Jackass Penguins on account of their braying call, these small, waddling waiters of the water have been renamed 'African Penguins' so that their feelings don't get hurt by those cruel zoologists. Political correctness and environmental awareness have finally joined forces, and as a result, the Jackass Penguin has become extinct. The human species of jackass, I regret to report, is still alive and well.

The other big attraction in Betty's Bay is the Harold Porter Botanical Gardens. This beautiful park was established on the slopes of the Kogelberg Mountains to protect and showcase the profuse world of Cape fynbos, and it is a great place to stop.

The town of Kleinmond is the next settlement on the R44, and it boasts the customary coffee shops, curio stands and the 'largest iron museum in Africa'! The five-star Arabella hotel, spa and golf estate can be found nearby.

Harold Porter Botanical Gardens

The Harold Porter Gardens, near Betty's Bay, are located in the Kogelberg Biosphere, at the heart of the Cape fynbos region. The grounds are interlaced with a lovely matrix of walkways which lead over bridges and past stupendous fynbos installations that will dazzle the eyes.

For the more adventurous walkers, there are also two mountain trails which are worth exploring. The Disa Trail runs up a kloof in the Kogelberg mountains, and the walk is spectacular when the orange Disa orchids are in bloom from mid-December to mid-January.

The Leopard's Kloof trail, however, is the real highlight of the gardens. This forty-five-minute walk leads up a steep river valley to an enchanting waterfall, hidden away near the top of the ravine. It is a well-constructed trail that has it all: grand views, a tumbling river cascade and thick indigenous forests. And, to top it all off, the walk culminates at a deep, dreamy swimming hole (complete with a tall, mossy waterfall). The path is very well maintained and active kids will love clambering up the rough-hewn ladders that lead over the big boulders and huge tree trunks which litter the kloof.

Harold Porter Botanical Gardens also has a garden restaurant and a nursery where you can buy plants. Get keys for the longer hikes at reception before you enter the Gardens.
- *Harold Porter Botanical Gardens: 028 272 9311*
- *National Botanical Institute website: www.nbi.ac.za*

FYNBOS AND THE CAPE FLORAL REGION

Technically, the term 'fynbos' only refers to fine-leaved plants, such as the various Erica species. Unofficially, however, the name has come to include the entire Cape Floral Kingdom, which includes Proteas, Rhus trees and Dune Milkwoods. Collectively, these plants form the smallest and most biologically diverse of the world's seven floral kingdoms.

The fynbos region has earned this distinction because it contains over 8 500 species of plants, all living in a tiny area of 90 000 square kilometres. 70% of these species are found nowhere else on Earth. In fact, the Cape Floral Kingdom is as biologically diverse as the entire continent of Europe.

The endless adaptation of the fynbos is a result of its determination to survive in a difficult micro-climate. Strong winds, winter rainfall and the nutritionally poor soil of the south-western Cape have all combined to create an unlikely home for this hardy family of plants, which grows like a blanket from the foothills to the sea. The fynbos has even adapted to the regular fires that sweep through the region every few years, and the heat of a passing fire is often required to release the seeds that will spawn a new generation.

Unfortunately, fynbos is very susceptible to foreign vegetation and can easily be pushed out by more assertive species. Rampant housing developments, pollution and wanton destruction of the fynbos has also taken its toll. Luckily,

Fynbos blooms in the Kogelberg Biosphere

fynbos is now heavily protected, and you can be fined for illegal picking and poaching of the plants. Even better is the news that the Cape Floral Kingdom is about to be declared a World Heritage Site of Outstanding Natural Significance, and this recognition will help conservation efforts enormously.

HERMANUS

The holiday headquarters of the Overberg Coast is unquestionably Hermanus. It is the largest town in the area and the local commercial hub. Despite its relatively large size, however, Hermanus is a reasonably pretty agglomeration of houses, hotels and hills, focused around the old harbour. Hermanus is also the place where many Captonians flee to in December, to get away from all the Inlanders.

Hermanus

Hermanus is a big holiday town, and is at its busiest in December. There are hundreds of B+Bs, lodges, backpackers and hotels to choose from. The city centre is full of restaurants and cafés. You can also try dining in their unique cave restaurant.

Hermanus has several excellent beaches, all highly rated for cleanliness and beauty. Unfortunately, only penguins and surfers can swim in the frigid waters, but the beaches are great for sun-tanning and building sandcastles. Nearby Onrus Lagoon and beach are also popular, with paddle boats, a fast-food kiosk and a restaurant with lovely views.

Hermanus has lots of outdoor activities for the non-slacker, such as horse riding, boating, diving, fishing and harbour cruises. The Rotary Club of Hermanus has also built an excellent scenic drive up to the top of a high hill outside town, and the views from the summit are outstanding. The road is tarred to the main view-point, and continues as gravel until reaching a dead end a few k's further on.

- *Hermanus Tourist Info and Whale Hotline:*
  028 312 2629
- *www.hermanus.co.za*

A highlight of Hermanus is the cliff walk; an outstanding promenade that runs along the rocks, looking out to sea. A casual stroll along this craggy parapet, with the waves dashing themselves on the splintered stone below, is good for the soul and the body. Besides, it's much better to look at the Hermanus sea than it is to swim in its icy waters.

The town's centre is focused around the old Market Square, across from the harbour. This area is lined with shops and restaurants (including all the big franchises). Estate agents, bookshops, surfware stores, curio emporiums and lots of other retail merchandise is freely available in this compact, pedestrian-friendly environment, and a regular flea-market is held across from the harbour entrance. Two museums (De Wet's Huis Photo Museum and Old Harbour Museum) can be found nearby.

Hermanus is also famous for its whales. Every year, from July to November, these aircraft-carriers of the mammal world swim along the cold waters of the Agulhas Coast as part of their breeding cycle. The Whale Route, which stretches from Hermanus to Plett, offers good whale-viewing opportunities both from the shore, and from chartered vessels that go out to sea. Hermanus, as self-appointed headquarters of the Whale Route, has even employed an official Whale Crier who clangs up and down the main road if there is a significant whale sighting.

The cliff walk at Hermanus

Stanford

From the urban delights of Hermanus, the R43 continues along the coast until it is deflected inland by the pristine coastal dunes of Die Plaat nature reserve. It then passes through the small town of Stanford, notable for the Birkenhead micro-brewery, which might be enough to persuade the thirsty motorist to stop for a cold one.

Stanford also has one of South Africa's few undeveloped market squares that is still regularly used by the local community. The buildings around this square are evocative of a bygone age, and parts of the village have been declared a national conservation area.

GANS BAY / GANSBAAI

I thought Gansbaai was a dreary-looking town. The day that I was there, steel-grey clouds hung over the industrial harbour and a cold wind was blowing off the sea. Sure, the main street had the usual stalwarts of a small town (cafe, take-away joint, video shop, pancake parlour), but there didn't seem to be any life in the place. Furthermore, it has no beachfront and you have to drive a way out of town if you want to swim in the sea.

But Gansbaai has an ace up its sleeve. It is the shark capital of South Africa. Now, I will not pass judgement on the practice of chumming the waters to attract sharks for the tourists, nor will I offer my opinion that anyone who wants to see a shark should stick to watching wildlife documentaries, and leave the real things alone. The only opinion I will hazard on this matter is that, if you want to dive with, fish for, or cruise among sharks, then Gansbaai is your best bet.

But it has other attractions besides the Great White: fishermen can get permits for perlemoen (abalone) and crayfish; hiking trails ramble through the surrounding countryside; there are several stone age cave sites in the area; and guided eco-tourism routes through the fynbos can be arranged.

The Birkenhead

Just outside Gansbaai, there is a gravel detour down to Danger Point. This suitably named headland is where the famous Birkenhead was wrecked in 1852. The Birkenhead was a ship carrying British reinforcements to the embattled Eastern Frontier of South Africa. Unfortunately, before she reached her destination, she struck an uncharted rock and quickly started to sink.

Much to the crew's dismay, many of the ship's lifeboats were found to be inoperable. To make matters worse, the seas were infested with sharks, and clinging clumps of seaweed seemed intent on dragging anyone who jumped overboard down beneath the waves. Escape from Neptune's clutches thus seemed highly improbable so, in the face of this disaster, the soldiers were called on deck and ordered into parade formation. If they were going to meet their maker, they would do so while standing to attention.

Out of 638 people on board the Birkenhead, 193 survived (including all the women and children). In fact, this was the first time that the cry 'women and children first' rang out over the creaking deck of a sinking ship. Those who lived to tell the tragic tale of the Birkenhead were quick to laud the tremendous discipline and fortitude with which the doomed troops met their watery fate. The story of the 'Birkenhead Drill' was thereafter heralded as the apotheosis of the British stiff upper lip, and became part of the Victorian military ethos. Silly sods.

Taking in the view of Gans Bay harbour

The trim, whitewashed houses of Elim Mission Station

ELIM

Like Genadendal [see Chapter 10], Elim is a mission station, belonging to the Moravian Church. Unlike Genadendal, however, Elim is still very much as it was when first founded in 1824, on the farm Vogelstruiskraal. All the land in town still belongs to the church, and homes are given only to paid-up members of the congregation.

With one foot still kept resolutely in the past, visiting Elim is like stepping into a time warp. The small town is laid out in several neat, parallel rows. There are no shops, chain stores or take-out joints. The houses are all simple, white-washed cottages with thatched roofs and jumbled gardens of wildflowers. While many of these homes were built quite recently, residents can only choose from one of three approved house plans, which date back about one hundred years, and this architectural restriction helps keep the town authentic.

As is to be expected, the focus of the town is the old church, which has pride of place in the centre of the settlement. This large but unfussy building is the spiritual home of this tight-knit congregation, and it boasts a lovely pipe organ and two ancient tower clocks that are driven by a single shaft. The mechanics of this time piece are Swiss and date back 235 years, making it the oldest working clock in South Africa.

Our tour guide, Emile, took us inside the church and explained that the congregation is seated in sections according to gender, marital status and age. This is so that the pastor can tell at a glance which members of the congregation are in attendance, and which are bunking. He also told us that marrying out of the community isn't really a problem as people tend to 'take a sheep from their own kraal'.

Next to the church is the beautiful old parsonage, and a leafy greensward surrounded by flowers and gently decaying buildings. An irrigation furrow leads to the old watermill, which has been restored to good working condition with the help of the Rembrandt Foundation, and is once again capable of crushing the community's corn and wheat. Nearby, a new library and day-care centre are evidence that things are changing in the little town, but the corner café where a young Emile bought his chips and sweets still stands proud. It is the only shop in town.

Nevertheless, like an advancing storm, the modern world is coming to Elim. A tarred road is currently being built that will link Gansbaai with Elim and Bredasdorp. This is part of the proposed asphalt link that will make the Agulhas Coast more accessible to tourists. Emile was a little bit concerned that the arrival of the road will destroy Elim's character and independence. I tend to share his fears.

And it's not just the new road that is ringing alarm bells. The regional council installed sewerage and water mains about six years ago, and the congregants of Elim are worried that the local government is about to demand that the town be handed over to them. This would cause problems for the desperately poor community members, who are given free housing in exchange for their meagre annual church fees.

Furthermore, if the land were taken away from the church, outsiders would be allowed to move into the peaceful valley and start building garish holiday homes wherever they liked. This would be the end of Elim's voluntary isolation, and the death of the town's unique personality. I think the whole place should be declared a national Heritage Site, before it's too late.

At the moment, tourist facilities are basic in Elim, which is only appropriate as it is still a working mission station and not a theme park. Nevertheless, there is a coffee shop, a corner café and a community-run B+B in the old parsonage.

When you get to Elim, stop at the small tourist info office and arrange a guided tour around town. This is not only more appropriate, it is also much more informative as the guides are knowledgeable and enthusiastic

about their village. While you are in the area, you might also want to take a walk through the nearby Geelkop Nature Reserve, which has several unique species of fynbos found nowhere else on Earth.

BREDASDORP

At first glance, there ain't much happening in Bredasdorp, especially on a Sunday. It's a large, dusty place, and it functions mainly as the gateway to Cape Agulhas, about 38km to the south, and Arniston, 25km to the south-east. But there *is* life in Bredasdorp, if you feel like looking.

The Shipwreck Museum is one unique attraction. It has an eclectic collection of period furniture, glass bottles and a separate maritime wing, full of ships' figureheads and other artefacts from the many vessels that came to a sodden end on the treacherous rocks and reefs of the Agulhas coastline. Sailing enthusiasts will be delighted by the exhibit. Those who are not so keen on boats would do better to visit the nearby centre of town for a cup of coffee and some *koek*.

The main Cape Agulhas tourism bureau is in the centre of Bredasdorp, and there is a Cape Nature Conservation booking office upstairs. From Bredasdorp, a tarred road leads South to Struisbaai and the Cape Agulhas headland.

Democracy flourishes on the farm fences of the Overberg

STRUIS BAY / STRUISBAAI – CAPE AGULHAS

Little more than a collection of fisherman's cottages, Struisbaai is located around a picturesque little bay, dotted with small sailing vessels bobbing in the sea. The houses are loosely arranged around the harbour, and tourist facilities are limited. A campsite, a couple of coffee shops and a general dealer are about all you'll find here. Do note, however, that there is not much else after Struisbaai and very few facilities at Cape Agulhas, so you'd better get what you need while you are in town.

The road from Struisbaai to Cape Agulhas is great. Humble cottages line one side of the road and, on the other side, the coastline is a jumble of green grass, ochre rocks and brooding sea. After a few k's the cottages stop and the iconic, candy-striped lighthouse of Cape Agulhas looms large on top of a small rise. The lighthouse can be toured, and also contains a museum.

Once past the lighthouse, keep following the signs for Cape Agulhas. This will lead you to a parking area and, from here, it's a short walk to the southernmost point of mainland Africa.

Although it is not as obviously dramatic as Cape Point, Cape Agulhas has a low-key power all its own and it's a very rewarding destination for any traveller to reach.

When you step out of the car, you will be struck by the austere beauty of the scene, compared to the hyperbolical grandeur of Cape Point. There are no mountains here, no curio shops, no restaurants and no grand walkways. Nevertheless, Cape Agulhas seems to resonate with the weight of the continent balanced on its shoulders. Turn your back to the land, and you are surrounded by sea and clouds and gulls and noisy silence. Turn away from the ocean, and you can imagine that you are gazing up the entire bulk of Africa, all the way to Cairo.

To emphasise the point, a concrete plinth has been erected which indicates your position at the end of the Earth, and the cartographic separation between Indian and Atlantic Ocean has been clearly signposted.

This cape was originally called L'Agulhas, after the Portuguese word for 'needle', as Bartolomeu Dias is said to have noted that the compass needle had moved several degrees once

The southernmost point of mainland Africa, Cape Agulhas

The day's catch dries on the washing line, Kassiesbaai

they rounded the headland, indicating that they had begun to travel northwards again.

But is Cape Agulhas really the southernmost point of Africa? Well, almost. Strictly speaking, the small South African territory of Marion Island in the Antarctic Ocean is the southernmost African landmass, but you would have to be a real stickler to deny Cape Agulhas its claim on the title. In my mind, this lonely, empty peninsula is the perfect culmination for the African continent, and the oceans seem to roar with approbation.

ARNISTON

Although it's on a dead-end road, the detour to Arniston is worthwhile. This tiny seaside holiday village boasts a lovely cliff walk along the sea, the roomy Waenhuiskrans Cave (which can only be reached at low tide), a nice beach, and a refurbished old hotel with al fresco dining on a marvellous patio.

The highlight of Arniston, however, is Kassiesbaai, an old fishing village that has been declared a national monument. This once-typical collection of simple, whitewashed cottages has been home to the coloured

fishermen and their families for over a hundred years. Most of the other villages of this ilk were destroyed by the apartheid regime, intent on separating the whites from their colourful compatriots. But, miraculously, Kassiesbaai somehow managed to escape the bulldozers and still stands as a testament to passive resistance.

Each day, just as the one before, the fishermen of Kassiesbaai go out to catch their evening meal and, in the evenings, the washing lines are often studded with glassy-eyed fish, hung out to dry in the sun. Kids play in the untarred streets and the old folk trundle around, chatting and cackling with their neighbours. All in all, it's a wonderful place in which to wander, and the local craft centre will appreciate your custom.

DE HOOP NATURE RESERVE

This large coastal reserve is administered by CNC, and it is a little-known gem with much to offer the visitor. The best way to explore this rugged and deserted coastline is to walk the three-day Whale Trail. But even if you are car-bound, many of the park's highlights are still accessible.

The walkway over the dunes of De Hoop Nature Reserve

Do note, however, that the last 50km to De Hoop are on gravel, and this may dissuade many from visiting. For those who do tackle the dirt, the rewards are ample.

The highlight of the park, and the first stop for any day visitor, is the monumental sand dunes that shoulder their way out of the plains and form a huge amphitheatre of chalk-white sand that sweeps down to a solemn sea. Since De Hoop is quite out of the way, this magnificent spectacle is not likely to be spoilt by a horde of holiday makers and, as you stumble down the long slope to the beach, you will probably find that the only signs of human habitation are the footprints that you leave behind in the silky sand.

De Hoop also has a rest camp for overnighting, and a game-viewing drive which usually offers up a herd of Eland and other ruminants. You can also drive down to the Sout River Mouth, which has created an extensive wetland with abundant birdlife.

MALGAS

Malgas is the only place south of the N2 where the aptly named Breede River can be crossed. But this is no ordinary crossing. Malgas is the home of the last man-drawn pont in South Africa. It's an extraordinary system, which has been in operation for many years, and is a unique, if sobering, transport experience.

The pont takes only two cars at a time, and is powered by nothing more than a cable, some chains and two sinewy men in orange overalls. This is how it works: A thick cable is suspended across the river and, once the cars are loaded, the two human motors take up their positions on either end of the pont. Both the men wear a harness, slung over their shoulders, which is attached to a thin, dangling chain. At a predetermined signal, the men flick these chains around the thick cable, take up the slack, and start to walk forward. Once the inertia is overcome, they continue walking slowly along the pont, dragging the heavy load across the river by the strength of their backs.

When one man reaches the end of the pont, he expertly unwinds his harness chain and walks to the opposite end of the floating platform. Once in position, he slings his harness chain around the thick cable again, and carries on pulling. And so they go, back and forth, until they have pulled the pont across the river. At the other side, they unload their cargo, take on two new vehicles, and pull the pont back across the Breede. The pont operates eight hours a day and costs R15 per vehicle.

This pont is a throwback to the days when

Manpower draws the Malgas pont across the Breede River

Malgas was the inland depot of the mighty Barry and Nephews trading empire, based in Swellendam. Once the Barry empire collapsed, Malgas fell into disrepair. Today, there is only a hotel, a small country store and a campsite in Malgas, but it is a serene and beautiful place, with gorgeous views out over the quietly impressive Breede River. If you are looking for a sedate getaway, Malgas could just be it. You can also hire a houseboat at Malgas and cruise along the Breede, fishing and swimming to your heart's content.

WITSAND – PORT BEAUFORT

Once a bustling harbour for the Barry and Nephews trading concern, Port Beaufort is now a humble gathering of cottages and fishermen's shacks, scattered around a pretty bay. Facilities for visitors are limited, but there is a seafood restaurant on the beach front, which is sure to offer the very freshest fish, and one or two small coffee and craft shops.

The real attraction here is the quiet coastal atmosphere and the vast white beach of Witsand, which stretches off into infinity.

Witsand is also known as the Whale Nursery of the Overberg coast, as many of these mammoth creatures calve in the cold waters off the bay. In season, Witsand boasts the highest concentration of Southern Right Whales on the South African coast, and this population seems to be increasing at a healthy 7% per annum. In 2002, 117 adult whales and 49 calves were counted in St Sebastian Bay alone.

Other kinds of marine life also thrive in the bay, and fishermen will be kept very busy hauling their catch out of the choppy waters. Charters and other fishing necessities are available. The tiny church on the outskirts of town was built by the Barry Dynasty, and is now a national monument.

STILL BAY / STILBAAI

The main appeal of Still Bay is its outstanding beach – a long, sheltered stretch of sand that seems to run for miles in either direction of the Goukou (formerly the Kafferkuils) river mouth. Still Bay is quite a large holiday town, certainly the largest since Hermanus, with several shopping centres, restaurants and the obligatory surf-ware shops.

Various nature reserves and quiet country villages can be visited in the area. The fishing is good and watersports are abundant. If you are historically minded, check out the ancient *Strandloper* fish traps, which are still maintained and used by the locals. These fish traps are visible only at low tide.

GOURITSMOND

Gouritsmond is another small fishing town with a pretty beach, a couple of shops and an exceptional location. It is the place where the long and winding Gourits River finally meets the sea.

The Gourits River is one of South Africa's more interesting waterways. It runs through several different biomes, and supports an amazing range of biodiversity. There is even a plan to create the Gourits River Mega-park, which would stretch from the river's source near

A windy laundry day at Kassiesbaai

Dwyka on the N1, all the way through the Klein Karoo to Gouritsmond. It's a huge undertaking, and hundreds of local farmers will have to get involved to make the scheme successful. But the fact that they are already talking about this twenty-year conservation project fills one with hope for the future.

Another interesting thing about the village is that it was once the home of South Africa's main nuclear testing facility. This hush-hush site was situated between Still Bay and Gouritsmond and, when the facility was quietly closed down in the last decades of the 20th century, a number of private land holders were allowed to buy up the land.

One of these was a Mr Rein, who established the Rein Nature Reserve on a lovely chunk of unspoiled coastline. The reserve welcomes day visitors, as well as overnight guests, and has all the facilities and activities you would expect. Unfortunately, Rein and other private landholders have uncharitably (and perhaps illegally) built gates across the beautiful gravel road that runs along the coast.

This is a great pity because the narrow sand road along the sea is quite superb. It runs so close to the ocean that the spray from the rocks will fleck your windscreen and, at times, the water almost reaches the gravel causeway. The deserted, rocky coastline is almost ominous along this road, and old fishermen's shacks (some abandoned, some restored) rear out of the fynbos, adding to the sense of abandonment. The eerie atmosphere of desolation is probably linked to those lost years when this whole section of the coast was closed off, so that the Nats could fool around with nuclear fission.

So, if you want to travel between Still Bay and Gouritsmond, do not take the coastal road marked on some road maps, as there is no thoroughfare. Instead, you will have to take the inland road which runs parallel to the coast.

VLEES BAY / VLEESBAAI

Vleesbaai really pissed me off. It's a pretty enough cluster of holiday homes built on the steep slopes of a small bay, but the clannish locals have recently turned their town into a gated community. Now, I am very familiar with enclosed communities on the urban streets of Joburg, but I wasn't prepared for an entire seaside village that has turned its back on the outside world. I didn't even know that was it legal to build a fence around an entire town, but that hasn't stopped the local xenophobes from cordoning off their village and employing a security guard to control the single access road in and out.

Unlike just about every other seaside town in South Africa, Vleesbaai is clearly a place that doesn't want visitors. There are no facilities here, no restaurants and no signs to the beach. Thankfully, South African law maintains that private beach ownership is illegal, and no one can build a fence across the sand. But the *verkrampte* residents of Vleesbaai have countered this ordinance by regulating access to the town itself. Sneaky, miserable bastards!

Agulhas Coast contacts:
- Kleinmond/Betty's Bay Tourist Info:
  028 271 5657
- Stanford Tourist Info: 028 341 0340
- Gansbaai Tourist Info: 028 384 1439
- Elim Tourist Info: 028 482 1806
- Cape Agulhas/Bredasdorp Tourist Info:
  028 424 2584
- www.capeagulhas.info
  www.capeagulhas.com
  www.lagulhas.co.za
- Cape Agulhas National Park and
  Lighthouse Museum: 028 435 6078/6222
- Malgas Hotel and River Cruises:
  028 542 1049
- The Arniston Hotel: 028 445 9000
- Witsand Tourist Info: 028 537 1010
  www.witsandtourism.co.za
- De Hoop Nature Reserve and Whale Trail
  bookings: 028 425 5020
- Rein's Nature Reserve: 028 754 1563
- Still Bay Tourist Info: 028 754 2602
  www.stilbaaitourism.co.za
- Oystercatcher Walking Trail (Mossel Bay
  to Gourits Mouth): 044 699 1204
- Gourits River Mega Park Tourism:
  044 279 1306/12/18
- Jeffrey's Bay Tourist Info: 042 293 2923
  www.jeffreysbay.info

Waiting for a soft-serve at Arniston Beach

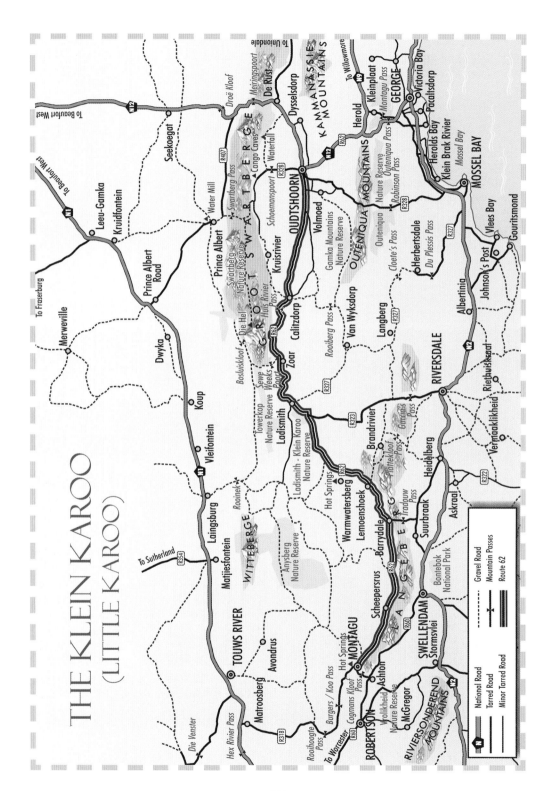

THE KLEIN KAROO
(LITTLE KAROO)

To Beaufort West

To Beaufort West

To Fraserburg

To Sutherland

To Worcester

To Uniondale

To Willowmore

Seekoegat

Leeu-Gamka

Kruidfontein

Merweville

Prince Albert Road

Dwyka

Koup

Vleifontein

Laingsburg

Matjiesfontein

TOUWS RIVER

Avondrus

Matroosberg

Die Venster

Hex River Pass

ROBERTSON

McGregor

Wolikheid Nature Reserve

Cogmans Kloof Pass

Burgers / Koo Pass

Ashton

MONTAGU

Scheepersrus

Hot Springs

Rooihoogte Pass

R318

R60

RIVIERSONDEREND MOUNTAINS

SWELLENDAM

Stormsvlei

R60

L A N G E B E R G

Bontebok National Park

Suurbraak

Askraal

Heidelberg

Barrydale

Tradouw Pass

Lemoenshoek

Warmwatersberg

Hot Springs

Ladismith - Klein Karoo Nature Reserve

Ladismith

Towerkop Nature Reserve

Anysberg Nature Reserve

Rooinek

W I T T E B E R G E

R62

Zoar

Seweweekspoort

Bosluiskloof

Die Hel

G R O O T S W A R T B E R G E

Swartberg Nature Reserve

Hot River Pass

Swartberg Pass

Water Mill

Prince Albert

R407

R328

OUDTSHOORN

Congo Caves

Waterfall

Schoemanspoort

Kruisrivier

Calitzdorp

R62

Rooiberg Pass

Van Wyksdorp

R327

Langberg

R327

Brandrivier

Plattekloof

Garcias Pass

R323

RIVERSDALE

N2

Albertinia

Vermaaklikheid

Rietbuiskaal

R327

Johnson's Post

Vlees Bay

Gouritsmond

Herbertsdale

Du Plessis Pass

Cloete's Pass

Gamka Mountains Nature Reserve

Volmoed

O U T E N I Q U A   M O U N T A I N S

Nature Reserve

Outeniqua Pass

Robinson Pass

R328

Herolds Bay

Klein Brak Rivier

Mossel Bay

MOSSEL BAY

Herold

Kleinplaat

Montagu Pass

GEORGE

Victoria Bay

Pacaltsdorp

K A M M A N A S S I E   M O U N T A I N S

N12

R62

Dysselsdorp

De Rust

Droë Kloof

Meiringspoort

174

Legend

National Road

Tarred Road

Minor Tarred Road

Gravel Road

Mountain Passes

Route 62

15. The Klein Karoo / Little Karoo

ORIENTATION

The Klein Karoo region runs from Montagu in the west to Oudtshoorn in the east. The main thoroughfare through the area is the R62, 'the longest wine route in the world', and it is about 250km long. Oudtshoorn is the unofficial capital of the Klein Karoo. Beyond Oudtshoorn, the R62 heads towards De Rust and down the Long Kloof to Humansdorp *[see Chapter 17]*.

From Oudtshoorn, you can:
➡ Go south on the N12, over the Outeniqua Mountains, to George and the Garden Route *[see Chapter 11]*. This will take you down the Outeniqua Pass *[see Chapter 17]*.
➡ Go north on the N12, through Meiringspoort *[see Chapter 18]*, to join the N1 at Beaufort West.
➡ Go north on the R328 towards the Cango Caves and the Swartberg Pass *[see Chapter 18]*. If you go over this grand pass, you will arrive in the delightful hamlet of Prince Albert. From here, the N1 highway is accessible on the R407 to Prince Albert Road. Alternatively, from this side of the Swartberg, you can do a round trip back to Oudtshoorn by taking the R407 to De Rust. This charming road joins up with the N12, and returns to Oudtshoorn via the grand Meiringspoort river pass *[see Chapter 18]*.
➡ Take the R328, down Robinson Pass to Mossel Bay *[see Chapter 10]*.
➡ Or you can turn west, towards Cape Town, by taking the R62 to Calitzdorp.

From Calitzdorp, you can leave the beaten track for an epic detour over the gravel Rooiberg Pass. This road doesn't lead anywhere specific, but it is utterly unspoilt and has

A burbling causeway on the Paardebont road

fantastic views on both sides. You can also reach the Rooiberg Pass from the Volmoed road, outside of Oudtshoorn. To do this, head past the tiny *dorp* of Volmoed and turn off onto a gravel track marked 'Paardebont'. This isolated road is shown on some maps, but only as a dead-end. The truth is that the road continues through dozens of farm gates before joining up with the Rooiberg Pass road. It's a haunting drive, and well worth the effort, but a solid suspension and good ground clearance is preferable. You'll also need time and a sense of adventure, as the possibility of getting lost is quite high.

At Zoar, further along the R62, you can turn off at the sign for Seweweekspoort. This is a spectacular but little-used access route through the Swartberg, into the Great Karoo. The gravel road eventually joins the N1 at Laingsburg *[see Chapter 18]*.

The R62 continues, over the beguiling Huis Rivier Pass, to Ladismith.

From here, the R62 leads through several other small towns until it reaches Montagu. Many alluring gravel roads branch off from this part of the R62, linking the farmlands with the main road, and these can be explored at your leisure. Cape Nature Conservation also has several reserves in the area.

From Montagu, you can:
➤ Take the beautiful R318 through the colourful Koo valley to join the N1 at Matroosberg, just above the Hex River Pass. This road takes in the lovely Burger's (or Koo) Pass and the Rooihoogte Pass, as it leads through a fertile fruit-growing area, dotted with farm stalls. From the Koo valley, there are also popular tractor trips up the Langeberg, which include a picnic or a *potjie* at the summit.
➤ take Cogmans Kloof *[see Chapter 16]* to Ashton and Robertson.
➤ From Ashton, you can turn east on the R60 to go to Swellendam *[see Chapter 10]*; or you can turn west on the R60 to go to Robertson.
➤ From Robertson, you can take the detour to the town of McGregor; or you continue with the R60 to reach the N1 at Worcester. From here you can return to Cape Town. The full story of the N1 will be covered in another book.

THE WORLD OF THE KLEIN KAROO

The Klein Karoo is a strange land, somewhat dry, somewhat fertile; a landscape of quiet delights, sandwiched between two great mountain ranges. For years, this part of the Western Cape was forlorn and forgotten by travellers, but now it is slowly gaining popularity, and with good reason.

The Klein Karoo may not boast the ceaseless fertility of the Garden Route, but it is a beautiful region with its own subtle charms. With its russet soil and red rocks, this is the kind of place that sorts the beach bunnies from the desert dreamers.

The Klein Karoo is actually a large valley, isolated from the coast by a line of mountains to the South, and cut off from the vast interior of southern Africa by the Swartberg to the north. At their narrowest point, the Klein Karoo plains are only a couple of kilometres across.

This is a land of heat and dust and details: small farmsteads simmering under the hot sun; corrugated iron roofs, glinting next to hardy vineyards; querulous ostriches dipping their heads over the barbed wire boundary fences; and small towns, each offering their own variation of down-home country comfort.

The Klein Karoo valley was first settled by white farmers in the late 18th century, as the trekboers trickled into the region and slowly spread along its dusty *leegtes*. At first, the farmers either entered through Cogmans Kloof, near Montagu, or over Attaquas Kloof from Mossel Bay. Later, several other routes were pioneered over the Outeniqua mountains from Oudtshoorn to George.

OUDTSHOORN

The unofficial capital of the Klein Karoo is Oudtshoorn. Once a small town in the middle of nowhere, Oudtshoorn became a booming metropolis in the early 1900s thanks to ostrich feathers. The elegant plumage on this distinctly inelegant bird became so popular with stylish European society that, for a short time, ostrich feathers were worth their weight in gold.

The ostrich is an ancient bird, thought to originate in Asia perhaps as long as 20 million years ago. Ostriches migrated into Africa around a million years ago and spread down the continent, moving about in large, strutting herds. From these wild ostriches came the meat, feathers, leather and impossibly large

Oudtshoorn

There are several ostrich ranches around Oudtshoorn, and all offer tours and opportunities for visitors to get up close and personal with these ungainly birds. Some farms encourage ostrich rides and even ostrich races. These activities are certainly not illegal, but many animal-rights activists have pointed out that the anatomy of an ostrich is not really built for carrying human cargo, and your little joy ride could snap their powerful legs.

If you would like to explore the human side of the feather boom, a walking tour booklet is available from the museums and info centre, which will guide you through the historical homes and buildings of old Oudtshoorn.

The beautiful C P Nel Museum, formerly the high school, has an excellent series of exhibits on feathers, fashion, ostriches and local authors (such as Pauline Smith). Of specific interest is the reinstallation of an old synagogue, built when the town supported a large Jewish population, which earned it the nickname 'Jerusalem of the East'.

An annex to the C P Nel Museum is the Le Roux townhouse, situated a couple of blocks away. This perfect little house museum is lovingly furnished in period style, and the enthusiastic guides will give you a pretty good idea of how the wealthy lived their life in the 'good old days'. When we visited, my parents recognised some of the fixtures from their childhood homes. If only my parents were as well-preserved as the townhouse!

Other interesting buildings to check out include Forster's Manor (also known as Forster's Folly). This is a superb example of a restored Feather Palace, originally built in 1902, and visitors are welcome to have a look around. It offers luxurious accommodation in eight en suite rooms and it is run by the local hotel school.

If you are a scholar of Afrikaner culture (and who isn't?!), drive to the other side of town to visit Arbeidsgenot. This is the home of C J Langenhoven, who wrote the original words of 'Die Stem' and several other much loved Afrikaans works of poetry and literature. Incidentally, the music to the dolorous half of our national anthem was written by the NGK Reverend De Villiers of Simon's Town.

Close to Oudtshoorn, in the foothills of the towering Swartberg Mountains, are the justifiably famous Cango Caves. Sixty minute tours through these dripping limestone caverns leave on the hour from nine to four, and a special ninety-minute Adventure Tour leaves at 09:30 and 15:30. The latter is recommended only for people who are NOT claustrophobic and who have a reasonable degree of fitness. Any old plodder will enjoy the regular tour.

Apart from the ostrich ranches, there are several other farms in the area which encourage visitors and offer tours, home-made produce and restaurants. Kids will like the angora rabbit farm, the butterfly farm and the nearby Cango Wildlife Ranch, which has white tigers, lions, cheetahs, flamingos, emus, wallabies, hippos, etc.

A big event on the Oudtshoorn social calendar is the very popular KKNK, or Klein Karoo Nationale Kunstefees (Little Karoo National Arts Festival). Held annually towards the end of March, this is the place to eat boerewors, do the langarm, listen to the top Afrikaans cabaret stars, and to indulge in a bit of boere-baroque kitsch from the large flea-markets. The KKNK is the Afrikaans counterpart to the English National Arts Festival, held in Grahamstown in July.

If you like gravel roads, take the detour from the Cango Caves towards the Rust-en-Vrede waterfall. This beautiful 74-metre plunge can be reached by following signs for Raubenheimer Dam from the Cango Caves road. From the waterfall, you can either turn back to Oudtshoorn, or continue on until you hit the N12 below De Rust.

- Oudtshoorn Tourist Info: 044 279 2532
- www.oudtshoorn.com / www.oudtshoorn.info
- Cango Caves: 044 272 7410 / www.cangocaves.co.za
- Cango Wildlife Ranch: 044 272 5593
- C P Nel Museum: 044 272 7306
- Bongolethu Township Tours: 044 279 4055
- Klein Karoo National Arts Festival: 044 203 8600
  www.kknk.co.za

An old lady laughs

Field of ostriches, ripening in the sun

eggs that were prized by early man and Queen Elizabeth alike.

Ironically, it was as a fashion item that the ostrich became a viable cash crop, and court couturiers of the 17th century liked to use ostrich feathers to decorate hats, dresses and fans. But ostrich feathers weren't so easy to come by, and early trend-setters, such as Marie Antoinette, had to rely on wild ostriches for their supply of plumes.

Then, as the middle-class grew, more and more people began aspiring to the fashions of the rich and famous. By the mid 1800s, graceful ostrich feathers had become *de rigueur* for the frocks and headdresses of the European bourgeoisie, and prices rose as wild ostrich numbers fell. So, in order to meet the supply, forward-thinking farmers in Asia, Australia, the Americas and South Africa started breeding tame ostriches.

The strategy was a success and prices rose dramatically as *fashionistas* snapped up the feathery crop. With the introduction of wire fencing and lucerne farming in the 1860s, ostrich cultivation became an important part of Oudtshoorn's agricultural output. The lanky, flightless birds seemed to like the hot, scrubby veld, and the lucerne fields thrived in the brackish soil. Oudtshoorn was on the way up.

The first 'feather boom' period lasted from 1870 to the 1890s. Then, after a brief lull in the ostrich market, a second boom period got underway at the turn of the century and ran from 1900 to 1914. It was this second boom that really left its mark on the town.

This was the era when 'feather barons', men who had grown wealthy from their birds' bumfluff, started building extravagant mansions in town and on their farms. The best furniture and fabrics were imported from Europe, and Oudtshoorn enjoyed a period of absurd prosperity.

While it may sound silly to say that the town prospered because some fat society matrons liked to wear a feather in their caps, it was true. And it was also a very competitive market. In order to stay ahead of their rivals in California and Australia, local farmers decided to get scientific, and sent an expedition to West Africa to track down the rarest and most valuable ostrich on Earth, the wild Barbary ostrich. The feathers of this thoroughbred bird had the thickest plumes, the most elegant droop and the highest price per kilo.

The Barbary was the Rolls-Royce of ostriches, so the South Africans captured several of these birds and began a cross-breeding programme with our local stock. The result was a tame ostrich that grew the 'Evans' plume: glossy, strong and curly. By 1913, South Africa was exporting 450 tonnes of ostrich feathers, worth £3 million annually. At the time, it was South Africa's fourth most valuable export, after gold, diamonds and wool.

Sadly, the little matter of World War One effectively ended the ostrich boom. After the horrors of this global conflict, fickle fashions turned away from the flamboyant ostrich feather and reflected a more sombre mood, both socially and economically. The popularity of motor cars also meant that women had to shift to more restrained head-gear, so that they could step out in their beau's convertible Model T. Finally, over-production and a badly organised industry couldn't sustain the high prices, and the whole plucking enterprise collapsed in a feathery heap.

Subsequently, the Feather Palaces were abandoned, and the town of Oudtshoorn began to drift back into its semi-desert somnolence. But ostriches still play a role in the region's farming. The excellent meat from an ostrich tastes like steak and is virtually cholesterol-free. Ostrich leather is hardy and attractive. And what home doesn't need a feather duster? So, even though many other crops are grown in Oudtshoorn, it is ostriches that still rule the roost.

CALITZDORP

Calitzdorp is the centre of the port wine industry of South Africa. These grapes thrive in the hot, dry climate of the Klein Karoo, and the poor soil and winter frosts are very similar to the Douro Valley in Portugal, where port wine originated. My ignorance of all things

viticultural has already been established in the section on the Wine Route, so I will just say that the port wines of the Klein Karoo are very popular for their intensity, depth and complexity.

Otherwise Calitzdorp is a snoozy little town with the added benefit of well-developed tourist facilities. Art galleries, curio shops, hiking trails, 4x4 routes, scenic drives and country cooking are all available. A hot mineral spring has also been tapped, and the homely Calitzdorp Spa is a popular resort.

LADISMITH TO BARRYDALE

After leaving Calitzdorp, the R62 leads along the valley floor as the mountains form two dark, parallel lines against the pale sky. While you drive towards the vanishing point, several tiny towns flash by: Zoar, Ladismith, Warmwatersberg, Barrydale. Each *dorp* has a collection of pretty little houses, an NG Kerk and a smattering of shops. Should you stop at any of them, you will certainly enjoy pottering around the main street, and might even unearth a retail gem in one of the roadside shops.

If you are feeling thirsty, go for a drink at Ronnie's Sex Shop. This establishment is actually a bar and curio shop, and started out life as plain, old 'Ronnie's Shop'. The owner's friends, however, kept painting the word 'sex' on the wall, and the new name stuck.

MONTAGU

Montagu is famous for three things: rock climbing, dried fruit and hot mineral springs. Although they were doubtless known to and frequented by the local tribes for centuries, the Montagu hot springs were only brought to the attention of the white people by a wounded man.

During a skirmish with the natives, a member of a local Boer commando had been hurt. Seeking relief, he soaked his wounded hand in a strange-smelling spring that bubbled up from between some rocks. To the man's surprise, the wound healed quickly, and word of

Montagu hot springs complex

complex and hundreds of homes were destroyed. Although Montagu did not suffer the extensive loss of life that the citizens of Laingsburg had to bear, it was as if the heart had been ripped out of the town. The shock and disbelief of the Montagu locals is well documented in the local museum, which has a touching exhibit on the fateful floods. The old newspaper clippings preserved in the museum also give the viewer an unwitting glimpse into the state of contemporary South African journalism of the 1980s.

Some time after the devastation, the land around the springs was bought by a private hotelier and the brand new Avalon Springs resort was built. A series of chintzy pools was created to hold the wonderfully warm water, and all the mod-cons of a classy health resort were established. The Montagu Springs were thus reborn.

Montagu

Montagu is a pretty town which, despite the 1981 flood and encroaching property developers, has managed to hang onto its village roots. The main road still has fields of crops ripening next to white-washed cottages, and the streets are full of old buildings that date back hundreds of years. The shops are iconoclastic, and only several of the major chains have penetrated the high street. All in all, Montagu is a charming spot that offers visitors sanctuary, scenery and some superb rock climbing.

For dried-fruit fanciers, Montagu is an excellent stop, and you will certainly stock up on dried apricots and apples, freshly prepared in the adjacent factory. But don't go overboard. Six months after my visit, I still had a 500g bag of dried mango sitting in my cupboard.

- *Montagu Tourist Info: 023 614 2471*
- *www.montagu.org.za*
- *Montagu Dried Fruit: 023 614 2682*
- *Protea Farm (Tractor rides to the top of the Langeberg from the Koo Valley): 023 614 2471*

the health-giving properties of the spring quickly spread.

Soon, Montagu started to attract invalids and neurotics who were always keen to try out a new cure. Later, a spa resort was built by the Victorians, who were intent on taking the water in style and comfort. This resort was developed over the years until, by the 1980s, the Montagu town council was in charge of a happy little holiday resort with steaming oval pools, criss-crossed by white stepping stones.

Then in 1981, on the same day that Laingsburg suffered its tragic flood, Montagu was swamped by rampant rivers. The hot springs

The Montagu Hot Springs at the Avalon Springs Resort

The manager and owner of the Avalon Springs Resort obviously takes his job very seriously. The grounds and service are impeccable and the pools are very well kept. But the rules! They are everywhere; stuck on bathroom mirrors, printed on boards in the parking lot, written on signs stuck all over the hotel lobby. It's all very Germanic.

Carping aside, the Springs are a pleasure to visit, as long as you obey orders. Day visitors will park in the approved bays and pay their admission at the counter, which also serves ice-cream and other goodies. You will then bypass the private pool, reserved for hotel guests only, and slip into the glorious water along with the other riff-raff in the public pools. A pool-side bar, fast-food outlet and a little putt-putt course may also be used by the non-residents.

The hotel also has a health spa, a pub, two restaurants and lush luxury suites, liberally decorated in an over-ripe shade of maroon. The vertiginous bar at the top of the hotel has great views, for those who don't mind heights. And each room comes with thick towelling gowns, which can be worn to the pool. This is why you will see a veritable procession of old-timers swaddled in their white robes, heading for the springs like a bunch of geriatric flashers queuing up for bingo night. Be warned: out of season, the resort attracts large numbers of pensioners, so if the thought of a pool full of old men in Speedo's is too much to bear, then this is not the place for you!

The springs are open to day visitors from eight in the morning until nine at night. Hotel residents and time-share guests have free access to the pool twenty-four hours a day. The pool is also accessible to guests staying at the adjacent Montagu Springs Resort and other private accommodation in the immediate vicinity. Just to clarify, the Montagu Hot Springs are on the grounds of Avalon Springs Resort, and the Montagu Springs Resort is actually next door. Got it?

• *Avalon Springs Resort: 023 614 1150*

ASHTON – ROBERTSON – BONNIEVALE

Once you have passed through the beautiful Cogmans Kloof road from Montagu, you are effectively back on the Cape Town side of the mountains. Rainfall increases and the soil is more flagrantly fertile. Robertson and Ashton are therefore the centre of a busy agricultural district.

Many of South Africa's best-known food brands (such as Koo and All Gold) had their start here, trading as humble farmers' co-operatives. Now, most of these co-ops have been bought out by stock-market money, and united under the über-brand of Tiger Foods. Nevertheless, much of the produce that goes into our tinned peaches, frozen peas and bottled bounty still comes from the surrounding countryside. Robertson also has a clearly marked wine route, and it offers an interesting alternative to the more common grape-growing region around Stellenbosch.

The Robertson area has a bird park, 4x4 trails and numerous hikes. And then there is the Soekershof maze and labyrinth, claiming to be the largest planted hedge maze in the world! Apparently, over 1 500 species of succulents and cacti can be found on the Soekershof property.

Near to Robertson is Bonnievale, another pretty little town, well known for its luxuriant rose gardens that spill out onto the road. It is also the home of TimJan Wonder Juice, an all-natural remedy that promises to cure just about any ailment, from stomach problems to snoring. Amazing what you can do with a bit of aloe and a whole lot of alcohol.

MCGREGOR

If you are driving between Cape Town and Montagu, you may be tempted to take the short detour to McGregor. It should be a humble little town: it has about a dozen untarred streets, maybe a hundred homes on large plots, and a nice line of mountains curving pinkly into the middle-distance. But this is a country town with pretensions, and there's something a little bit smug about McGregor.

Once McGregor was just a little outpost, famous for making the whipstocks which were used to control the oxen which, in turn,

A road cuts through the heart of the Klein Karoo

controlled the pace of white colonisation. When the ox-wagon went the way of, well, the ox-wagon, McGregor was a town without an industry, and the town floundered for many years. Then it was 'discovered' that McGregor lay at the junction of two ley lines.

Ley lines are channels of natural energy that criss-cross the Earth. Locations where they intersect are supposed to be spiritually enriched, and these cosmic junctions have been associated with immemorial places like Stonehenge and Rustler's Valley, near Clarens in the Eastern Free State.

In McGregor, the convergence of ley lines has manifested itself in a host of wellness, healing and therapy centres. Massage treatments, mineral cleansing, karmic irrigations, shamanistic psychoanalysis and every other kind of alternative therapy is on offer in discrete spa's and retreats all over town. Many Capetonians now own property in town so that they can be close to their crystals and, where Capetonians go, cheese and wine shops are soon to follow.

If stroking your karma isn't your cup of herbal tea, a visit to McGregor can be enlivened with a lovely drive on the Road to Nowhere. This gravel road is actually a mountain pass that wasn't. Originally intended to link McGregor with Greyton on the other side of the Riviersonderend Mountains, the road builders ran out of money halfway through. So, now the Road to Nowhere hits a dead-end in the cliffs about 13km out of McGregor, at which point you have to turn around and head back to town. The scenery is luscious, but I don't know if it's worth going all the way to McGregor for a scenic cul-de-sac; unless you are already in town to have your aura serviced.

Klein Karoo Contacts:
- Klein Karoo Regional Tourist Info: 044 873 6314/55
- Klein Karoo Wine Route: 028 572 1284 www.route62.co.za / www.scenicroute.co.za
- Breede River Valley Regional Tourist Info: 023 347 6411
- Calitzdorp Tourist Info: 044 213 3775 www.calitzdorp.co.za
- Calitzdorp Spa: 044 213 3371
- Gamkaberg Nature Reserve: 044 213 3367
- McGregor Tourist Info: 023 625 1954
- Robertson Tourist Info: 023 626 4437 www.robertson.org.za
- Robertson Wine Valley Tourist Info: 023 626 3167 / www.robertsonwinevalley.co.za
- Birds Paradise: 023 626 3926
- Soekershof maze and labyrinth: 023 626 4134 / www.soekershof.com
- Bonnievale Tourist Info: 023 616 3753
- Tiger Brands Canning Factory Tour (by appointment): 023 615 1120
- Breede River Winelands Regional Tourist Info: 023 615 1100
- The Brandy Route / South African Brandy Foundation: 021 887 3157 www.sabrandy.co.za

Mother and son, Bonnievale

The CP Nel Museum, Oudtshoorn

The flamboyant wallpaper of a feather palace, Oudtshoorn

A homestead left to crumble on the Klein Karoo plains

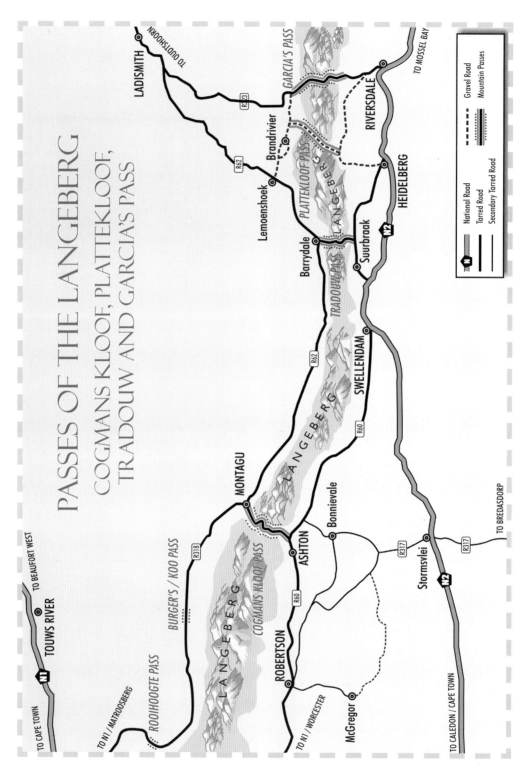

PASSES OF THE LANGEBERG

COGMANS KLOOF, PLATTEKLOOF, TRADOUW AND GARCIA'S PASS

16. Mountain Passes over the Langeberg

ORIENTATION

The Langeberg (meaning 'Long Mountains') is a range of peaks that stretch 200km, from Worcester to George. There are only a few ways that wheeled traffic can cross the Langeberg mountains:

➡ There is Cogmans Kloof, between Ashton and Montagu.
➡ The little-used gravel track, variously called Plattekloof or Gysmansberg, between Brandrivier and Heidelberg.
➡ Tradouw Pass, between Suurbraak and Barrydale.
➡ And Garcia's Pass, between Riversdale and Ladismith.

COGMANS KLOOF

The mountainous barrier between the Overberg and the Klein Karoo was first cracked at Cogmans Kloof, between present day Robertson and Montagu. But this useful passage was not discovered by intrepid explorers. It was revealed as a result of a native war party.

By the turn of the eighteenth century, a pass had already been established into the Roodezant, and the Land of Waveren (present-day Tulbagh) was being farmed with great success. Then, in 1701, a Khoikhoi tribe called the Koekemans spilled out of the Langeberg (about 100km to the east) and attacked a Dutch military outpost. The invaders were presumably repulsed and pursued back to their gap in the mountains. The pass had been revealed and the name stuck. Cogmans (Koekemans) Kloof quickly became a useful access route through the Langeberg.

In 1725, the first farms were granted in the Montagu valley, on the far side of the kloof, but

Kalkoenkrans tunnel, Cogmans Kloof

access to the Cape remained difficult. Farmers who wanted to take their goods to market had to struggle through Cogmans Kloof, head up towards Tulbagh and then scramble down the Roodezant Pass to the Cape.

This circuitous route was made even more daunting by the fact that Cogmans Kloof wasn't much of a pass. It wasn't even much of a road. Cogmans Kloof was actually just a muddy track that followed the banks of the Kingna River as it carved a narrow valley through the magnificent red rocks of the Cape Fold Mountains. Letting the river do all the work

185

The Cogmans Kloof road sweeps along the valley floor

seemed like a good idea to the early transport riders, but the route had its drawbacks.

The Cogmans Kloof 'road' crossed the Kingna River eight or nine times during its passage through the kloof. When the water was high, the road was impassable. When the river was low, the drifts became muddy quagmires that trapped wagons like flies on sticky paper. To make matters worse, there was one thrusting piece of rock, called Kalkoenkrans, which extended out into the river. At this point, the wagon drivers had no choice but to splash through the water until the obstacle had been cleared.

The farmers of the Montagu valley kept asking the Cape government to improve the track, but help was not forthcoming. Occasional attempts were made by the local councils to create a better road, but these were invariably destroyed whenever the river ran high. Then, in 1867, a severe flood swept away twelve people. Another bad flood occurred in 1868. The British authorities were finally prompted into action.

The problem was that there were just not enough convicts around. Convict labour was a mainstay of road construction in the Cape Colony, as free labourers (who, ironically, weren't) tended to push the prices up. The bean-counters dragged their feet for a few more years, until it became clear that a proper road had to be built, with or without prisoners. The ever-present Thomas Bain got the call in 1873, and he quickly staked out a safe course that ran

above the river's floodplain, avoiding the numerous crossings.

Although Cogmans Kloof is technically a *poort* (which follows a river through a mountain), rather than a pass (which climbs over a mountain), it was still difficult to build. Bain's routing required a lot of cutting and blasting through the incredibly tough rocks. Nevertheless, he and his foreman persevered and, by 1876, the road was nearly finished.

Only one little problem remained – Kalkoenkrans. This narrow ridge of rock still forced wagons off the nice new road and into the river bed. The only solution was to build a tunnel through the bloody thing. Back then, tunnel building was a primitive art, but Bain was up for the challenge. However, his supplies of dynamite had run out, so Bain used unreliable gunpowder to blast away at the rock until, finally, he had blown a hole 16 metres long and five meters high through the Kalkoenkrans. It is one of the earliest road tunnels in SA. The newly completed Cogmans Kloof road opened in 1877.

Bain's original road was improved in 1931 to cater for the increased traffic but, by 1952, it had again grown too small for the zooming motor cars. A new road was built and Bain's tunnel was enlarged. Today, Bain's original road can still be seen running on the opposite bank of the river, resolutely propped up by his characteristic dry-stone retaining walls. Bain's old Hodges Bridge is also still standing, white and tidy, just next to the new Boy Retief Bridge, which carries the modern road.

The old road is closed to traffic nowadays, but it has stood the test of time. When he built it, Bain declared that it would survive any future flood that may come down the Kingna River. In 1981, on the same day that Laingsburg was devastated, Montagu also experienced its worst flood in living memory. The Montagu Springs complex was destroyed, and the new road was extensively damaged. Bain's old road, however, was unharmed, and traffic was diverted onto the hundred-year-old roadway while the new road of 1952 was repaired.

Oh, and next time you drive through the Kalkoenkrans Tunnel, look up and you will catch a glimpse of the British blockhouse built during the Anglo-Boer War to prevent the marauding Afrikaners from reaching Cape Town.

PLATTEKLOOF / PLATTEKLIP / GYSMANSHOEK

The next access route over the Langeberg was the old Plattekloof road. This pass ran from Heidelberg (on the N2) to the middle of nowhere, most closely represented on my current road map by a little dot called Brandrivier.

It is a strangely neglected pass that never really caught on, perhaps because it was not easy to find and did not take you anywhere useful. The pass still isn't easy to find but, if you have an off-road vehicle, you can safely drive along this little-used pass.

It's probably a good idea to approach Plattekloof from the Klein Karoo side, as there are a couple of rickety old signposts pointing the way. To do this, take the R62 to Lemoenshoek and leave the tar, following signs to Brandrivier. The gravel road splits without warning after a few k's, but don't worry, the two branches rejoin before the turn-off to the pass.

On this forgotten route, the landscape is dusty and dry, and the road seems deserted. Several old farmhouses doze in the sun. Scrubby vegetation spools down the hills. Then, just when you're about to give up hope, there is a precarious little sign that points right to Kortfontein, Karetberg and Gysmanshoekpas.

Plattekloof/Gysmanshoek is a very pretty pass. It has no extreme gradients and doesn't go very high. It starts with a gentle ascent up the slopes of the Langeberg mountains, which offer great views over the sparse Klein Karoo plains. The road then summits a low nek and descends

An rare sign of habitation on the road to Plattekloof

into a hidden valley, running parallel to the main peaks. Here, the fynbos grows thick and the dashing Duiwenhoks river runs along the valley floor. The road soon drops down to the little stream and follows it, until both the road and the river emerge from the mountains into the Overberg. Once you're out of the pass, keep going until you hit an unmarked T-junction. To your left is Riversdale, to your right is Heidelberg. Take your pick. I turned towards Riversdale and finally re-joined the tarred R323 just below the Korenterivier Dam.

The history of the old Plattekloof Pass is obscure. Several important travellers mention it in their memoirs, including William Paterson and Carl Thunberg, but it was never very popular. The Divisional Council improved the old pass in 1841, and again in 1860 when it was renamed Hudson's Pass. In the 1870s, the opening of Tradouw and Garcia's passes made Plattekloof obsolete and the road fell into disuse. Still, you can't keep a good road down and the present-day Gysmanshoek Pass is said to follow the old Plattekloof route quite closely.

Strangely, Gysmanshoek does not appear in any commercially available road atlas, and Jose Burman gives an entertaining account of finding this remote pass in a state of decay. However, I found the roadway in good condition. Perhaps the secret to this discrepancy can be found on the breezy slopes above the pass. The hidden little Duiwenhoks valley is actually quite well known in paragliding circles, and several launch sites have been cleared out of the fynbos. The paragliding clubs might be the ones who rehabilitated the road, I don't know. But if you like taking the road very much less travelled, try Gysmanshoek Pass from Brandriver to Heidelberg. It's a charmer.

TRADOUW PASS

In the 1860s, Swellendam was booming, Barry and Nephews' trading empire was in full bloom, and the little harbour at Port Beaufort was bustling. Unfortunately, farmers in the Klein Karoo had to travel all the way to Cogmans Kloof (50k's to the West) or Plattekloof (30k's to the East) to get their goods over the mountains to Swellendam. The traders at Swellendam were similarly frustrated when trying to get their wares into the Klein Karoo. A distance of thirty or forty kilometres may not sound like much today, but the average speed of an ox-wagon was never more a couple of k's per hour, and the extra distance cost the farmers a good few days in each direction.

Enjoying the view from Tradouw Pass

Under pressure from the wealthy Barrys, and encouraged by the local farmers, parliament finally consented to build a new pass. It was to run through Tradouw Kloof, thus linking the towns of Swellendam and Barrydale (named after the aforementioned Barry dynasty). Trusty Thomas Bain was sent out to survey the route, and he pegged out a thirteen-kilometre pass that climbed up the steep valley carved through the mountains by the Buffeljags River. He moved on site in 1869 and the pass was opened in 1873. It was initially called Southey's Pass, but the old 'Tradouw' title was more popular. The road was reconstructed in 1979.

In its day, Tradouw was one of the main roads to the interior and the diamond fields of Kimberley. Today, it is a little-known pass that has outlived its usefulness. Nevertheless, it is a gorgeous drive, with a large viewing area that repays your stop with a sweeping view out over the river gorge below. It is also a bitter-sweet pass, as the body of kidnapped Dutch tourist, Marlene Koenigs, was found here in 2003. Ironically, Tradouw is a Khoikhoi word that means 'the ravine of the women'.

GARCIA'S PASS

Just as the people of Swellendam wanted more direct access to the Klein Karoo, so did the people of Riversdale. The Civil Commissioner, Maurice Garcia, was inclined to agree, and petitioned parliament accordingly. Since they already had convicts working on Tradouw Pass, not too far away, parliament agreed that the captive work force would be transferred to Riversdale as soon as their work on Tradouw was finished.

Once again, Thomas Bain picked up his theodolite and staked out a winding path that crept up the slopes of the Goukou River Valley (also called the Kafferkuils, in the old parlance). Work began in 1873, and was finally completed in 1877.

Garcia's was not a simple pass to build, as the Kloof had steep sides with little soft material on which to support a perpendicular road surface. This required lots of blasting and very high retaining walls, which can still be seen today. Because of the difficulty of the work, Bain's initial budget for the pass had been very optimistic and the expenses kept on mounting.

To ensure that the pass was completed, Bain did a sneaky thing. Instead of working slowly and methodically from one side of the mountains to the other, he quickly built a very rough road over the entire pass. Once this was done, the authorities had little option but to keep spending until the road was completed. All in all, Garcia's Pass came in a whopping ten times over budget from Bain's original estimate of £3 000.

Garcia's Pass was modernised between 1958 and 1963, and many of Bain's original twists and turns were straightened out by the realignment. These dislocated gravel bends can still be seen, branching off from the tarred road and hugging the walls of the shallow valleys, before rejoining the new route once again. The vast retaining walls are also impressive, as is the scenery.

The town of Riversdale, at the base of the pass, is a small country village which contains the Julius Gordon Africana museum (antique furniture). Nearby is the Sleeping Beauty Peak, which is supposed to look like a reclining figure, but only reminded me of my father's prodigious profile.

Sharp bend on Tradouw Pass

PASSES OF THE OUTENIQUA MOUNTAINS:

ATTAQUAS KLOOF, DUIWELSKOP / KLOOF,
CRADOCK KLOOF, MONTAGU, ROBINSON, OUTENIQUA,
PRINCE ALFRED'S, LONG KLOOF, BAVIAANSKLOOF

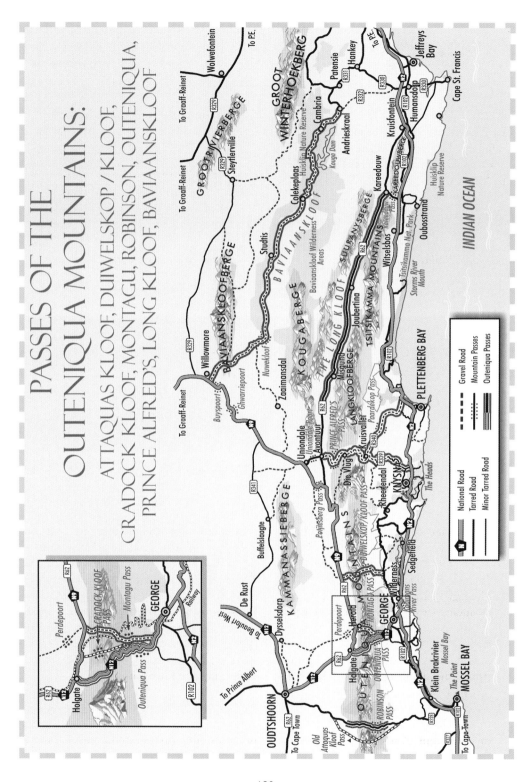

ORIENTATION

The Outeniquas are a beautiful range of mountains that pick up where the Langeberg leave off, and run unbroken all the way to Plett. The name comes from the Khoikhoi phrase meaning 'people carrying honey', because the heather-covered slopes of the mountains harboured a thriving bee population.

Over the years, explorers and engineers have forged quite a few passages over this concatenation of mountain peaks. These mountain passes provided access from the coast to the Klein Karoo and the Long Kloof.

Here is a list of your options, in chronological order:

➡ Attaquas Kloof runs from Mossel Bay to Oudtshoorn. This old pass is now a private 4x4 trail.

➡ Duiwelskop Pass is another privately run 4x4 trail, and runs from the farm Louvain, on the N9, to Kleinplaat Forest Station above Woodiville.

➡ Cradock Kloof runs from George, over the mountains towards Oudtshoorn. This was the first of four passes (one rail, three road) to use the Y-shaped valley behind George as an access route into the Klein Karoo. Cradock's Kloof has long been impassable and is now a hiking track.

➡ Montagu Pass is the second pass over the mountains from George. It is a good gravel road, and is the oldest unaltered road pass in the country.

➡ Robinson Pass, on the R328, was built to replace the crumbling Attaquas Kloof. It connects Mossel Bay with Oudtshoorn and the road is tarred.

➡ The Outeniqua Pass is the latest pass over the mountains from George. It is tarred, and part of the N12 national route.

➡ Further afield is Prince Alfred's Pass (R339). This long gravel passage connects Avontuur to Knysna, and provides access to the Long Kloof.

➡ The Long Kloof leads from Avontuur to Humansdorp. It is actually a river valley that cuts through the mountains, and used to be an important part of the Cape Wagon Road [see Chapter 8]. The road is now tarred.

➡ Baviaanskloof is a rough gravel track through a pristine wilderness area. It runs parallel to the Long Kloof, from Hankey to Willowmore.

ATTAQUAS KLOOF
(probably pronounced Atta-kwass)

The first and most important of the Outeniqua passes was Attaquas Kloof, above Mossel Bay. This pass was originally a prehistoric elephant path, and was later used by the local Attaqua Khoikhoi. The first wagon passage of the pass was recorded by Isaac Schrijver in 1689, as he hacked his way through the thick foliage.

For a few years, curiosity and greed led people over this rough track into the unknown interior, but these were largely adventurers and no one chose to settle on the far side of the Outeniquas. In 1756, however, as the relentless pursuit of new lands drove prospective farmers ever onwards, the first four farms on the northern side of the mountains were granted. The bottle had been uncorked, and the *witblitz* of humanity started drifting into the Klein Karoo.

For one hundred years, Attaquas Kloof remained the main rocky highway across the mountains, a vital link of the Old Cape Wagon Road. Occasionally, they tried building better passes, but the rugged Attaquas Kloof passage stuck it out, despite minimal improvements. Finally, Montagu Pass opened up the mountains above George in 1848, and other well-engineered routes followed. It was all over. Attaquas Kloof dropped out of popular memory, and became a hiking trail.

Now, the old track has been re-established and is being run as a private 4x4 trail. The route runs through several farms and it can currently be tackled in sections, each with its own difficulty rating. Attempts are now being made to unite the whole Attaquas Kloof road, complete with farm stay-overs. It would be great to have the Old Eastern Highway back together again, and all the other sections are still in use. Let's hope they succeed.

DUIWELSKOP / KLOOF

The next road up and over the Outeniquas was Duiwelskop. This fearsome sounding pass led from the head of the Langkloof down to the forests around Kleinplaat, north-west of Knysna.

The first Duiwelskop route was probably laid out in 1772. It was a badly made track that went straight up and straight down two consecutive mountainous humps, with little fanfare and less finesse. This approach was borne out of calculated madness as the sides of the mountain are very steep, and wagons have a very high centre of gravity. This means that they would topple over if driven laterally across the slopes, causing the wagon and oxen to tumble into oblivion. The only solution was to keep the wagon on an even keel by heading straight for the summit.

After Montagu Pass above George was opened to a rapturous response, Knysna citizens quickly started petitioning the local council to rebuild Duiwelskop. But funds were not forthcoming. Both Andrew Geddes Bain and his son, that ever-present Thomas, inspected the route and declared it workable, but the cash-strapped council still sat *shtum*. Finally, in 1864, they stumped up a measly £300 for Bain (the younger) to construct a rough 'Boer Road' over the pass. In 1867, Bain's new Passes Road made Duiwelskop largely redundant, and the old pass fell into disrepair.

But the road lives on! The old Duiwelskop Pass is now accessible as a privately run 4x4 route, which starts at the farm Louvain. The

Taking a stroll on the Duiwelskop 4x4 route, deep in the Outeniqua Mountains

current road over Duiwelskop follows an approximate route that incorporates the original track, Bain's later 'Boer Road', and a third path that was built during the Anglo-Boer War.

When I drove the pass, recent rains had left the road very rough and rocky. As the driver, I was fine with this, but my passengers did not entirely appreciate the bouncy ride. If you thinking of doing this trail in your SUV, a high ground clearance is essential and low-range is a very strong preference. Also, people with a fear of heights should be left behind, as the road is very exposed on the severe slopes. The views, however, are worth it, and thick, wild fynbos lines the track in feathery profusion. But don't pick the Proteas!

Once over the mountains, drive through the pine plantations to the forestry station at Kleinplaats. Leave the key here, and continue down to colourful café at Woodiville. From Woodiville, you will join Bain's Passes Road: right will take you to George and left will take you to Knysna.

CRADOCK'S KLOOF

After the new British settlement of George was founded in 1811, the citizens started clamouring for their own route over the mountains. Mossel Bay and Attaquas Kloof was a long detour, and Duiwelskop was not an appealing alternative. The town's founding fathers were sympathetic to the plight of their citizens, and the first Landdrost of George, one Mr Van Kerwel, managed to get some money out of Governor John Cradock, after whom he proposed to name the new road.

Full of bureaucratic confidence, Van Kerwel gaily went ahead and built a brand-new pass over the Outeniquas in a couple of months. His alacrity was to be commended, but his road-building was not.

Cradock's Kloof became known as the worst pass in the Colony. It was very steep, and the rocks formed themselves into huge, broken shelves that had to be climbed like steps. The ascent took three days with double spans of oxen. The descent, however, was quicker. Much quicker.

The procedure was very technical. First, most of the oxen were taken off the span to make the wagon more manageable. Then, everyone held tight to the ropes of the *remskoene*. And off they went, skidding down the mountain until they (hopefully) reached the bottom.

I like the quote of one contemporary traveller who said that the pass was 'fit only for baboons, and for baboons which have the advantage of youth and activity'. When chief engineer Charles Michell tried to galvanise the government into putting some money towards the shoddy roads of the colony, he used Cradock Kloof as an example of how bad things had become. Cradock Kloof was eventually replaced by Montagu Pass in the 1840s, and Van Kerwel's road was reclaimed by the mountain.

Then, in 1936, those little munchkins from the Afrikaner youth movements celebrated the centenary of the Great Trek by marking out the old Cradock Kloof wagon route with white stones. I'm not sure why. I suppose their motivation was as simple as wagon road+voortrekker=good. Whatever the reason, it was a good idea, and these stone cairns can still be seen heading up the valley. Cradock Kloof Pass is now being used as a hiking and mountain bike track.

MONTAGU PASS

Charles Michell, chief engineer at the Cape, was a persistent campaigner for better roads in the colony. Luckily, the head of the newly formed Central Road Board, John Montagu, was in complete agreement. Their first joint venture was to be Montagu Pass, from George to Oudtshoorn.

Michell planned the route himself, but the experienced Henry Fancourt White was imported from England to supervise the work. Construction was started in 1844 with a couple of hundred convicts and some free labour, and with much blasting and battering, a ten-kilometre road was

The stately Montagu Pass climbs the mountains above George

slowly cut up the side of a large cleft in the mountains behind George.

Upon completion, the new Montagu Pass was opened with great fanfare and to universal acclaim. It was comfortable, well surfaced, and the steepest section had a gradient of only 1:6. It was a pass that could be safely travelled by any wagon, over and over again. Everyone considered it £35 000 well spent.

The remarkable thing is that, 150 years after it was built, the old gravel road is still open to traffic. And it hasn't changed a bit, making it the oldest unaltered mountain pass in South Africa. This has earned Montagu Pass the well-deserved status of a national monument.

At the bottom of the pass stands another national monument – the old, abandoned Toll House. Many of the early mountain passes had a toll house, putting paid to the idea that toll roads are a modern connivance. And, like today, these toll concessions were all put out to tender and awarded to an individual, who then became responsible for the road's maintenance and repair. Some of these toll keepers did a good job, and their roads persevered. Others misappropriated the funds, and the roads quickly became ruins. We wait and see which kind of collectors are in charge of our nation's modern highways...

Historically, Montagu Pass is very rich, and the various well-tended signposts give you real flavour of the old days. For example, 'Boshoff se draai' is a tricky turn that a braggart *tou-leier* named Boshoff failed to negotiate. 'Grogdraai' is a corner near a little spring from which the horses drank, while the transport riders did the same from their bottles. 'Amanda's Grave' marks the final resting place of Amanda Pienaar, who requested a burial at the spot where her husband proposed. 'Die Noute' is the narrowest part of the pass, and 'Regop Trek' is slightly exaggerated name given to the steepest section of the road.

Montagu Pass also has two other national monuments along its course: The Keur River Bridge, a rustic stone archway built by Michell, and the ruins of the Old Smithy. Both are signposted and the bridge is quaintly attractive. At the sign for the Old Smithy, however, all I found was a couple of local ladies who were having a *braai* among the trees. They were kind enough to offer me a *dop*, though.

ROBINSON PASS

Mossel Bay was once the coastal terminus of the Eastern Highway before the road headed North over Attaquas Kloof. In 1848, Montagu Pass opened, and traffic quickly adopted the neatly engineered road as opposed to the rough elephant track that was Attaquas. This meant that, although it was still the main port of the region, Mossel Bay was somewhat cut out of the loop. The town's fathers scrambled into action, looking to find a replacement for the crumbling Attaquas Kloof route.

They finally identified a likely bridle path, called Ruytersbosch Pad, just east of Attaquas Kloof. The Mossel Bay Divisional Council committed some money and, after much nagging, the government agreed to share the expense. Despite this spirit of co-operation, the first attempt to build a pass quickly failed. Enter Mr Thomas Bain.

In 1867, fresh from his efforts on the Prince Alfred Pass near Knysna, Bain was sent to Mossel Bay to create an alternative to Attaquas Kloof. The Robinson Pass was opened in 1869, named after some arbitrary Inspector of Public Works, and was tarred in the early 1960s.

OUTENIQUA PASS

The first motor cars in the George area appeared around the turn of the 20th century and their numbers steadily grew over the years. So, when the first national road plan was being drawn up in the 1930s, it became apparent that the old Montagu Pass, which had carried animal-powered traffic for eighty years, could not be upgraded to modern specifications.

Legendary road engineer PA de Villiers looked at many alternative routes, and finally planned a brand-new pass which would carry motor cars safely over the Outeniquas. Construction began in 1942, during the Second World War, when several hundred Italian POWs were conscripted from the Cape and put to work.

It was a considerable job. The wide carriageway required rock cuts 20m deep and fills more than 30m high. The reluctant Italian labour-force was, understandably, not entirely up to the task and, when the war ended, the Italians happily went home, having completed only one-tenth of the pass. A few hundred local 'African' workers were then sent for, and got on with the job. The pass was opened in 1951.

The road cuts around a spur on Robinson Pass

By 1990, the lack of passing lanes had made progress down the pass frustrating. Long queues snaked behind the slow-moving trucks, and impatient drivers diced with death each time they tried to overtake on blind corners. Over the next six years, the pass remained open to traffic, while various alterations were made to make the road more practical. This upgrade was successfully completed, and today the road offers many passing lanes, gorgeous views over the green coastal plain and some grand viewing areas. It's particularly worth stopping at the Four Passes viewsite, from where you can see the white stones marking the original Cradock Kloof Pass, the brown scars of Montagu Pass and the railway pass, all snaking up the opposite side of the Y-shaped valley.

PRINCE ALFRED'S PASS

Sometimes called the grand-daddy of the Cape's mountain passes, Prince Alfred's is certainly a long and confident access route. Originally intended to help people get in and out of Knysna, Prince Alfred's was planned by Andrew Geddes Bain and built by his son, Thomas. It opened in 1868 and was named after Queen Victoria's son, who was in South Africa for an elephant hunt.

Prince Alfred's is a very long pass, about 70k's from beginning to end, and it leads through some exquisite scenery. The first half of the road had to be hewn out of the dense forests around Knysna, and this part of the road still runs through indigenous woods, which cloister hiking trails and cycle paths beneath their leafy bowers.

About 40k's from Knysna, the road hits a junction. If you turn right, you will travel over the gravel Gates of Eden Pass and down to the N2, a few dozen k's outside Plett. This route used to be called Paardekop, and was part of the old road from Plett to George. If you keep going straight, you will head up towards the main section of Prince Alfred's Pass.

Once clear of the forests, the pass finally begins its ascent up the flanks of the Outeniquas. It is a memorable drive, as the gravel road gently curves up the wall of a vast, green amphitheatre, before finally cresting the mountains and entering the Klein Karoo near the town of Avontuur.

From Avontuur, you can turn left towards the N9 and Oudtshoorn, or right to enter the Long Kloof, which leads down to the sea near Humansdorp.

THE LONG KLOOF / LANGKLOOF

Not to be confused with the Langberg near Swellendam, the Long Kloof is a long, narrow valley wedged between the Kougaberge in the North and the Tsitsikamma mountains in the South. It runs from Willowmore, in the Klein Karoo, to Humansdorp, near Port Elizabeth.

In its day, the Long Kloof was a vital link in the Cape Wagon Road. Today, it is the quiet extension of R62 from Oudtshoorn

The Long Kloof itself is a fertile valley that produces a good variety of fruit, mainly apples. There are many working farms in the area, much as there were in heyday of the Old Wagon Road, and several of these offer farm tours, tractor rides and farm stalls. There are several small towns in the Long Kloof, such as Joubertina and Kareedouw, which offer a small selection of general stores and eating places. Kareedouw has a particularly nice church built out of golden sandstone, which is worth checking out.

BAVIAANSKLOOF

Although the Long Kloof functioned as the main thoroughfare from the Klein Karoo to Algoa Bay for well over one hundred years, there were a couple of rugged alternatives through the mountains. One of these has now become a popular 4x4 route through Baviaanskloof.

Thankfully, Baviaanskloof (Baboon's Ravine) is still a public road, so you don't need any permits or permission. It leads from Hankey (near the N2) to Willowmore on the N9. If you have the time and an SUV, this is a fantastic drive through a pristine wilderness area. A word of caution, however. Only a fool would try to do this road in a single day. As I did!

Instead, spend at least one night in the Baviaanskloof Wilderness Area. The various campsites (all administered by CNC) are beautifully located, and you will be missing much of the untamed scenery if you just stick to the 'main' road. Besides, the road is rocky and corrugated in places, and progress is often slow, so you won't be making good time.

Any 2x4 or 4x4 vehicle with good ground clearance can accomplish this route. Nevertheless, the road is lonely and standard recovery equipment should be taken along: a spare tyre, a working jack, water for the radiator in case of overheating, that kind of thing. I know whereof I speak because I got a flat on this road, and had to lie on the ground struggling with a stubborn lock-nut, while the baboons had a screaming fight in the bushes next to me. I learnt an important lesson that day. Don't rush the good stuff!

There are no towns or supplies of any kind between Hankey and the N9, so make sure you have everything you need before you enter the stunning Baviaans River valley. You'll need your cozzie too, as the road crosses the river several times and there are plenty of places to stop for a swim in the cool water. A couple of upmarket lodges have been established on either side of the wilderness reserve.

While you're in Hankey, pay your respects to Saartjie Baartman, the Hottentot Venus. She was a Khoikhoi woman with enormous buttocks who was taken to Britain in the 19th century and exhibited as an oddity. In 1816, after years of being displayed to callous crowds, gawping royalty and sneering scientists, Saartjie died in exile, and her voluptuous body was stuffed and mounted as a museum piece.

Despite many requests to have her sent back to South Africa, 'The Hottentot Venus' remained on display in a dusty glass box, until she was finally returned to us in 2002. Her remains have now been ceremoniously buried in Hankey, where she was born around 1789.

Outeniqua Mountains Contacts:
- Duiwelskop 4x4 Route / Louvain Guest Farm: 044 888 1726 / 083 287 6927 www.louvain.co.za
- Attaquas Kloof Nature Reserve: 044 874 2184
- Attaquas Kloof 4x4 Trail: 044 695 3175 083 660 0227
- Langkloof Tourist Info: 0427 41221
- Hankey Tourist Info: 042 284 0543
- Patensie / Gamtoos Valley Tourist Info: 042 283 0437
- Baviaanskloof Wilderness Area: 042 283 0882 / 049 839 1090 042 273 1530
- www.baviaans.net / www.baviaans.co.za

The beautiful gateway to Baviaanskloof Wilderness Area

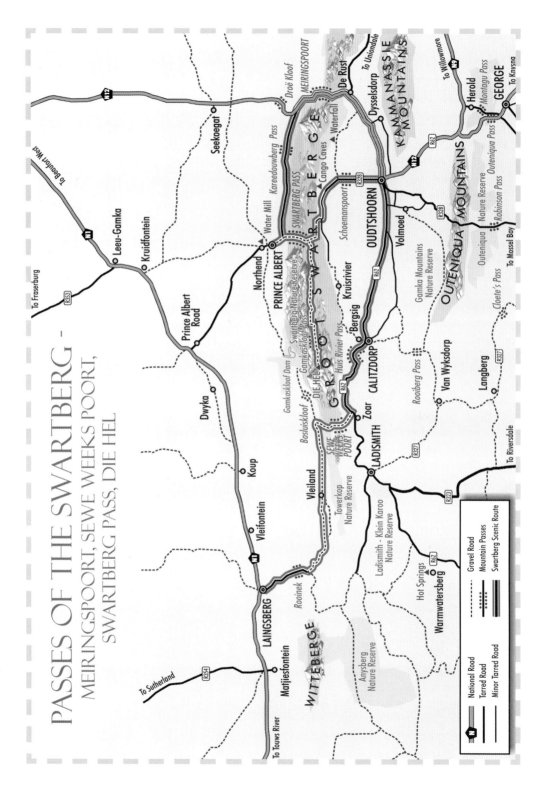

PASSES OF THE SWARTBERG -
MEIRINGSPOORT, SEWE WEEKS POORT, SWARTBERG PASS, DIE HEL

Legend:
- National Road
- Tarred Road
- Minor Tarred Road
- Gravel Road
- Mountain Passes
- Swartberg Scenic Route

To Beaufort West
To Fraserburg
To Sutherland
To Touws River
To Uniondale
To Willowmore
To Knysna
To Mossel Bay
To Riversdale

Seekoegat
Leeu-Gamka
Kruidfontein
Prince Albert Road
Dwyka
Koup
Vleifontein
Vleiland
Matjiesfontein
LAINGSBERG
Northend
PRINCE ALBERT
Water Mill
Droë Kloof
De Rust
Dysselsdorp
Herold
GEORGE
OUDTSHOORN
Volmoed
Kruisrivier
Bergsig
CALITZDORP
Zoar
LADISMITH
Van Wyksdorp
Langberg
Hot Springs
Warmwatersberg

Kareedouwberg Pass
SWARTBERG PASS
MEIRINGSPOORT
Swartberg Nature Reserve
Gamkaskloof Pass
Gamkaskloof Dam
Bosluiskloof
SEWE WEEKS POORT
DIE HEL
Huis Rivier Pass
Schoemanspoort
Cango Caves
Waterfall
Rooiberg Pass
Gamka Mountains Nature Reserve
Outeniqua Nature Reserve
Robinson Pass
Outeniqua Pass
Cloete's Pass
Montagu Pass
Towerkop Nature Reserve
Ladismith - Klein Karoo Nature Reserve
Anysberg Nature Reserve
Rooinek

GROOTSWARTBERGE
KAMMANASSIE MOUNTAINS
OUTENIQUA MOUNTAINS
WITTEBERGE

R353
R354
R328
R62
R327
R323

18. Mountain Passes over the Swartberg

ORIENTATION

The Swartberg must be one of the most fearsome mountain ranges in South Africa. They cut off the Klein Karoo from the Great Karoo in the north, and they run unbroken from Touws River to Willowmore. The crest of the range is above Oudtshoorn.

By the 1800s, there were farmers in the Klein Karoo and there were farmers in the Groot Karoo, but in between the two there was a bloody great mountain range that just wouldn't be conquered. This was a problem for the Groot Karoo farmers, because they had to travel all the way to Cape Town to get their produce to market. Klein Karoo farmers also suffered, because they had no way of trading their fruit and vegetables with the wool-rich Karoo lairds only a few dozen aerial kilometres away. But the landscape had spoken and, for the moment, there was just no way over the Swartberg.

Out of all the mountain ranges in South Africa, I think the Swartberg is the most impressive. Steep sides, a fierce countenance and stormy clouds make this spine of rock very powerful. The Swartberg clearly mean business, and they contain some of the clearest evidence of the colossal forces that were at work when the Cape Fold Mountains were being formed. Bedding plains, dozens of meters thick, have been folded and bent, like the pages of a phone book dropped on its side. Mighty sheets of red rock have been raised up and buckled into a petrified vista, which looks like a raging sea frozen in stone.

There are only four routes that traverse the Swartberg mountains: one for the railway and three for cars. Only one of these road passes is tarred.

Meiringspoort is a well-designed tar road that runs along the floor of a river valley. It cuts through the Eastern side of the Groot Swartberg range, and is part of the N12 from Beaufort-West to Oudtshoorn.

Seweweekspoort is a gravel track that runs through another river valley, on the Western side of the range. It leads from Zoar, on the R62, to Laingsburg on the N1.

The Swartberg Pass is a man-made masterpiece, and the only road that goes over the mountains instead of through them. It is a gravel track, from Oudtshoorn to Prince Albert, and it vaults over the central part of the Swartberg range. From Prince Albert, you can continue (on tar) to the N1.

At the summit of the Swartberg Pass, there also is the option for a detour down Gamkaskloof Pass to one of the most isolated spots in the country, Die Hel. This incomparable road runs along the top of the Swartberg mountains before reaching a dead-end in the Gamkaskloof valley. It is an unforgettable experience for those who don't mind heights.

MEIRINGSPOORT

A poort is a mountain pass that actually runs along the floor of a river valley, through the heart of the mountain, so to speak. The gradients of a poort are usually quite mild, as the river has already done several million years of earth-moving for you. Unfortunately, any road which runs close to a river bank is subject to flooding, and this has been the bane of many poorts around the country.

Meiringspoort had its start as a transport route in 1800, when two local farmers laid out a bridle path that ran along a river valley from the Oudtshoorn side of the mountains to the town of Prince Albert. In 1856, it was decided to expand the road, and two budgets were submitted: one for a rough 'boer' road, and another for a proper roadway. To no one's surprise, the cheaper boer road was commissioned and the miffed engineers set to work, muttering something like 'next time the river comes down in flood and washes the road away, don't come crying to me'.

The rough road through the poort was opened in 1858, and tons of wool immediately started trundling down from the Great Karoo, through Oudtshoorn, to the port of Mossel Bay. Things were looking good. Unfortunately, the engineers were right to have reservations about the low-level road, and regular floods kept closing the pass for months at a time.

Despite all the closures, the road remained a vital link between the Little and Great Karoos, and it was constantly being rebuilt and improved. In the 1950s, the original gravel and stone drifts were replaced by concrete causeways, and the road was tarred in the early 1970s.

Sadly, a tarred surface and fancy new low-water bridges did not stop the floods and, in 1997, a big deluge took out most of the road. Meiringspoort was rebuilt over three years, at a cost of R70 million, and was reopened only in 2000. But the reconstruction is superb.

Today, a drive along Meiringspoort is a pleasure. There are a number of spacious rest areas with kiosks, craft markets, toilets and *braai* facilities. The views are remarkable as you drive along the valley floor looking up at the rumpled, red rocks. On either side of the car, the peaks of the Swartberg loom so high that you need a sun roof to see the summit.

If you are going to make a pit stop while in the poort, the main rest area offers a tourism bureau and a pretty waterfall, which is a short walk away. This is worth checking out in the rainy, winter season. Another notable rest area contains what is possibly South Africa's most arbitrary national monument: Herrie se klip. This the place where venerable Afrikaner poet, C J Langenhoven, carved the name of his pet elephant (Herrie) into a rock. While this may

have counted as a major cultural event in the old days, I can't help but think that the National Monuments Council was starting to run out of things to proclaim. If, however, you are a Langenhoven fan, this rock's for you.

SEWEWEEKSPOORT
Like Meiringspoort, Seweweekspoort is a natural passage through the belly of the mountains. This one follows the Huis River, from Laingsburg on the N1 to Zoar on the R62. Unlike Meiringspoort, however, Seweweeks has never been tarred and remains a dusty backroad, unused and unloved.

That's a pity, because Seweweeks is even more impressive than Meiringspoort. The twisted piles of rock tower above the narrow sand track, and you can't help but feel insignificant as the car skitters along the confined valley, eked out of the mountains by a deceptively feeble river. When you stop the car to take in the solitude, the stone seems to bulge and groan with the illimitable stress of the aeons, and beauty and drama are eternally united in the mountain side.

Seweweekspoort sure ain't a short-cut, but it is a road that will reward the curious driver with a little-seen geomorphological gem.

SWARTBERG PASS
Both Meiringspoort and Seweweekspoort were river-bound passes that were prone to regular flooding. Understandably, the citizens of

The twisted rock strata in Seweweekspoort

Ostrich sculptures on the far side of the Swartberg

Oudtshoorn and Prince Albert kept demanding an all-weather pass over the summit of the Swartberg, which would stay open all year round.

For many decades, this was simply impossible. The Swartberg were just too extreme. Then, they called in Thomas Bain to have a look, and even he was troubled by the angry mountain. He tried staking out four different routes before finding a suitable passage for his road, and he finally submitted his proposals to parliament in 1879. The construction tender was awarded to a private contractor, Jan Tassie, in 1881.

Unfortunately, as was so often the case, the contractor went bankrupt in 1883 and Bain had to take over, with his customary gang of convicts in tow. Despite extremely difficult working conditions, and severe flooding in 1885, the pass was completed and officially opened to traffic in 1888. It was the last mountain pass that the prolific Thomas Bain ever built.

Today, the pass is much as Bain left it. The surface is gravel, the geometric standards are way below modern road specifications and the views are staggering. In fact, I will hazard the opinion that the Swartberg is probably the most scenically breathtaking pass in the country.

The adventure starts north of Oudtshoorn, as the tarred access road leads past the Cango Caves and through a delightful valley, called Schoemanspoort, up to the mouth of the Pass.

Do note the battered old sign that warns against trying to tow a caravan over the pass. It's not a good idea.

From here, the road climbs steeply along the rippled mountain flanks, offering gorgeous views out over the Klein Karoo plains. The road then summits between two thrusting peaks, and leads out onto a narrow plateau with a few picnic tables and grand views on all sides. Remains of the old Toll House and a memorial plaque to Thomas Bain are also nearby. Shortly after the summit, you will see an enticing sign that points the way to Die Hel. This is an extensive but rewarding detour, which is detailed below.

Next comes the most famous section of the Swartberg Pass: the hairpin bends. These switchbacks are a common feature of European road passes but were not often used by our local *padmakers*. Our passes tend to take the long way round, tracking the contour lines as they wind in and out of the foothills. On top of the Swartberg, however, Bain found that there was little room to manoeuvre, and he had to build a series of three sharp bends that turn back on themselves as they descend. After the hairpins, the road straightens out somewhat and leads down a mighty cleft in the mountains, which bottoms out at a clean little brook called Eerste Water. Oxen used to drink from this brook before or after tackling the steep road ahead, and the remains of one of the old convict stations can be seen close by.

The famous hairpin bends on the Swartberg Pass

The Swartberg Pass can be safely tackled in most cars, although mist and rain may reduce visibility, and snowfalls can occur in winter. But, whatever you do, take it slow. This is a pass to be savoured.

GAMKASKLOOF / DIE HEL

Hidden inside a narrow valley, folded away within the Swartberg Mountain massif, is Gamkaskloof. Literally, this translates as 'Lion's Ravine', but the valley is much better known by its derogatory nickname, Die Hel.

For 150 years, Die Hel was arguably the most isolated community on the subcontinent. Surrounded by mountains on the north, south, east and west, residents of this tiny community were entirely cut off from the outside world. When they wanted to leave their valley and go into town, they either had to walk out over the mountains, or ford the Gamka River through a rocky kloof. Likewise, when they wanted to bring something back, such as a bed or a stove, it had to be carried in on the back of a farmer, or harnessed to a donkey.

Gamkaskloof was therefore a largely self-sufficient community, made up of a handful of pioneer families who had started moving in from the late 1700s. Most people would have avoided such a remote settlement, but the *Klowers* were an iconoclastic bunch, attracted by the freedom that comes with isolation. Many of the original families stuck it out for generation after generation, until the surnames Mostert, Cordier, Swanepoel, Nel and Marais rang through the annals of the valley, like Dlaminis in a Swaziland phone directory.

Life was peaceful here, and the people of Gamkaskloof marched to the beat of a different drummer. In their narrow enclave, tucked away in the formidable fastness of the Swartberg Mountains, the *Klowers* felt safe and free to make up their own rules. Sure, life was hard and creature comforts were largely unknown, but the valley people were happy and prosperous in their humble way.

So, for many years, this lonely community tended their farms, which spread out along the narrow valley floor. They farmed sweet

Gamkaskloof / Die Hel

Accommodation in Die Hel is suitably unusual. Cape Nature Conservation is slowly restoring all the old homes in the valley, and you can now choose to spend the night at the Headmaster's House, Tant Lenie's old cottage or one of the other local dwellings. There is no electricity in Die Hel, but gas fridges and cookers are supplied. Contact Oom Sannie at the Swartberg CNC office to make bookings.

The only way to reach Die Hel is from the top of the gravel Swartberg Pass. Just after you crest the summit, you will see a sign that points to Gamkaskloof / Die Hel. You will also note that the sign points out that Die Hel is 50k's away and those 50k's = two hours. Don't think that you know better than this sign. You can't safely complete the journey in less, so make sure you give yourself enough time to get down to Die Hel and back up again before it gets dark. In any case, I wouldn't recommend going to Gamkaskloof for a day trip. It's just too much driving, and an overnight stay is the only way to savour the fresh air and clear night skies.

One final note about Die Hel; do not attempt the journey if you don't like heights. The roadway is narrow and exposed throughout its length, and the final descent into the valley is nothing short of perpendicular. This last stretch of road, called Eland's Pass, does not have any retaining walls, no guard rails, and very sharp hairpin bends. Those with vertigo or acrophobia should definitely not venture down the snaking road to the valley floor.

I know this to be the case because, when I was in Die Hel, I was asked to drive two fellow guests out of the valley. These lovely people, Ken and Margaret, had struggled to drive down into die Hel and were frozen with fear at the thought of having to tackle the road a second time. It was so bad that, during the night, Ken had seriously resolved to leave his car and walk out. Luckily, we dissuaded them from this drastic course of action, and drove their sedan out of the pass without any problems.

Ken and Margaret, who were ready to walk out of Die Hel

Hanepoort grapes, made jams and preserves, and collected wild honey. Slowly, as the families grew in number, a school and a church were also built, using the local mud bricks and reeds from

The road climbs to the top of the menacing Swartberg

the river. By the 1930s, there were probably 120 people living in Gamkaskloof, oblivious to the dictates of the twentieth century.

Then, the outside world caught up with Gamkaskloof. First, the Boer commander, Denys Reitz, stumbled into the valley around the turn of the 20th century, while hiding from a British force during the Anglo-Boer War. He recounted his experiences among the locals in his popular book *On Commando*, and piqued the interest of his readers with romantic accounts of a forgotten community, cast adrift in a mountainous backwater.

Then, government came to Gamkaskloof in the form of a local tax collector and stock inspector. One of these men is credited with giving the valley its more-familiar name, 'Die Hel', apparently bestowed on the idyllic valley because the collector thought it was hell to trek down into the kloof to do his regular livestock checks. The *Klowers* hated the name but it endured, thanks to the successive waves of journalists and photographers who descended the precipitous slopes, eager to get an interesting story.

These articles were usually unflattering and supercilious. They characterised the *Klowers* as backward, in-bred hicks with anachronistic clothes, language and customs. Even modern novels, such as Andre Brink's *Duiwelskloof*, have indulged in these stereotypes, much to the chagrin of the *Klowers'* descendants. So, not only did the locals have to be hardy and stoical, they had to be thick-skinned too.

Despite the occasional cover story in *Rooi Rose*, the *Klowers'* little piece of paradise was still too remote to be incorporated into the real world, and life continued apace. People still had to hike over the peaks to reach Oudtshoorn or Prince Albert, and this journey was only undertaken in the event of sickness, for commerce or when an unattached *Klower* had to find someone to marry.

Then, in 1962, everything changed. In that year, the government decided to dam the Gamka River, thus effectively stranding the little community of Gamkaskloof. To make amends, they decided to build a long-overdue road down into Hell.

Armed with nothing more than a bulldozer and a handful of workmen, Koos van Zyl was given the mandate to carve a road from the summit of the Swartberg Pass, along the rolling alpine plains, and down a steep switchback pass to the valley floor. It was dangerous work, and Koos often complained that he had nearly fallen, bulldozer and all, *'gat oor kop, Die Hel in'* (arse over head, into the Hell).

Ironically, this new access route into the valley quickly turned into an escape route out. Within twenty years, everyone had left Gamksakloof. The last farmer to abandon his land was Piet Swanepoel, in 1991.

Under the cloudless Karoo skies, the abandoned homesteads started crumbling, and

The remains of the first car in Gamkaskloof

farms that had been in the same family for generations became overgrown. It seemed like Die Hel was dead. Then, a consortium of doctors from nearby towns decided to buy up a few of the farms, and established a private conservancy at one end of the valley. More recently, Cape Nature Conservation bought up most of the other farms and incorporated them into the Swartberg Nature Reserve. Finally, Annetjie Joubert, a native *klower*, decided it was time to move back home. Her family farm had not been sold to CNC, much to the conservation authority's consternation, and Annetjie returned to her ancestral land to start up a private lodge and a restaurant, called The Devil's Kitchen.

Joubert is now the only genuine local living in Gamkaskloof. A few other original *Klowers* are also still around, but they are living in the relative modernity of Oudtshoorn, Prince Albert and Calitzdorp.

PRINCE ALBERT

On the other side of the Swartberg Pass is the picture-perfect town of Prince Albert, situated at the southern edge of the Great Karoo plains. It is a classic Karoo *dorp*; pristine old homes line the streets with corrugated iron roofs and shady *stoeps*, and a fully operational system of furrows channels water into the flowering gardens.

Despite the Karoo heat and the gritty dust, this is a little town with an appealing air. The local characters are warm and distinctive, and dozens of weather-beaten faces watch the passing parade with mild interest. The schools seem to be busy and kids walk around town, popping in at the ancient general dealers for an ice-cream or an orange soda.

The historical centre of the town is the Fransie Pienaar Museum. Located in an old house on the main road through town, this remarkable assemblage of antiques, bric-a-brac, books and loads of other junk was collected by the renowned pack-rat, Ms Fransie Pienaar herself. The house was actually secured by the citizens of the town to store her burgeoning collection, and it kinda became the local museum by default.

Although it looks a bit like a junk shop, the museum is full of interesting odds and ends, and the local tourist bureau is right next door. Here, you can book for the other attractions of Prince Albert, such as the guided historical walks, the ghost tours and the 4x4 excursions into the arid Karoo heartland beyond the town.

The main street of Prince Albert contains quite a few attractive little restaurants, which offer pancakes, sandwiches and other wholesome country fare.

Other Useful Phone Numbers:
- Swartberg Nature Reserve: 044 279 1739
- Gamkaskloof / Die Hel: 044 279 2746 / 044 802 5310 / 023 541 1736
- The Devil's Kitchen (Die Hel): 023 541 1107/737
- Bo-Plaas Guest Farm (Die Hel): 044 874 7130
- Prince Albert Tourist Info: 023 541 1366 www.patourism.co.za
- Fransie Pienaar Museum: 023 541 1172

Public transport in Prince Albert

19. Appendices

REFERENCES / FURTHER READING

Travel books are constantly being revised and updated. Consult your bookstore for all the latest travel titles. All books listed below are first editions, unless otherwise specified. Some of these titles are now out of print, but may be available from second-hand book dealers.

General Travel and Accommodation

- AA Accommodation Guides: Self-catering getaways / Hotels, lodges and B&B's. Published annually by the AA of South Africa.
- Bulpin, T.V. 1992. Discovering Southern Africa, 5th edition. Muizenberg: Southern Book Distributors
- Burman, Jose. 1975. Cape Drives and Places of Interest. Cape Town: Human and Rousseau
- Burman, Jose. 1978. Coastal Holiday. Cape Town: Human and Rousseau
- Burman, Jose. 1964. The Garden Route. Cape Town: Human and Rousseau
- Erasmus, B.J.P. 1995. On Route in South Africa. Johannesburg: Jonathan Ball
- Klurman, Melissa. 2002. Fodor's Southern Africa (guidebook), 2nd edition. New York: Fodor's Travel Publications
- Maclay, George (editor). 1987. Off the Beaten Track. Cape Town: AA The Motorist Publications
- Newbould, Steve (editor) 2003. The Tourism Blueprint Reference Guide to Nine Provinces of South Africa, 2nd edition. Cape Town: The Tourism Blueprint
- Olivier, Willie and Sandra. 1999. Exploring the Natural Wonders of South Africa. Cape Town: Struik Publishers
- Raynierse, Cecile (editor). 1988. Illustrated guide to the Southern African Coast. Cape Town: AA The Motorist Publications

General History

- Burrows, Edmund H. 1988. Overberg Outspan. Swellendam: Swellendam Trust
- Burrows, Edmund H. 1994. Overberg Odyssey. Swellendam: Swellendam Trust
- Gall, Sandy. 2001. The Bushmen of Southern Africa – slaughter of the innocents. London: Chatto and Windus
- Mostert, Noel. 1992. Frontiers – the epic of South Africa's creation and the tragedy of the Xhosa People. London: Pimlico
- Mountain, Alan. 2003. First People of the Cape. Cape Town: David Philip Publishers
- Mountain, Alan. 2004. Unsung Heritage – perspectives of slavery. Cape Town: David Philip Publishers
- Oakes, Dougie (editor). 1988. Illustrated History of South Africa – the real story. Cape Town: Reader's Digest Association
- Oberholster, J. J. (translated by B.D. Malan). 1972. The Historical Monuments of South Africa. Stellenbosch: The Rembrant van Rijn Foundation for Culture
- Raper, P. E. 2004. The New Dictionary of South African Place Names. Johannesburg: Jonathan Ball Publishers
- Sleigh, Dan (translated by André Brink). 2004. Islands – a novel. London: Secker and Warburg
- Van Waart, Sue. The Hell – Valley of the Lions. 2000. Pretoria: J.P van der Walt and Son

Natural History / Geology / Ecology

- Berger, Lee and Hilton-Barber, Brett. 2004. Field Guide to the Cradle of Humankind, 2nd edition. Cape Town, Struik
- Beyer, Judy and Duggan, Alan (editors). 1997. Illustrated Guide to Game Parks and Nature Reserves of Southern Africa, 3rd edition. Cape Town: Reader's Digest Association South Africa

206

- Bristow, David. 1988. *The Natural History of South Africa*. Cape Town: Struik Publishers.
- Burman, Jose. 1962. *Safe to the Sea – The Rivers of the Cape Peninsula*. Cape Town: Human and Rousseau
- Du Toit, Alex L. and Haughton, S. H. 1954. *Geology of South Africa, 3rd edition*. London: Oliver and Boyd
- Jacana (editors). 1998. *Cape Town, the Cape Peninsula National Park and Winelands - Eco-Guide*. Johannesburg: Jacana Education
- Jacana (editors). 2003. *The Garden Route - Eco-Guide, 3rd edition*. Johannesburg: Jacana Education
- Viljoen, M.J. and Reimold, W.U. 2002. *Introduction to South Africa's Geological and Mining Heritage*. Johannesburg: Geological Society of South Africa / Mintek

Road History / Mountain Passes
- Burman, Jose. 1963. *So High the Road – Mountain Passes of the Western Cape*. Cape Town: Human and Rousseau
- Burman, Jose. 1988. *Towards the Far Horizon – the story of the ox-wagon in South Africa*. Cape Town: Human and Rousseau
- Floor, Bernal C. 1985. *The History of National Roads in South Africa*. Pretoria: National Transport Commission
- Forbes, Vernon S. 1965. *Pioneer Travellers of South Africa 1750-1800*. Cape Town: A.A. Balkema
- Marincowitz, Helena. 1989. *Swartberg Pass – masterpiece of a brilliant road engineer*. Oudtshoorn: Bowles
- Marincowitz, Helena. 1990. *Meiringspoort – scenic gorge in the Swartberg*. Oudtshoorn: Bowles
- Marincowitz, Helena. 1992. *Montagu Pass and other passes over the Outeniqua mountains*. George: George Museum Society
- Meyer, Ilse. 1999. *The Prince Alfred's Pass - spectacular and diverse*. Oudtshoorn: Bowles
- Mossop, E. E. 1927. *Old Cape Highways*. Cape Town: Maskew Miller

- Ross, Graham. 2002. *The Romance of Cape Mountain Passes*. Cape Town: David Philip Publishers
- Storrar, Patricia. 1984. *A Colossus of Roads*. Cape Town: Murray and Roberts / Concor

Outdoor activities
- Levy, Jaynee. 1993. *The Complete Guide to Walks and Trails in Southern Africa, 3rd edition*. Cape Town: Struik Publishers
- Olivier, Willie and Sandra. 2003. *Hiking Trails of South Africa*. Cape Town: Struik Publishers
- St Pierre-White, Andrew. 2003. *The Complete Guide to 4x4 Trails and Expeditions in Southern Africa*. Somerset West: International Motoring Publications

Maps and Road Atlases
- AASA. *Road Atlas of South Africa*
- Globetrotter. *Road Atlas of South Africa*
- Juta Gariep. 2003. *General School Atlas*
- Map Studio. 2001. *Tourist Atlas – Eastern Cape*
- Map Studio. 2002. *Tourist Atlas – Western Cape*
- Map Studio. *Road Atlas of South Africa*
- Oxford University Press South Africa. 2001. *Senior Atlas for Southern Africa*

Facing the future in Factreton, Cape Town

USEFUL PHONE NUMBERS AND WEBSITES

Tourist Info and Accommodation:
- Central Tourism Info Hotline: 083 123 6789
- Western Cape Tourism: 021 426 5639/47 www.capetourism.org
- Eastern Cape Tourism: 041 585 7761 043 701 9600 / www.ectourism.co.za
- www.southafrica.net / www.southafrica.info
- www.infoafrica.co.za
- www.go24.co.za
- www.sacape.co.za
- www.southerncape.co.za
- www.wheretostay.co.za
- www.sa-venues.com
- www.places.co.za
- www.aatravel.co.za
- www.saexplorer.co.za – with maps
- www.routes.co.za – with maps
- www.coastingafrica.com – backpackers
- www.backpacking.co.za – backpackers
- www.btsa.co.za – backpackers
- www.tourismgrading.co.za

Special Interest:
- Birdlife SA: 011 789 1122 www.birdlife.co.za
- Mountain Club Of South Africa: 021 465 3412 / www.mcsa.org.za
- Museums of South Africa: www.museums.org.za
- South African history: www.sahistory.org.za
- National Biodiversity Institute: www.nbi.ac.za
- Geological Society of South Africa: 011 492 3370
- Hiking trails: www.linx.co.za/trails
- South African Heritage Resource Agency: www.sahra.org.za
- Department of Environmental Affairs and Tourism (DEAT): www.environment.gov.za
- Wildlife and Environmental Society of SA: www.wildlifesociety.org.za
- South African Weather Service: www.saweather.co.za

- Wines of South Africa: www.wosa.co.za
- Wine Guide: www.platteronline.com

Transport:
- Avis Rent-a-car: 0861 021 111 011 923 3660 / www.avis.co.za
- www.bazbus.com – backpacker's bus
- www.greyhound.co.za – bus liners
- www.translux.co.za – bus liners
- www.spoornet.co.za – trains
- www.flysaa.com – airline
- www.kulula.com – airline
- www.1time.aero – airline
- www.nationwideair.co.za
- Johannesburg International Airport: 011 921 6262
- Airports Company of South Africa (ACSA): www.airports.co.za

Local Search Engines and ISPs
- www.google.co.za
- www.aardvark.co.za
- www.ananzi.co.za
- www.mweb.co.za
- www.iafrica.com
- www.news24.co.za

Local Newspapers and Periodicals:
- www.iol.co.za – Independent Newspaper Group (including Cape Argus, Cape Times)
- www.mg.co.za – Mail and Guardian weekly newspaper
- www.sundaytimes.co.za – Weekly Sunday paper
- www.getawaytoafrica.com – Travel Magazine
- www.driveout.co.za – 4x4 Trail Guide
- www.winemag.co.za – Viti-cultural magazine

General Reference:
- www.wikipedia.org – Open source, on-line encyclopaedia
- www.aasa.co.za – Automobile Association of South Africa website
- www.transport.gov.za – SA Department of Transport website

CONSERVATION AUTHORITIES

SAN Parks

The South African National Parks Board is a remarkable organisation. It is the custodian of many millions of hectares, and it protects some of our most precious natural resources. As conservationists, they do an amazing job. As hoteliers, they are getting better all the time.

Daily conservation fees are payable for each person entering a SAN Park, whether as a day visitor or as an overnight guest. To keep costs down, citizens of the SADC countries can apply for a Wild Card. This grants the holder free entrance into any SAN Park reserve for a full year. Family cards are also available. Foreigners are not eligible for a Wild Card, and have to pay higher Conservation fees to boot. Sorry for you!

- SAN Parks (central reservations): 012 428 9111
- SAN Parks (Admin): 012 426 5000
- SAN Parks Joburg Office: 011 678 8870
- SAN Parks Cape Town Office: 021 426 4260
- SAN Parks Durban Office: 031 304 4934
- www.sanparks.org
  (note that www.sanparks.co.za is run by an independent booking agent)

South African
NATIONAL PARKS

Cape Nature Conservation:

I'm a bit annoyed with Cape Nature Conservation. When I started researching this book, I approached them and asked for free accommodation. They responded to my request with ill-concealed arrogance. Apparently, CNC is a rather schizophrenic organisation. First, they told me their resorts were small and not really geared for overnight guests. Then they said they would rather pay money to advertise in travel magazines, than allow writers like me free access to their reserves in exchange for publicity. They also warned me that I could not publish any pictures of their reserves unless I paid them a wad of cash for the privilege. It seems like Cape Nature Conservation has succumbed to the general Capetonian malaise of gouging anyone remotely affiliated to the media.

Nevertheless, CNC does look after many beautiful wilderness areas and nature reserves scattered around the Western Cape.

- Cape Nature Conservation (central reservations): 021 426 0723
- Cape Nature Conservation (enquiries): 021 483 4615
- www.capenature.org.za

Sunsets are glorious from the top of Table Mountain

Caraville Vacations

While researching this book, I travelled extensively around South Africa. My extended trip would not have been possible without the generous assistance of Caraville Vacations and their affiliate hotels. Caraville is a very useful organisation, offering a central reservations number for dozens of highly-rated hotels, lodges and self-catering resorts around the country. They can also arrange car hire, adventure tours and other special-interest travel services. For overseas visitors, they have convenient offices in Great Britain and Germany. Below is a list and brief description of the places that kindly offered me their hospitality while I was driving around the Western Cape.

• Caraville Central Bookings: 086 066 0030
  031 266 0030 / www.caraville.co.za

Cape Town Lodge – Cape Town City Bowl

The Cape Town Lodge is a particularly good hotel, with an excellent location in the heart of the City Bowl. It is a well-run, understated but luxurious hotel, which is popular with businessmen and French tour groups. But don't let that put you off. Their family rooms are good value, and you can walk from the hotel to just about any part of town. The roof-top pool is very *larney*, and the service is excellent.

Round the Bend River Lodge – near Swellendam

If you want to try something a little bit different, book into Round the Bend. This is actually the rest camp for Felix Unite rafting excursions on the Breede River, but you can stay here even if you aren't booked on one of their trips. The setting on the banks of the Breede is very pretty and peaceful, and the large thatched dining area serves hearty meals. You may have to share the bar with a rowdy crew, fresh from their river adventure, but it is an interesting alternative to a traditional hotel. A few words of warning: it's not easy to find, the bathrooms are communal, and sleeping quarters are in quaint thatched huts with a canvas flap instead of a door. On the night that I stayed over, the wind was blowing so hard through the canvas that it kept lifting the duvet off my bed.

The Point Hotel – Mossel Bay

The Point Hotel is the linchpin of the Saint Blaise headland and it's a great place to stay. This upmarket hotel is run by a motivated manager and a friendly staff, but the secret of its success is that every room has a sea view. In fact, every room has a balcony which hangs out over the sea, and the spray from the waves speckles the sliding door to your room. I caught my breath every time I looked out of the window.

Knysna Hollow Country Lodge – Knysna

The tranquil yet luxurious Knysna Hollow Country Estate is a large, comfortable retreat a few minutes outside of Knysna. Rooms are in spacious, thatched, semi-detached units. Furnishings are crisp and fresh, and the double-volume shower is a revelation!

Lily Pond Country Lodge – Plettenberg Bay

This outstanding guest house is rather exclusive. It only has room for twelve guests in six rooms, and it offers personal service and excellent cuisine. Lily Pond is run by a Dutch couple, Niels and Margaret, who first came to South Africa on holiday several years ago. They liked the place so much, they decided to stay. My kind of people. The lodge is built around a series of large ponds, and it is a quiet oasis on the edge of the dark forest. Niels is the host and speaks five languages. Margaret does all the cooking herself. The German couple I dined with said it was the best food they had eaten in South Africa, and this was no mean compliment.

The Windsor Hotel – Hermanus

The Windsor Hotel is a classic. It's one of the oldest hostelries in Hermanus and it's a charming place to stay, especially if you are in one of the sea-facing rooms that has an unrestricted view out over the rocky shoreline. It is a wonderfully unpretentious, old-fashioned hotel that reminded me a bit of Fawlty Towers (just the layout, not the service).

Thylitshia Villa – Oudtshoorn

A cosy, family run B+B on the outskirts of Oudtshoorn, Thylitshia Villa is also a working wine and ostrich farm. Accommodation is in plush converted stables, and home-cooked meals are served in the old farmstead next door. The whole scene is relaxed and restful, as any country getaway should be.

Montagu Country Hotel – Montagu

The Montagu Country Hotel, in the old town centre, is probably the best example of an Art-Deco hotel in South Africa. The confident pink façade of the building sets the mood, and its passionate owner, Gert Lubbe, has taken every effort to furnish the interior with beautiful period furniture and fixtures. The Victorian annex has four luxury suites, which lead onto a beautiful wrap-around *stoep*. Service is exceptional and the hotel has its own beauty therapy rooms, herb gardens and mineral spring. If you're really good, Gert might even show you his enviable collection of vintage and veteran cars.

SELECTED CHRONOLOGY OF MOUNTAIN PASSES FROM CAPE TOWN TO PE

(re-printed with the kind permission of Graham Ross)

1653: Wagenpad na't Bosch 'constructed' – and maintained.

1658: Roodezand Pass to Tulbagh Valley pioneered by Pieter Potter.

1660: Piquinierskloof pioneered by Jan Dankaert.

1662: Elands Path/Gantouw pioneered by Hendrik Lacus.

1666: Kirstenbosch road extended to Constantia Nek/Cloof Pas.

1682: Houw Hoek Pass pioneered by Olof Bergh.

1689: Attaquas Kloof pioneered by Isaac Schrijver.

1693: Constantia Nek road extended to Hout Bay.

1699: Olifants Pad (Franschhoek) in use.

1705: Banghoek/Helshoogte Pass in use.

1752: Kaaimans Gat Pass pioneered on horseback by Beutler.

1772: Duiwelskop Pass, possibly by farmer Jacobus van Beelen.

1772: Paardekop Pass: a bridle path in use.

1772: Plattekloof Pass pioneered by Thunberg.

1772: Prince Alfred's Pass: a bridle path in use.

1778: Kaaimans Gat Pass pioneered for wagons by Van Plettenberg.

1803: Cogmans Kloof in use.

1803: Paardekop Pass and Little Long Kloof used by wagons.

1811: Palmiet River: Die Oudebrug, first bridge outside a town.

1812: Cradock Kloof Pass, by Landdrost Adriaan van Kervel.

1812: Trek-aan-Touw Pass in use.

1819: 'Cats Pad', by farmer S J Cats of Franschhoek.

1824: Hottentots Holland Kloof in use.

1824: Jan Joubert's Gat stone bridge, on Franschhoek Pass.

1825: Franschhoek Pass, by Major William Cuthbert Holloway.

1830: Sir Lowry's Pass, by Charles Cornwallis Michell.

1831: Houw Hoek/Cole's Pass, by Major Charles Michell.

1836: Attaquas Kloof: improvements by Charles Michell.

1841: Plattekloof Pass reconstructed

1845: The 'Hard Road' across the Cape Flats.

1847: Houw Hoek Pass reconstructed by Andrew Bain.

1848: Kloof Neck, Cape Town.

1848: Montagu Pass, by Henry Fancourt White.

1849: Zuurberg Pass, by Central Roads Board.

1854: Helshoogte Pass: Bang Hoek Pass reconstructed on new route.

1858: Meirings Poort, by Adam de Smidt.

1859: Meiringspoort: flood repairs.

1860: Hudson's Pass: new name for Gysmanshoek Pass through Plattekloof, improved by Divisional Council.

1860s: Viljoen's Pass, Grabouw.

1862: Phantom Pass, by Thomas Bain.

1862: Seweweekspoort, by Mr Apsey and Adam G. de Smidt.

1862: Knysna River: stone causeway by Thomas Bain.

1864: Duiwelskop Pass: a 'country road', by Thomas Bain.

1867: Prince Alfred's Pass, by Thomas Bain.

1867: Avontuur – Uniondale Pass over Gwarna Range, by Thomas Bain.

1867: Van Staden's Pass, by Thomas Bain.

c1868: Swart River Pass (The Passes Road), by Adam de Smidt.

1869: Kaaimans and Silver River Pass (The Passes Road): De Smidt.

1869: Robinson Pass, by Thomas Bain.

1871: Hoogekraal Pass (The Passes Road), by Adam de Smidt.

1871: Touw River Pass (The Passes Road), by Adam de Smidt.

1872: Cogmans Kloof, by Thomas Bain: first section opened.

1873: Tradouw Pass, by Thomas Bain.

1877: Cogmans Kloof, by Thomas Bain: tunnel opened.

1877: Garcia's Pass, by Thomas Bain.

1877: Koo/Burgers Pass, by Divisional Council.

1877: Thompson's/Rooihoogte Pass, by Divisional Council.

1881: Gouna Forest Road, Knysna, by Thomas Bain.

1882: Groot River Pass, by Thomas Bain.

1882: Homtini Pass (The Passes Road), by Adam de Smidt.

1882: Karatara River Pass (The Passes Road), by Adam de Smit.

1882: The Passes Road, by Adam de Smidt.

1883: Bloukrans Pass, by Thomas Bain.

1885: Storms River Pass, by Thomas Bain.

1885: Coastal road from Cape Town reached Humansdorp.

1886: Baviaanskloof, by Thomas Bain.

1887: The Passes Road handed over to Divisional Council (includes Swart, Kaaimans/Silver, Touws, Hoogekraal, Karatara and Homtini (Goukamma) River Passes, and the Phantom Pass), by Adam de Smidt.

1888: Swartberg Pass, by John Fitz-Neville and Thomas Bain.

1888: Victoria Road, Sea Point to Hout Bay, by Thomas Bain.

1896: Huis River Pass, by Ladismith and Calitzdorp Divisional Councils.

c1903: Houw Hoek Pass reconstructed on 'railway' route.

1905: White's Road, at Wilderness, by Montagu White.

1911: De Waal Drive, by Union Government PWD.

1922: Chapman's Peak Drive: gravel construction, by Robert Glenday (of the Union Public Works Department.)

1927: Boyes Drive constructed.

1928: Uniondale/Avontuur Poort road, replacing 'Bain's Pass'.

1928: Rooiberg Pass (south of Calitzdorp), as relief works.

1936 or 1937: Boesmanskloof Pass, near McGregor: never completed.

1951: Outeniqua Pass constructed by Italian POWs and Cape Province Roads unit (bitumen surface).

1951: Kaaimans River curved bridge on N2.

1952: N2: George–Knysna constructed by Cape Province Roads unit (bitumen).

1953: Cogmans Kloof reconstructed on new alignment (bitumen), and Cogmans Kloof tunnel enlarged, by Divisional Council.

1953: N2: Cape Town–George: bitumen surface complete.

1956: Storms River: P O Sauer Bridge on N2/13. The all-asphalt link between Cape Town and Port Elizabeth was established with the construction of the Storms River bridge.

1958: Sir Lowry's Pass reconstructed, by Simpson Construction.

1958: De Waal Drive reconstructed, dual carriageway.

1958: George–Oudtshoorn R25 National Road: construction complete.

1962: Otto du Plessis Road and Eland Pass, from top of Swartberg Pass to Gamkaskloof (Die Hel), constructed by Prince Albert Divisional Council (gravel).

1971: Port Elizabeth Bypass: freeway: 1963–1971 (four contracts).

1971: Van Staden's Gorge bridge on N2/14.

1974: Widespread flood damage.

1976: Houw Hoek Pass (N2): dual carriageway reconstruction, HHO/S&L.

1981: Laingsburg floods.

1983: Bobbejaans River bridge on N2 toll road.

1983: Bloukrans River bridge on N2 toll road.

1983: Groot River bridge on N2 toll road.

1984: Sir Lowry's Pass: upper portion reconstructed by HHO/S&L.

1988: Huguenot toll tunnel (N1) in Du Toit's Kloof opened.

2003: Chapman's Peak re-opened, December 2003

GLOSSARY OF SOUTH AFRICAN WORDS

For any international readers, I have included a short glossary of useful local words that may have appeared in this book. Many of these words have an Afrikaans origin, and may confound those who have accents with limited vowel sounds.

ag: multi-purpose exclamation of surprise, pity, anger or defeat, often linked with the word 'shame', pronounced with an uvular fricative (the sound you make when clearing phlegm from your throat)

baai: a bay, also a casual way to say 'goodbye', pronounced 'buy'

bakkie: a pick-up truck, also a small container, pronounced 'bucky'

berg: a mountain or a mountain range *(berge)*

bergie: an uncomplimentary name for unruly Cape Town locals

boer: a farmer, can also refer to any *verkrampt* Afrikaner

boerewors: literally 'a farmer's sausage', an essential ingredient for a *lekker braai*

bos/bosch: bush-lands or forest, also what happens when you go crazy

boot: a car trunk

braai: a barbeque, the national pastime

bru: a Joburg term of affection, derives from the Afrikaans for 'brother', can be used in any sentence in place of a full stop, variations include 'bro' or 'bra'

burg: a town or a city

cafe: a convenience store, often connected to a dodgy take-away, pronounced 'kaff-ee', not the same as a 'cafay' (which is a place that sells over-priced coffee)

cheers: goodbye, also what you say after a *dop*

chips: what Americans call French Fries, also an exclamation that means 'watch out!'

cold-drink: soft-drink, soda or pop, pronounced 'coal-drink'

cozzie: a swimming costume

dankie: thank you, often used in conjunction with *skat*, pronounced 'dunky'

drif: a drift (the ford across a river), also an alcoholic drink that you add to Coke

dof: stupid, pronounced 'dohff',

dop: a drink, usually alcoholic, often preceded by the words 'wanna go for a'

doos: literally 'a box', also used to describe an unpleasant person, pronounced 'do-us'

dorp: a small, dozy town, or any place outside of Joburg

dummy: what Americans call a 'pacifier', what we call Americans

full stop: what Americans call a 'period'

gat: literally 'a hole', can be extrapolated to refer to the entire arse

goef: a swim, usually followed by a *kip*

groot: big or great, a stark counterpoint to *klein*

hoek: a corner or a district, also a punch in the face

hol: a hole, often used in conjunction with *poep*

howzit: a quick way of saying 'hello, how are you?'

izzit?: a quick way of saying 'is that so?'

ja: Afrikaans for 'yes', contagious word that is picked up by most visitors within two weeks, pronounced 'yaw'

jou ma: literally 'your mother', usually followed by a genital descriptor

just now/now-now/now: a South African's way of saying 'later', we don't have a word for 'now'

kak: multi-purpose word, can be used to express surprise, disbelief, anger and friendship, pronounced 'kuhk', often used in conjunction with 'don't *tune* me…'

kaal: naked or bare, often used in conjunction with *gat*

kip: a nap, the best thing to have after a *braai*

klap: a slap or a smack, sometimes linked to snot, pronounced 'kluh-p'

klein: small or little, pronounced 'klayn', opposite of *groot*

kloof: a ravine or cleft in the rocks, pronounced 'kloo-uf'

koek: cake, pronounced 'cook'

kop: a head

koppie: a rocky hill

kraal: a cattle enclosure, pronounced 'krah-ul'

krantz: a rocky ridge or cliff

larney: smart or expensive, can refer to an object or an entire person

lekker: nice, pleasant, also a sweet or snack, pronounced 'leh-kuh'

lift: an elevator

mielie: corn on the cob

mlungu: a supposedly affectionate term for 'whitey', but I'm never sure

melktert: a milk tart, the national dessert of apartheid

mond: a mouth, river or facial, pronounced 'mohnt'

mozzie: a mosquito, I hate them!

man: a person (usually male), can also be used to end any sentence, pronounced 'mehn' or 'muhn'

nek: literally 'a neck', also a low saddle of land that connects two mountain peaks

oke: a person, a mate, 'bloke' without the 'bl', pronounced 'oak'

oom: an uncle, can also be used as a generic term for any old bugger

ou: old, also a generic term for 'person', pronounced 'oh'

ouma: granny

pad: a road, pronounced 'putt'

padkos: literally 'road food', nosh for the car

pap: corn meal, a staple food of Africa, also means 'flat' as in tyre, pronounced 'pup'

plaas: a farm, pronounced 'pl-arse'

poep: a fart or, if pushed, a poo

poephol: the thing that most politicians talk out of

pomp: pump, can be used as a noun or a verb

poort: a river valley that cuts through a mountain

poppie: literally 'a little doll', also refers to an empty-headed bimbo

rivier: river, pronounced 'rif-ear'

robot: what we call traffic lights, don't ask me why, might have something to do with perceived technological complexity when they were first installed in the 1930s

rooi: red, the colour of the Englishman's neck, pronounced 'roy'

rusk: a thick, baked biscuit which is good for dunking, often made by Ouma

sarmie: a sandwich, also called a 'zarm'

shame: an all purpose expression, can mean anything from 'how cute' to 'how terrible', usually bracketed by the words *ag* and *man*

skat: term of affection, equates to 'darling', 'sweetie' or 'lovey'

sies: term of disgust, equates to 'yucky' or 'gross', pronounced 'sees' or 'sihs'

slap: soggy, usually used to describe *chips* make in a *cafe*, pronounced 'slup'

stoep: a covered veranda attached to the house, good for sitting on

strand: a beach, pronounced 'strunt'

swart: black, the colour, pronounced 'swyart'

takkies: sneakers or trainers

tannie: auntie, also generic term for any old bat, pronounced 'tunny'

trap: to walk or hike, literally 'steps', pronounced 'trup'

trek: literally 'to pull', also to migrate

tune: to chat or say *howzit*, also what you do to a radio

uitspan: outspan, to unharness the oxen from their span, also a once-controversial brand of export oranges

vallei: a valley, pronounced 'fuh-lay'

veld: grassy plains, the open spaces of southern Africa, pronounced 'felt'

verkrampt: literally 'cramped', reactionary, conservative, grumpy, the national condition before 1994

voetsek: bugger off!, pronounced 'foot sack'

vrot: rotten, pronounced 'frrroht'

wit: white, pronounced 'vit'

witblitz: literally 'white lightening', a powerful drink, brewed in back-yard stills

Committed to preserving the cape floral kingdom, while helping all to benefit from its riches

The cause of nature conservation has always been dear to Avis. It is the natural beauty of the countries in which it operates that attracts the tourists who account for a significant part of its business. Avis has for many years provided financial as well as practical support for a variety of nature conservation initiatives, among them the World Wildlife Foundation.

In South Africa, the World Wildlife Foundation focuses on the prevention of degradation of the South African natural environment, the conservation of diversity and the sustainable use of natural resources. The World Wildlife Foundation has initiated new projects in the country every year since it expanded to South Africa. Many of these projects run for several years and a few have run as long as the World Wildlife Foundation has existed in South Africa.

The Fynbos Programme is one such project. As the smallest, yet richest of the world's six floral kingdoms, the sustained conservation of the Cape Floral Kingdom (or fynbos) is of critical global significance. A phenomenal 9 000 plant species make up this kingdom, 6 000 of which are found nowhere else on earth.

Committed to conserving the fynbos ecoregion and its adjacent shores, the World Wildlife Foundation played a pivotal role in the establishment of the Cape Action Plan for People and the Environment. This programme has showed demonstrable success in its ability not only to secure the conservation of the biodiversity of the cape floral region but also to deliver sustainable economic benefits to the people of the region through the tourism that the fynbos region draws. A real opportunity exists in the Cape Floral Kingdom to create the conditions for the emergence of a new type of conservation management where biodiversity conservation can be meshed with social challenges.

Avis has long been associated with the project, having to date sponsored vehicles to the Programme in addition to offering its vehicles to the World Wildlife Foundation at cost prices. Avis has long been the country's leading car rental system with over 110 locations throughout Southern Africa and a rental fleet of 12 000 vehicles. Its acknowledgement as the best car rental system in South Africa for the third consecutive time in 2004 by the Association of South African Travel Agents bears testimony to a company committed to sound corporate citizenship and driven by its belief that people will always be more important than cars.

We try harder

A cosy log cabin nestles in the thick forest under a deep blue sky, Tsitsikamma National Park

A seamless expanse of sea and sky, view of Camps Bay from Lion's Head